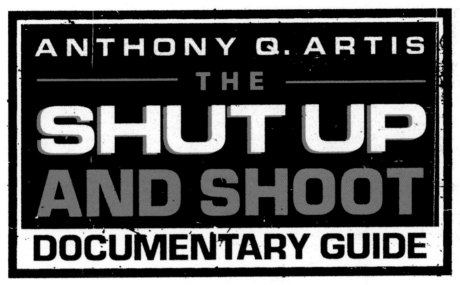

ANTHONY Q. ARTIS
THE
SHUT UP AND SHOOT
DOCUMENTARY GUIDE

2ND EDITION

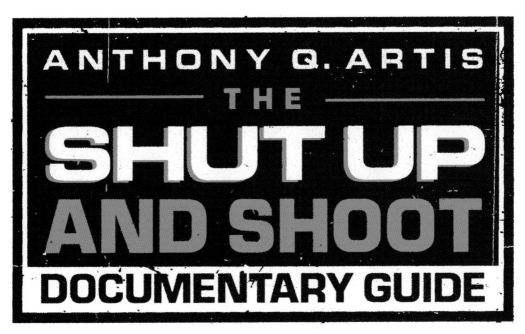

ANTHONY Q. ARTIS
THE
SHUT UP
AND SHOOT
DOCUMENTARY GUIDE

2ND EDITION

A
DOWN & DIRTYDV
PRODUCTION

Focal Press
Taylor & Francis Group

NEW YORK AND LONDON

First published 2007 by Focal Press

This edition published 2014 by Focal Press
70 Blanchard Road, Suite 402, Burlington, MA 01803

and by Focal Press
2 Park Square, Milton Park, Abingdon, Oxon OX14 4RN

Focal Press is an imprint of the Taylor & Francis Group, an informa business

Notices
Knowledge and best practice in this field are constantly changing. As new research
and experience broaden our understanding, changes in research methods,
professional practices, or medical treatment may become necessary.

Practitioners and researchers must always rely on their own experience and
knowledge in evaluating and using any information, methods, compounds, or
experiments described herein. In using such information or methods they should
be mindful of their own safety and the safety of others, including
parties for whom they have a professional responsibility.

Product or corporate names may be trademarks or registered trademarks, and are
used only for identification and explanation without intent to infringe.

Library of Congress Cataloging in Publication Data
Artis, Anthony Q.
The Shut Up and Shoot Documentary Guide / Anthony Q. Artis.–Second Edition.
    pages cm
Previous edition title: The shut up and shoot : freelance video guide : a down &
dirty DV production.
    Includes index.
1. Documentary films–Production and direction. 2. Video recordings–Production
and direction. I. Title.
    PN1992.94.A77 2014
    777–dc23
    2013039188

ISBN: 978-0-240-82415-4 (pbk)
ISBN: 978-0-240-82444-4 (ebk)

Typeset by Alex Lazarou

Printed and bound in India by Replika Press Pvt. Ltd.

This book is dedicated with love and gratitude

To my son, Tai, let this book stand as a testament that you can do anything you set your mind to, whenever you're ready to do it.

To my wife, Sonya, who always has my back, front, and sides and keeps my feet on the ground. Without all of your sacrifice, encouragement, and faith I would have never even started, let alone completed, this project.

And to my elementary teachers Ms. Fletcher and Ms. Klein, who many years ago told a skinny little Black kid from Baltimore that he could write . . . and he believed them. Your faith in me gave me faith in myself and the heart to help others discover and nurture their own talents against the odds. I'm forever grateful to you both.

Praise for *The Shut Up and Shoot Documentary Guide*

"I vouch for this book . . . extremely helpful for the newborn documentary filmmaker."

—**Albert Maysles,**
Grey Gardens, Salesman, Gimme Shelter

"Anthony Artis' book is the best, most informative, and entertaining book about making documentaries that I have come across."

—**Lloyd Kaufman,**
President of Troma Entertainment
and creator of The Toxic Avenger

"As my teacher, Anthony Artis taught me how to cut production down to the bare essentials to get it done . . . Without this foundation I would never have been able to keep up at the White House."

—**Arun Chaudhary,**
First Official White House Videographer
and author of First Cameraman

"Anthony Artis' **The Shut Up and Shoot Documentary Guide** *is a good primer for the entry-level documentary filmmaker, presented in a breezy, down-to-earth vernacular style."*

—**Thomas White,**
Editor of Documentary Magazine,
a publication of the International Documentary Association

"A superb addition to the 'how to' subsection of your library, Artis' tome is concise, while containing useful, accessible information on every aspect of documentary filmmaking, all with a doggedly hands-on attitude. Five stars."
—**Empire Magazine**

"The book is a very easy, straightforward read with plenty of graphics to demonstrate proper and improper techniques. It is also extremely user friendly in its layout . . . It will be helpful to you for many, many years to come."
—**Microfilmmaker Magazine**

"Anthony Artis has consolidated years of practical, professional experience into the quintessential blueprint for documentary filmmakers. I have used the techniques in this book on my documentary and narrative film projects, knowing that budget should never stop a filmmaker from seeing his or her vision through. I highly recommend this book if you want to turn your limitations into assets. Now shut up and shoot!"

—**Pete Chatmon,**
Writer/Producer/Director PREMIUM and 761st

"Plain and simple, nuts and bolts on making documentary films. It's told in a conversational manner with no wasted or minced words and, most importantly, no BS! Few books of this type would mention how important it is to take care of your crew and how that can dramatically improve the outcome of your film. Definitely told from an insider's point of view with useful and practical info that won't go over your head."

—Cliff Charles, DP,
When the Levees Broke,
ThePeoplesDP.com

"The practical approach promised in the title is delivered fully by the text. Artis exposes the pitfalls that can swallow a beginning filmmaker and offers straightforward advice to avoid them."

—Jonathan Luskin,
Flying Moose Pictures, San Francisco.

"The book is comprehensive and detailed. Indeed the most comprehensive practical (I do hate the word 'guerrilla', a filmmaker is surely at the end of the day just a filmmaker!) guide to documentary filmmaking I have ever come across! ... It has three principle outstanding qualities that you seldom find individually let alone together in the same book. The first is how comprehensive it is; the second is how intensely practical it is; and the third is how clear it is . . . But remember that this book will not tell you how to make a great film or indeed a good film. Or indeed even pretend to. But it will give you clear and practical guidance on how to make your film. And without such guidance it is hard to even get started. This book will help you do so much more than that!

—Nik Powell,
Director of the National Film and
Television School in London

"While focused first and foremost on documentaries, this is an utterly indispensable resource for anyone who wants to get their films made, on any budget . . . Smart, fun, and on your side, Shut Up and Shoot is packed with good stuff you'll otherwise have to learn the hard way."

—Bill Camarda,
from the December 2007 Barnes and Noble Newsletter

To Pete who helped to water this seed and to Maxie who helped to plant it. Watching you both do your thing up close gave me the courage to step out on a limb to do my own thing. (First one to the top, reach back.)

To Mom, Gwen, and Sharon, who all believed in me before I believed in myself. Thanks to my Dad for my twisted sense of humor. It's become an effective tool in my teaching toolkit.

I'm very thankful to all my filmmaking colleagues who agreed to be interviewed for the Down and Dirty DV Project. Thanks for sharing your expertise, wisdom, and time on this project. I learned so much from all of you in the making of this project. I know that so many others will do the same.

A big thanks to the entire NYU Tisch School of the Arts Production Center, faculty and administration, and the Doc Committee. Everyone's constant support, enthusiasm, helpful answers, and candid feedback inspired me to make this book a better tool for students. To Lou LaVolpe, your encouragement and advice have been invaluable.

Thanks to all the filmmakers and fans who crewed and modeled for the illustrations in this book. I couldn't have pulled any of this off without you all watching my back and making me look good every step of the way.

To my oldest friend, Darren Hackett, the man who introduced me to the film game and who was brave enough to take the first crack at editing this book in its roughest, self-published incarnation. Not only did you introduce me to filmmaking, but you showed me how to actually *be* a writer. (Shut up and write.) I will be eternally grateful for both.

To Dan "The Man" Shipp, we've come a long way from those all-night edit sessions for *Storybook Theatre*. Thanks for still having my back and still making me look good all these years later. I promise, the best is yet to come . . . and this time we're getting paid!

To Dave DiGioia, who taught me half of what I know and didn't even know he did. You've had an incredible impact on how I shoot, direct, and produce video. Not only did you school me to the video game, but you taught me how to be a video professional. And no, I ain't giving you any royalties, but you'll always have my eternal gratitude. Much love.

And of course I gotta thank my Focal Peeps for helping me pimp this book and get it out to the masses of the Down and Dirty DV Nation. Elinor, Rockin' Robin, Cara,

Dawnmarie, Joanne, Dennis, Peter, The Notorious Scotty B, Becky, Sheri, Big Jim and company, you guys are aaalllright! I appreciate the trust you gave me on this project and your putting up with all my changes and additions to additions.

To my literary agent, Jan Kardys, your sincere generosity, guidance, and support helped make this the best possible publishing experience. You're one of the people that give agents a *good* name. Thanks to you and all of my publishing peeps for pushing me to take this from a little, homemade, self-published book to a bona fide, worldwide, live publication. (This is why *we're* hot!) Much love and guerrilla gratitude. Let's keep putting out hotness.

So many other people have contributed to this project in ways big and small, tangible and spiritual, that it'd be impossible for me to name and thank them all here (although you wouldn't know it from the long list of credits). Please forgive me if I overlooked any of you in my rush to press. My coworkers, friends, and family have all been so incredibly supportive through the years that I've been *living* this project. I'm truly grateful and blessed to have such a film-family and family-family behind me.

Lastly, a special thanks to all the students I've instructed over the years and to all the fans who have stopped me in the street or reached out to me from all over the world to tell me how this book has helped their filmmaking. Cruce and Debra, Miguel, Lorien, Chip, Floyd, Steve, Vallerie, Susan and all the rest—people like you are the only reason I do this. I've learned as much as I've taught. And I've been inspired as much as I've inspired. You all help me remember why I got in this crazy business in the first place: I had no clue what I was getting myself into! LOL

So many of you have such a creativity, passion, and sincerity about filmmaking. It's been my main inspiration in writing this book and it's contagious. Hold onto that whatever you do. If you ever get lost along the way, just go back to the mindset you started with on that very first thrilling project and take it from there. I hope this book helps you somewhere on your filmmaking journey.

I love and thank each and every one of y'all. No joke.

CONTENTS

GETTING THE MONEY

GETTING THE GEAR

CHAPTER 4—LIGHTING 149

CHAPTER 5—SOUND RECORDING 183

SOUND TOOLS OF THE TRADE

RECORDING TECHNIQUES

MORE VISUAL STORYTELLING TOOLS

CHAPTER 7—INTERVIEW PREP 247

BEFORE THE INTERVIEW

MAKING THEM LOOK GOOD

WORKING WITH SUBJECTS

CHAPTER 8—CONDUCTING INTERVIEWS 264

INTERVIEW QUESTIONS

INTERVIEW TECHNIQUES

GETTING IT OUT THERE

THE CRAZY PHAT BONUS WEBSITE

www.focalpress.com/cw/artis

The Crazy Phat Bonus Website contains:

Link to Online Camera Guide
Sample Release Forms
Storyboards
Documentary Shoot Checklist
Craft Service Checklist
Live Event Gig Sheet
Warm Cards
Links to Resources
Video Tutorials
And More!

This Ain't Your Mama's Film Book

Since I first wrote this book at the height of "The DV Revolution", the state of filmmaking has evolved considerably. The revolution is over and digital video won. No longer the ugly step-child of film, video is now the Cinderella of the ball and everybody and their mama can now afford a decent camera. The problem of accessibility has been conquered. The new problem is that not everybody and their mama knows  how to make that camera "do what it do" (as the kids like to say) and tell a compelling visual story that looks and sounds professional. That's where this book comes in.

And so there's no confusion, let me be perfectly clear: This is not a book for people who want to *study* documentary filmmaking. This is a book for people who want to *make* documentary films—right here and right now. There are many good books that you should also read that cover the history, development, and nuances of documentary filmmaking in great depth. But this ain't one of those books. This book is for people who are done *talking* about the films they want to make and who are ready to shut up and shoot.

It's an ultra-user-friendly reference guide to basic documentary production from the technical specifics of camerawork, lighting, and sound to the practical intangibles of hustling up a crew, conducting interviews, and stealth shooting. While it's documentary specific, most of the advice and techniques in this book can be applied equally to narrative projects or event video. It's written casually with healthy doses of humor, lots of pictures, and all in plain English (with a little slang thrown in just for fun). In other words, this ain't ya mama's film book.

Why I Wrote This Book and Who I Wrote It For

As a young, broke film student I often found myself combing through thick and overwhelming film books with illustrations and terminology so advanced that it sometimes seemed like they were actually *trying* to confuse me. The equipment they showed was often beyond the reach and level of a novice. (That's a nice Ultra Max 5000 Crane—now could you teach me about something that costs *less* than half a million dollars that I might actually use on my film?!) Even more aggravating, the information that was most relevant to me was always scattered between a bunch of unnecessarily long words, technical terms, and crazy scientific diagrams that were completely over my head and mostly useless to me at that early stage.

I'd sometimes read the same paragraph three times over and *still* not get the concept or why it was important. (Granted, I wasn't the brightest kid in the class, but

I wasn't the slowest either, so I know I was not alone.) On the flip side, the less formal film books I bought were just too general and short on specifics to be of much use. Ultimately, I'd get frustrated and end up learning many concepts through the more painful process of trial and error for lack of a simple explanation that would help me get started.

I knew that there was a whole science and intricate technology behind everything and that as I specialized I might eventually have to learn the science behind terms such as "footcandles," "decibels," and the aptly named "circle of confusion," but I just didn't *care* in the beginning. It was a simple case of information overload. Starting out, I just wanted basic information to help me turn my ideas into films. I wanted straight, easy-to-find answers about the *core* things I needed to know to make my films look and sound more professional. I rarely found those answers and hardly ever in a single book. It didn't stop me from learning filmmaking in the end. It just forced me to learn many things the hard way.

Years later as a film instructor at NYU, speaker and production consultant, I began to train many students who were just as intimidated and confused as I was then. These novice filmmakers were making all the same mistakes I had once made, and they were suffering through all the same pains and frustrations that I had felt. They didn't lack intelligence or ability. What they lacked most was **simple, practical, beginner instruction** to give them a foundation (and sincere interest) in the more complex nuances of cinematography, storytelling, and filmmaking science. They were trying to cram the whole technical, historic, and philosophical aspects of filmmaking into their head all at once before they even shot a single frame of film or video. While some teachers still favor this approach, they fail to recognize that it just doesn't work for many students. And if it doesn't work for the *students* . . . it doesn't *work*.

So after years of talking about it, I finally shut up and wrote a book that breaks the complex process of filmmaking down into simple manageable, bite-sized chunks of practical instruction and advice for filmmakers of all budget levels who just want the specific basics to get them started. I have not tried to cram in every nuance of documentary or visual storytelling theory or even any pretense of film history in this text. This is just a clean and clear film production primer.

However, as best as I could, I've tried to illustrate everything, give step-by-step procedures, and offer all the practical advice and wisdom that I wish I had had at the start of my own filmmaking journey. Peppered throughout this book you will also find the candid advice of other notable and new documentary filmmakers that have "been there and done that," so that you might learn from even more people who have blazed the same trail.

The end goal of this book is to cut through the clutter to save you hours of heartache and countless dollars, and to enable you to successfully overcome the obstacles of filmmaking whether you are an aspiring film student looking to shoot your first project or a

This book provides simple practical beginner instruction in plain language and illustrations.

veteran filmmaker looking for a quick reference guide to some of the areas with which you're not as familiar. In short, this is an illustrated jump start for filmmakers who are ready to *execute* their vision now and don't have a lot of time to read between the lines.

The Down and Dirty Filmmaking Approach

What is "Down and Dirty" filmmaking? In the simplest terms, it's a filmmaking mindset that bucks the outdated idea of raising production value through bigger budgets and more expensive resources. If you've got the money, you can get more professional equipment and crew, but if you've got a Down and Dirty mindset, you can get more professional results from *any* equipment or crew.

When I first began to learn filmmaking in the early 90's, it was a struggle for me just to cover tuition, rent and living expenses. So pulling together a reasonable budget to shoot a film project on top of that was a real challenge. As a result, my budgets then were pretty sad—food for the crew, film stock, processing and a few necessary props, but not much else. As a result of being profoundly broke, I quickly learned to borrow, co-op, substitute, fabricate, replace, alter, trade, or cheat whatever resources I couldn't afford. Every dollar I spent was always "on the screen", because there simply wasn't enough money to put anywhere else. By necessity, broke filmmakers are often more resourceful filmmakers.

So, regardless of your budget level, I am all about maximizing your resources by teaching you how to enhance and get the best use out of the things you *do* have and *can* afford, and how to substitute or workaround the resources you don't have. It's about focusing all of your filmmaking efforts on improving the final result onscreen, rather than the tools and methods used to achieve it. It boils down to the fine art of doing more with less. Let me break it down in pictures:

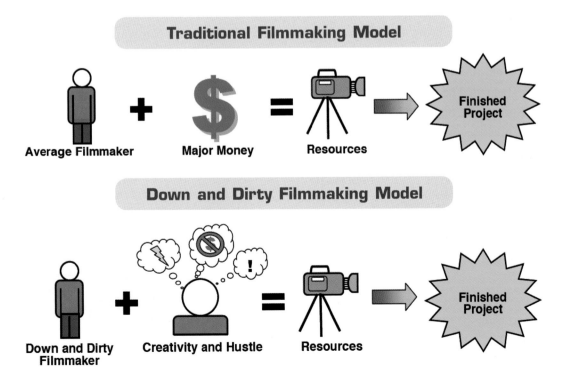

> *Down and Dirty DV's core principle: it doesn't take money to make films. It takes resources.*

The Down and Dirty DV Project

Much more than just this book, Down and Dirty DV is my personal labor of love. Everyone learns differently, and at the end of the day, filmmaking is a visual and hands-on process, so I've dedicated the last decade of my life to developing a variety of concise and easy-to-use instructional filmmaking resources that are both educational and entertaining. Apart from this book, I've written the follow up text *The Shut Up and Shoot Freelance Video Guide*, created a variety of filmmaking courses on lynda.com, released the *Indie Film Boot Camp* 6-DVD box set, and put out more than 80+ hours of candid filmmaking advice via my filmmakers podcast, *The Double Down Film Show*, so if you like what you read here check out even more resources on DownAndDirtyDV.com.

I've assembled all of these projects in my "spare" time. (Which is pretty much a joke since I was working full-time, have a wife and two energetic kids, and spent at least two hours commuting each day!) In the end, I had to write this book, co-host a podcast, and create video courses all the same way I shoot video—by being practical and maximizing my limited time and resources for all they're worth. More than half of this book was written guerrilla-style and underground (literally) on the subways of New York City during my daily commute. I sincerely hope you enjoy and learn from the effort. I've done my best to give you a solid jump start in the film game and help you avoid the most common mistakes that trip people up.

That's it. The back door to film school is now open. I hope you will enjoy this 2nd edition of *The Shut Up and Shoot Documentary Guide*. I've done my best to keep it real, practical, and helpful. It's my fondest wish that each and every person who reads this new edition of the book will be empowered to overcome the intimidation and obstacles to filmmaking (real and imagined) and successfully execute their vision as so many other aspiring filmmakers all over the world have already. Remember, the only thing that really matters is what's in your heart and what's on the monitor. Everything else is just static, baby.

Happy guerrilla filmmaking!

Peace, Love, and Video,
Anthony Q. Artis
Down and Dirty Filmmaker
8:40 a.m. Friday, Sept. 20, 2013
Manhattan-bound F-Train, New York City

Get Down and Dirtier...

- Film books, DVD's and online courses.

- Live training at your school or business.

- Camera buyer's guide, podcasts and blog.

DownAndDirtyDV.com

The first documentary I ever remember seeing was *Scared Straight* by Arnold Shapiro. It was about a program for juvenile delinquents that took groups of law-breaking teenagers into a state prison for a day to be "mentored" by a group of hardcore convicts serving minimum life sentences or longer. (I should point out here that prison mentoring is a *whole lot* different than regular old mentoring.)

I was about 9 or 10 years old and it was billed as a major TV event. They told parents to watch it with their kids. It was shown uncut and uncensored on primetime TV with a bunch of warnings about the language and subject matter. And it scared the living hell out of me! From that day to this, I largely credit that documentary for keeping me out of trouble with the law. It was the first of many docs that changed the way I came to look at the world around me. (Coincidentally, I ended up working for Arnold Shapiro two decades later, but I never got to go on a prison shoot. Bummer.)

I've always found documentary content to be more compelling than the fantasy narrative films that were offered up to me as a young person. You simply can't make up a narrative story that is as fascinating as films like *Scared Straight*, *Man on Wire*, or *The Devil's Playground*. And it's pretty hard to come up with characters that are as quirky and interesting as those in *The Cruise* and *American Movie*. And I think all the great screenwriters in the world would be hard-pressed to invent fiction that would move people and elicit as much emotion as films like *Lalee's Kin*, *When the Levee's Broke*, or *Grizzly Man*.

At the end of the day you can always dismiss powerful fiction as the work of someone's imagination or an exaggeration of the real events. Powerful *documentaries* on the other hand, grab you by the collar and force you to seriously contemplate societies, ideas, and human realities that you might otherwise never acknowledge or think twice about. (How would you know that right along side the gang culture of L.A. is a whole other underground culture of make-up-clad, clown dance groups who "battle" each other with hyperkinetic dance moves unless you saw the documentary *Rize*? . . . You wouldn't.)

In the best case scenarios, I truly believe this medium has the power to change the world–sometimes in big ways, but usually one person at a time, in a thousand little ways, from helping people confront their own serious illnesses (*A Healthy Baby Girl*), to showing urban communities a new way to break cycles of violence (*The Interrupters*), or helping people achieve personal fulfillment by examining the true meaning and source of happiness. (*Happy*). And to me, that's about as good as filmmaking gets–having a real impact on the real world. There's a big world out there in desperate need of understanding, change, and inspiration and documentary gives us the power to help make it happen. If not us, then who? . . . Look around you. We're *it*, baby! Time to shut up and shoot.

CHAPTER 1
PREPRODUCTION

Plenty of people have bright ideas. Plenty of people are geniuses, but will never know it, because they don't <u>execute</u>.

—Fat Joe
from the documentary **Paper Chasers**

Shut up and shoot.

—Anthony Q. Artis

Know this: Filmmaking is not magic or rocket science. All the crafts and practices of filmmaking can be learned. Pretty much anyone can be a filmmaker (or even a rocket scientist for that matter). All you've gotta do is *study and learn* what the task involves, then methodically do it, step-by-step, and at the end of the day you will have a film (or a rocket). Whether or not your first efforts take off is another story, but you will be well on your way to success if you study, practice, and–above all else–persist at it.

Filmmaking, especially in the digital age, is *constantly* evolving. The tools and practices of the industry are all continually changing and you need to stay up to be Down and Dirty. If you weren't in film school, once upon a time, it would've really sucked to be you, but right now you have many options in addition to film school to learn and hone the craft. I say use them all... You'll need them.

Film Books

You're already off to a great start with this book, but you need more books. In my personal filmmaking journey, books have been invaluable to expanding my knowledge and understanding of filmmaking. Film books come in many flavors and styles. Some are simply collections of inspirational filmmaking anecdotes, some are technical blueprints, some are more academic and philosophical, and others are in-depth case studies. I have found they all have something to offer. Ask fellow filmmakers what they recommend.

Film Books

(At DownAndDirtyDV.com you can find a collection of specific film books I recommend.)

DVD Extras

DVD extras are probably the best thing to happen to film education in a long time. It's truly miraculous that we can now stream movies–in HD even. But one thing that was lost in the trade-off are behind-the-scenes DVD extras. Whenever possible, try to watch the DVD versions of your favorite movies that include director commentary and other extras that detail the filmmaking process. Apart from telling you specifics about their production methods, you can learn a lot about how a real crew functions and how the film actually came together from idea to distribution. Moreover, many of these DVDs also contain storyboards, set and costume sketches, director's early

DVD Extras

works, research material, scripts, crew interviews, deleted scenes, and other previously unseen elements of the filmmaking process. Try watching a movie once, then look at the making-of documentary (doc) and all the extras, then watch it again with the director/crew commentary. After that, you'll never look at that film the same way again. Every time you look at it, it will be like taking a mini-film studies course.

Podcasts

The newest entry to filmmaking instruction is podcasting. If you're not down with podcasting yet, you really need to get down, because you're sleeping on some amazing free resources. In short, podcasts are audio and high-quality video clips that can be downloaded, saved, and played on your computer or your iPod or other portable media player. There is of course my own Double Down Film Show Podcast, which I highly recommend. And there are also many other great audio and video shows out there that can help you understand the filmmaking process, if not teach you in outright step-by-step lessons. The filmmaking podcasts out there include feature interviews, tutorials, call-in Q&As, news, Web links, interviews, product reviews, trailers, shorts, and even feature-length films. See the Resources section on the companion website for a list of filmmaking-related podcasts.

Podcasts

Workshops

In major cities all over the country there are filmmaking workshops, panels, and classes that will help you learn the craft of filmmaking. These range from scriptwriting classes to hands-on workshops to Q&A panels about industry issues. Time and price also vary from one hour to one year or free to thousands of dollars. There is something out there for everyone from kids to old-school video veterans. Filmmaking organizations typically sponsor panels and workshops, but there are also commercial and

Workshops

college workshops to help every level of filmmaker expand their skills and knowledge. Down and Dirty DV offers short guerrilla filmmaking workshops, but there are plenty of other workshops out there with different focuses. Poke around on the net, ask fellow filmmakers, and comb your local college course listings.

Online Learning Sites

One of the more recent learning resources to mature is the realm of online skills learning. Specifically sites such as Lynda.com, CreateLive and FilmSkills.com all offer in-depth tutorials on everything from DSLR shooting to editing and special FX software to how to light. If you like this book, I recommend you check out *my own* Fundamentals of Video courses on Lynda. com, which cover many of the same topics in this book.

Lynda.com

Instructional DVDs

Books are cool, but ultimately filmmaking is a visual process that's easiest explained in pictures. There are a number of DVDs out there (seemingly all with the subtitle "film school in a box") that will help walk you through the technical aspects of the filmmaking process step-by-step. From lighting tutorials to

Instructional DVDs

camerawork to non-linear editing, there's probably a DVD product out there to teach almost every aspect of filmmaking. If guerrilla is your style, check out the Down and Dirty DVD Series at DownAndDirtyDV.com.

Filmmaking Web Sites

There are endless filmmaking blogs and Web sites online. You can look up do-it-yourself (DIY) projects, case studies, articles, tutorials, get your filmmaking questions answered, join an online filmmaking community, research equipment and prices, and on and on. Sites such as Vimeo's Video School or CyberCollege.com offer free and low-cost

Web sites

filmmaking instruction in the form of online tutorials and instruction. See the Resources List on the companion website for more film-related Web sites.

Magazines

Magazines are a great way to stay down with the latest trends and practices of the industry: in-depth case studies, equipment reviews, tutorials, and interviews with today's filmmaking movers and shakers. Some mags, such as *StudentFilmmakers* and *DV*, are offered free to qualified people in the industry. As far as I can tell, qualifying usually involves giving up your e-mail address and filling out a brief survey once or twice a year. It's a fair trade-off and beats the cover price.

Magazines

Crewing

Any place where people are making films and videos is a great place to learn the process up close and personal. If you are willing to work for free, there are infinite opportunities to work on film and video crews. (I call this OPM Learning, because the only thing better than learning from your own mistakes is learning from Other People's Mistakes on Other People's Money.) Crewing is cheaper and less stressful and painful with many of the same first-hand learning benefits of working on your own film.

Crewing

More important, you will have informal teachers and you will meet and feel out people who you can later recruit to work on your own projects. I've worked for no money a hundred times over, but I've never worked on a project "for free" in my life. The knowledge, skills, and contacts I've acquired while helping fellow filmmakers with their efforts have been invaluable to me. I never think of it as *working* for free, but *learning* for free. In the best case scenarios where there is a real budget for crew and you have some experience under your belt, you will actually be getting paid to learn. Production Assistant, Craft Services, and boom operator are all excellent positions for observation. Check your local film organizations, college bulletin boards, and Web sites like Mandy.com or Craig's List for film crew announcements.

Doing

It doesn't matter whether you study all or none of the previous resources first, at some point you are going to have to actually make like Nike and *just do it*. This is the hands-down most effective way to learn. Don't worry that you don't know everything (you never will). Don't worry that you're not as good as that other kid (you will be later). Don't wait until you can afford a better camera (it's just a tool).

Doing

Don't worry that it's gonna suck (it probably will). Stop BS-ing yourself and everyone around you and just shut up and do it! The real learning process begins the moment you commit to a project and hit the record button. I've had one simple goal on every project I've shot, and that is to make it suck *less* than the last project. When you take this approach a magic thing happens over time . . . you go from sucky to mediocre to good and maybe, just maybe, if you take your video vitamins and say your prayers, someone will call your work "great." But you'll never know if you don't actually start doing it, screwing it up, and getting better at it. No professor, course, book, or DVD can teach you all the things you will learn by actually hitting the streets with a camera and doing it. Straight up. Guerrilla.

WHY MAKE A DOCUMENTARY?

ALBERT MAYSLES, DIRECTOR/DP

mayslesfilms.com

(Grey Gardens, Gimme Shelter, Salesman, Lalee's Kin, etc.)

Very simply put one of the great needs—maybe certainly one of the greatest needs in our world—is for us to know one another, to know what's really going on in the world around us and to feel a commonality of need and purpose with other people. People of different walks of life, other nations, other ethnic backgrounds, economic statuses, different philosophies, and religions . . . We need to find a common bond with the rest of humanity and the documentary allows us to do that. I think it's the most effective way of connecting with another person's life. You film somebody in a particular situation that is the same or different from that of the viewer, and that viewer feels a connection with that person and that person's experience—an engagement with the life around that person, who is the viewer. And it's what we need. As I think of it, it's a documentary filmmaker's way of making a better world.

If you go into documentary filmmaking, you are making a connection with life itself. And you have an opportunity to inform people in such a connective fashion. You know the word "entertainment" is an interesting one. A documentary is an entertainment, but not as a diversion, which is the first definition in entertainment, but in engaging. You're engaging that person by making a good documentary and that's a wonderful form of entertainment.

I've always had a great deal of confidence in the value and even in the eventual popularity of documentary as a form of filmmaking . . . Also, I've felt that eventually just as we say, "the truth will out," so there will be a very strong trend toward nonfiction, away from fiction, because the nonfiction has already within it a source of truth that is difficult for fiction to match. And so, that's what's happening now. There was a movement in the direction of documentary. I just hope that that movement flourishes and becomes stronger and stronger as people make good documentaries and we don't rely on so-called "reality television" and that way of recording reality in a way that's really kind of documentary, but not really.

Basic Steps of Documentary Preproduction

1. Brainstorm ideas and develop goal(s)
2. Research story
3. Choose interview subjects
4. Choose equipment package
5. Make budget
6. Write production plan
7. Hire crew

Introduction

A good shoot begins long before production with extensive preparation, otherwise known as **preproduction**. Carefully planning out what you will do and double-checking your equipment will help ensure that you get it right the first and perhaps *only* time. Proper preparation will also greatly boost your confidence when it's time to shoot, particularly if you're new to filmmaking. Just say the tongue-twister to the right three times and never forget it.

> ✔ *Proper preparation prevents a poor performance.*

Documentary Goal

Regardless of whether you're making a documentary feature, short, news story, reality show, or even shooting a wedding, you should always start with the same basic questions: What's the focus? Why are you making this project? What story do you want to tell? What topics will be explored? What information do you hope to convey to your viewers? What aspects of your topic are most compelling? Are there new angles to explore on your topic? In short, ask yourself what **story** do you want to tell and why? You should to be able to make a statement such as:

- I want to make a documentary about the birth of modern video games, because most people don't know the fascinating story behind the people who started it all.
- I am making a video project about the history of my church to inform new members and preserve the story of the founders for future generations.
- I am documenting the underground culture of squirrel fighting to expose the exploitation of rodents to a prime time news audience.

The primary purpose is for you to get a clear grasp of what it is you want to do, then gear everything else toward that goal. These are some of the first questions you should ask yourself, because your ultimate goal will affect many of your decisions during preproduction.

> ✔ *Determine the goal of your doc first in order to focus your preproduction in the right direction.*

Use the Internet, personal contacts, trade organizations, books, magazines, and newspapers to begin researching your topic, then track down potential interview subjects. If you don't spend a lot of time on the Web, you need to start. There simply is no single greater, cheaper, or more convenient source of *starting point* information for documentaries than the Internet.

Once you pick a topic, grab a cup of coffee and spend a few hours online scouring everything you can find. If you haven't already determined your goal or the focus of your documentary, this process will help you brainstorm and clarify exactly what aspect(s) of the broader topic you want to examine. The chart below illustrates just some of the information you could easily find on three diverse topics depending on where you decide to look.

	SKATEBOARDING	POLITICS	DEATH PENALTY
News Web Sites	■ Products ■ Recent events ■ Photos/video ■ Major skaters	■ Recent events ■ Major figures ■ Photos/video ■ Upcoming events	■ Statistics ■ Upcoming executions ■ Photos/video
Personal Web Sites	■ Tricks and tips ■ Most popular skaters ■ Fan perspective	■ Public opinion ■ Activist movements ■ Upcoming events	■ Pro/con activists ■ Protests ■ Essays
Blogs and Podcasts	■ Fan perspective ■ Tricks and tips ■ Popular products	■ Latest rumors ■ Insider info ■ Public opinion	■ Public opinions ■ Inmate POVs ■ Advocate POVs
Trade/Professional Organizations	■ Upcoming events ■ New developments ■ Pro skater perspective	■ Organizations' political stance ■ Upcoming events ■ New initiatives	■ Law enforcement opinion ■ Statistics

Also check a *major* public library and sites like Amazon.com or Netflix.com to see what films and books already exist on the topic and what approaches have been taken to the material in the past. Try to gauge what was successful and why. Did these previous works exhaust the subject or are there still new angles, stories, and perspectives to be mined?

> ✔ *Remember — the Internet is just a <u>starting</u> point for brainstorming and research.*

THE IMPORTANCE OF RESEARCH

It's important that you try to keep an open mind during this phase of preproduction. You want to gather all the potential directions you could take before settling on an approach. Once you've done your preliminary "brainstorming" and research you'll be ready to further define exactly what your documentary should and should not cover.

By mentally separating the normal from the extraordinary in your observations, you will know what's interesting and worth shooting and what's routine and boring. Potential characters, themes, and, most important, *stories* will begin to emerge. Think about how these will play onscreen. Has the general public seen these stories and people before? From what angle were they presented? Is there enough compelling material to hold an audience's interest? What *new* ideas or questions will you examine in your doc?

Research is simply forming the answer to these questions *before* you dive in. If you skip this vital step, you may easily find yourself wasting countless hours and budget dollars pursuing people, themes, and events that will never see the light of day. The better you know your story ahead of time, the more focused and successful your efforts will be.

I know fellow filmmakers who have spent months shooting hours of video of some subject only to discover in the end that the material has no useful or coherent narrative thread. There is no focus, no compelling new info, no real characters . . . no story. All they have is some bits and pieces of interesting footage that don't add up to Jack. (And you know his last name!)

PREPRODUCTION   9

✔ *Research and study your topic beforehand to determine which aspects are most worth shooting.*

RESEARCH AND FACT CHECKING

SAFIYA SONGHAI, PRODUCER/JOURNALIST

safiyasonghai.com

(Diamonds: The Price of Ice) and Assoc. Prod. (Brown vs. Board of Ed.)

The main thing with researching documentary is to not approach it like you did your senior English paper. Don't just *stay* on the Internet and think that those are sources that are reliable, because many times they're not . . . How do you present something and say, "This is official. This is true?" Now you might have one professor at a prestigious university who states something as fact. Don't take that as the whole truth and stick with that one man's approach to it. You can present it, but you definitely have to show a balanced picture.

The best way to do research is to just take a camcorder and go to as many people as you have access to and really just interview them. First person primary sources are the best way to make sure that your information is valid and is truly coming from the horse's mouth.

In addition to that, just make sure if they offer statistics, that you can back up those statistics. If someone says, "35% of the people do X" you can go and dig up that information in journals, in newspapers . . . If they're saying that 35% of women who have this problem are XYZ, then you have to go find that. And if you can't find it, you can choose to let the statement stand as is, but you should let the audience know that you weren't able to find evidence of that subject's assertion. Because many times people know that their authority and their expertise will make it so they can say anything and you're not going to research it. You really just have to follow up with reliable sources.

You have to look at their standards for journalistic excellence or fact finding in particular periodicals or any type of media. People can be very convincing in their accounts. You may be listening to their story thinking, "Man, this is amazing! This is gold!" You just have to research and dig deeper to make sure that the gold that you have is not *fool's* gold.

INTERVIEW SUBJECTS

The people you select to appear onscreen will ultimately make or break your documentary. Choosing interview subjects is to documentary productions what casting is to **narrative filmmaking**. The only difference is that docs have *real* characters instead of character actors.

A compelling character can really make a project. In fact, many of the most successful documentaries are **character studies**. *American Movie* (about a filmmaker), *Crumb* (about a comic strip artist), and *The Cruise* (about a NYC tour guide/poet) are all notable documentary character studies. All of these docs are built around the unique perspective of a compelling central character. These docs would be entirely different creations if they were to just focus on their respective general subject matters: filmmaking, comic strips and tours of New York City without the unique perspective of these colorful individuals. You can't separate the two and still have the same film, if you'd even have a film left at all.

But don't get it twisted. You can't just point your camera at someone interesting and make a good character study doc. You still need to manage structure, pacing, story development, and approach the same as you would for any other doc, but the most important core element will always be the character(s) at the center of it all.

While your project may not be a character study per se, the people you ultimately choose to speak on your topic are still equally crucial to the success of your doc. The better your subjects communicate and express themselves verbally, the more articulate and interesting your piece will be. So what else makes for a good interview subject?

The Ideal Character/Interview Subject

- ❏ Candid and forthcoming
- ❏ Able to speak coherently about topic
- ❏ Unique perspective
- ❏ Knowledgeable about topic
- ❏ Passionate about topic
- ❏ A recognized expert
- ❏ Clear viewpoint

If you can check off three or more of the above, you've probably got a decent candidate on your hands. If you crap out and choose a poor character, it only means you've wasted your time, and resources and you'll have to find another subject or cut that segment from your finished piece. You may have plenty of hard drive space, but time and resources are always limited. Research and choose wisely.

✔ *Choose interview subjects who are compelling and knowledgeable about your topic.*

EXPOSITORY

- ❏ Attempts to persuade
- ❏ Strong viewpoint
- ❏ Omniscient narration
- ❏ Images support the words

Examples

When the Levees Broke, Too Big To Fail

OBSERVATIONAL

- ❏ Filmmaker is just observer
- ❏ Little to no narration
- ❏ No direct interviews
- ❏ Usually minimal crew

Examples

Grey Gardens, Brick City, Banging in Little Rock, Senna

PARTICIPATORY

- ❏ Attempt to persuade
- ❏ Often personality driven

Examples

Super-size Me, Bowling for Columbine, Blue Vinyl, Paper Chasers

DRAMATIC

- ❏ Often have recreations
- ❏ Uses actors and narration
- ❏ Narrative style lighting

Examples

Man on Wire, The Thin Blue Line, Slavery by Another Name, Zoo

APPROACH AND STORYTELLING

The one thing that separates documentaries from each other, especially those dealing with the same subject matter, is **approach**. Approach is just a general term that refers to how you choose to tell the story on screen. What tone, storytelling techniques, and elements will you use? For example, will the subject of your documentary read narration or will you hire an actor? Or will you forego narration entirely and use **screen captions** to tie elements of your story together? Or will you just let the action speak for itself without any embellishment?

Will you be an onscreen character in the documentary like Michael Moore (*Fahrenheit 9/11*) or Morgan Spurlock (*Supersize Me*)? Will there be re-enactments in your piece? If so, how will they be stylized to distinguish them from the rest of your footage? Are you going to include an animated segment? Will your doc be shot "naturally" with no artificial lighting? The answers to all of these questions will form your doc's *approach*.

Your combined storytelling choices such as using animation, titles, color, shooting style, etc. all make up your approach.

Think it out. Experiment. Look at other documentaries and analyze how different filmmakers approached their subject. The possibilities are as endless as your imagination. Even though there have been countless documentaries on Tupac or teen pregnancy or corporate pollution (often using much of the same source material), yours can be made compelling and unique with a new *approach*. The story may have been told before, but you have your own perspective, focus, and a unique voice that the world has never heard before. Your storytelling style *is* your approach. It may include any of the following or more. Mix and match, research, and invent new ways to tell your story.

> ✔ Decide on an approach and storytelling techniques that are most effective for your material and style.

What's Your Approach?

- ❏ Narration (*Fahrenheit 911*)
- ❏ Reenactments/recreations (*The Civil War*)
- ❏ Animation (*Bowling for Columbine*)
- ❏ Direct or natural cinema (*Grey Gardens*)
- ❏ Filmmaker as part of story (*Paper Chasers*)
- ❏ Interviews (*The Fog of War*)
- ❏ Confessionals to camera (*Blue Vinyl*)
- ❏ Archival footage (*Eyes on the Prize*)
- ❏ Archival photos (*4 Little Girls*)

CONCEPT AND STORYTELLING

SAM POLLARD, PRODUCER/EDITOR
(4 Little Girls, Jim Brown All-American, Eyes on the Prize II, When the Levees Broke, etc.)

As a producer, part of my job is to figure out what the material is, which is all in my head. So, now I have to translate all these ideas from my head to communicate to a cameraperson and a sound person to shoot that stuff . . . Really, the ideas, the concepts are all in my brain, as a producer, and I have to make them become real when someone goes out to shoot the material . . .

The key thing as a documentary producer is to develop the concept. To find the subject is number one. Then after you find the subject, what's the concept? What's the theme that this subject is going to help you tell? The third thing is, how to tell the story. What is the story and how to tell it?

So, for example, I'm leaving on Tuesday to go to Minnesota to shoot on a pig farm, with a lady and her husband. The lady's a singer and the husband's a farmer. So, I have to figure out what the story is. The story is how they met, their lives on the farm, the pros and cons of her singing career, and being married to this farmer who has this very big farm. So, that's the story I'm gonna tell. I have to figure out what to visualize to help tell that story. Okay, so I'm gonna go out and shoot the pig farmer early in the morning feeding the pigs, sunrise, the waving fields, planting corn, planting soybeans. Then parallel, back at the house, the wife is rehearsing, practicing her singing, playing the piano, and warbling to the mirror.

Then, maybe there's a scene with the husband and the wife together out in the fields; then, an interview with both of them in the house; then, single interviews with each individual so I can get their own particular, personal backstories. It's good to shoot stills, if they have scrapbooks, pictures of them together and them separately . . . , so I'm thinking about the story and how to visualize it.

THE PRODUCTION PLAN

Once you determine the goal and approach of your piece, you can begin to put together a **production plan**, which includes all of the specific elements you will need to realize your documentary. The production plan simply answers the overall question: "How can I make this happen?" To answer this big question, start with your goal then ask yourself a series of smaller questions such as:

1. What specific aspects of the topic should be covered?
This will determine your sources and depth of **research**.

2. Who is most qualified to speak on this topic?
This will determine your choice of **interview subjects**.

3. Where does the action of this topic take place?
This will affect your choice of **locations**.

4. How will I tell this story? Style? Structure?
This will determine your **approach**.

5. Where will this documentary end up? Theaters? TV? DVD?
This will help determine your **equipment package**.

6. Who will I need to help me make it?
This will dictate the size of your **crew**.

. . . and all of these questions will affect your **budget**. So when all is said and done, your production plan should contain specifics on:

❏ **Research**
❏ **Interview subjects**
❏ **Locations**
❏ **Approach/style**
❏ **Budget**
❏ **Crew**
❏ **Equipment package**

Armed with this information, you will have a clear blueprint for producing your documentary and formulating a budget. Now you are ready to begin to make it happen.

> ✔ *Prepare a production plan that spells out all the elements needed to make your doc happen.*

HOW TO RAISE MONEY

HINTS FOR EMBARKING ON THE FUNDRAISING JOURNEY
MICHELLE COE

The original version of this article was published in The Independent Film and Video Monthly.

Probably the most common can-of-worms question pressing the emerging filmmaker is, How do I find money for my film? It's never a simple question to answer, since film/video funding and financing involves a lot of time, research, skill, and perseverance. As competitive as the market is today, there is money out there, and with a little creative thinking it just might be yours.

The term "fundraising" implies that funds are given to you with no expectation of a financial return or ownership in the project. Sources include grants from government (federal, city, state) agencies or arts councils, private foundations and corporate giving programs, as well as those from individual donors. Film "financing," on the other hand, involves lenders who expect a financial return or ownership of rights to the project on a certain level. Some forms of financing might include individual investments, foreign or domestic pre-sales to distributors, licensing fees from broadcasters, and co-productions with studios or other production companies.

Determine Your Approach
Things to Consider:

Your project. Do you have a commercial feature film, or a social issue documentary? Narrative feature films usually have a difficult time obtaining grants; and short films often cannot compete in the marketplace to warrant investors.

Your timeline. If you intend to apply for grants, their funding cycle may not coincide with your production timeline. Developing trust with individual donors or investors takes time as well, unless you have someone else making those connections for you. Truthfully, any form of money-raising is going to take time, so be sure to allow for it.

Your "Fundability" or "Salability"
Does your project have commercial appeal to a broad audience that would do well in the marketplace and thereby attract investors? Is there a social issue angle that some nonprofit foundations would embrace? Do you have a prior project, or track record, that demonstrates success?

Get to Know Your Project
One of the most difficult steps in the fundraising process can be describing what your film is about. Even if you have a script and the story is clear: how do you compellingly convey not just what happens, but the underlying issues that the film presents? In short: why is your film important and unique and why, within the overcrowded marketplace of media, will audiences want to see it? Then, how will you assure prospective donors that it will actually be made—and seen?

Whether you apply for grants or approach individual donors or investors, the better presented your project is the greater the likelihood you'll end up with a check. While each funder or company requires specific elements they need to know about your film, every project should have the basics:

- a synopsis (three versions: one-line, one paragraph, and detailed)
- a detailed treatment (basically, a plan of how the story will visually be told)
- bios of key personnel
- the project's budget
- a fundraising plan
- a distribution plan
- a sample reel of past work and/or footage of the project
- the script (if applicable)

It is very important, even in this early stage, to consider where your project will ultimately end up. While a theatrical release or broadcast on HBO may be your goal, the truth is many projects are never picked up for distribution. Don't limit your project's life by not addressing how you will reach your audience if the project does not get sold to a major company. The people supporting your project—be "they" a foundation or an investor—will want to know this, and being prepared will only make you a more attractive prospect.

Helpful Hints
Be Concise. Writing that synopsis may be a difficult task, but if it's too wordy or doesn't get to the point, you may lose some people.

Assemble a Strong Team. Bringing on a producer with a track record may improve your chance of actually getting the grant; emerging artists are more of a risk. An accomplished producer or a board of advisers can assure a funder that the project will see completion and look professional.

Note Your Successes. It's important to mention other grants or contributions already received. Commitments from other entities or individuals are always reassuring to a prospective contributor.

Think of the Bigger Picture. Why is it important that your project be made? Why are you the one to make this film? Why should the funder, out of all of the applications they have received, support this particular project?

If your writing skills (grants or otherwise) are not strong, seek an experienced grantwriter or producer to help fine-tune things. Your local film organization will likely have membership directory or règumè bank to consult.

Determine the Fit: Who to Ask, Where to Send It

Nonprofit Fundraising: Foundations & Government Grants
Do your research carefully. There are a number of arts-oriented private foundations as well as state and city arts and culture grants that fund film and video projects, but they are extremely competitive, and even then the grants only cover a small portion of the project's costs. But here is where you need to think outside the box. Understanding your project inside and out can help you emphasize certain social angles to which a private foundation might respond: while they may not specifically fund media, they do have a mission statement that your project in some way may fulfill. Study the foundation's website and read their guidelines carefully.

Once you're confident that your project is a match, determine the best way to approach them. Some funders are open to phone call inquiries, others ask for a brief Letter of Inquiry, in which you introduce yourself and your project, and state how it fits into their funding goals. Others may just instruct you to complete their downloadable application and submit by the next deadline. Never write a generic proposal and send it out randomly. Proposals must be tailor-made to fit the funder's mission.

Fiscal Sponsorship

Most foundations will only fund nonprofit organizations, so if this is the route you plan to take, you will likely need to align yourself with a fiscal sponsor, or an organization that will lend their 501(c)(3) IRS tax-exempt status to your project. Not only are you eligible for most grants, but you now offer a huge incentive for individual donors: a tax write-off on their contribution. A number of film organizations are set up to offer this service to artists. (To clarify: The organization does not produce the film, nor do they own the copyright. Being sponsored by a nonprofit also does not mean you cannot eventually sell—or profit from—the film.)

Your fiscal sponsor can lend your project credibility, especially if you are a first-time filmmaker. Ultimately, you should choose an organization whose mission matches yours and who you think might be able to bring other resources to the project: Can they assist with crew or suggest interview subjects? Can they help promote the film in their newsletter? Can they provide a venue for meetings or events? Do they have equipment rentals, or even mentorship programs?

Take the Money, But Only If . . .

Once you've gotten a contribution or grant, be sure you know what is expected of you in return. Fundraising guru Morrie Warshawski advises clear communication with donors, and reading the fine print. "[While a granting agency] may not expect financial return, they may have other expectations for other types of things (i.e., free DVDs, a mention in the credits, etc.)" He notes that the lines between financing and fundraising are beginning to blur: "Some donors, like the National Endowment for the Humanities, ask that you pay back that grant if you see a profit; others, like ITVS, are not grants at all but have an application process similar to that of a grant."

Where to Find Them

The Foundation Center (foundationcenter.org)—A comprehensive resource of grants and funding entities online, in print, and in person through facilities (New York, Washington, DC, Cleveland, San Francisco) and Cooperating Collections Networks in other US cities.

Your local media arts center or film organization—They often post deadlines for grants, both local and national. They may also offer equipment/services grants. Also, if you're shooting your film in another city, out-of-town productions may be eligible for local grants, provided you use local crew and resources.

Approaching Individual Donors

Most independent films (in fact, every first film) would not have been made without the help of friends and family, in cash donations as well as in-kind goods and services. With grants getting tougher to come by, this cannot be stressed enough. People support people, not just projects. Know who believes in you, and start from there.

You can approach individuals though donor appeal letters via mail and email, by having your supporters host fundraising house parties, and by presenting benefit events. Some people who end up donating to your project might work for companies that offer matching gifts: the amount that they donate to your project (via your fiscal sponsor) will be matched—in some cases by 3 to 1!

Helpful Hints

Keep Events Simple and Affordable. While events are a great way to raise awareness about the project, they can take up a major amount of time and resources. Work with your community to get items donated (i.e. the venue, food and drink, printing of invites, etc.). Otherwise, any income will be used to pay off the event, as opposed to help pay for your project.

Be Patient. Once you send out a donor appeal letter or have a few meetings, donations may not rush in right away. Don't be discouraged; checks may come unexpectedly to you in the mail over the next few weeks, even months.

Stay in Touch. Be sure to send out regular announcements to keep everyone abreast of your project's progress—you wouldn't be doing this without their support! Fundraising is not just about money, but about building a community of people who have (at least) one thing in common: their enthusiasm for your film and for you.

Reality Check: Be Prepared to Support Your Own Project. More than likely you will be the one contributing the majority of funds to your project, so try to save as much money as you can before moving forward.

Financing Through Individual Investors

Individual donors and investors are often found via personal relationships and word-of-mouth. A donor who gives to your project may know of other prospective donors and may pass your name along to them.

An investor will make a contribution or buy a share of the film's equity, and some may require involvement in negotiating the sale of the film, or that they play more of an executive producer role. Film is generally a very risky investment, and individuals may find they can benefit more from a tax break on a sizeable donation than they could on an investment of a film that, due to unpredictable market and audience demands, may never be sold or make a sizeable profit. To lessen the risk, an investor may also have certain demands of the project before they actually invest (i.e. attachments such as "name" talent, a distribution deal, etc.).

Be sure all expectations and conditions are clearly outlined in a contract before any money is exchanged. Here is where having a reputable entertainment attorney is a must. You will need to set up legal entity (limited liability corporation, limited partnership, sole proprietorship, etc.) and draw up necessary contracts. Contact your local film organization for referrals.

Industry Financing

Never randomly send out your project proposal or script. Always make contact ahead of time. Some production companies or broadcasters won't accept unsolicited material and require that an agent or lawyer send it in. Others ask for a one-page query letter detailing your project, including a brief synopsis and a description of any attached elements such as financing, cast, and key personnel.

You can also approach a sales agent or a producer's representative to take on the project. The rep assesses the feasibility of pre-sales, co-production or other forms of financing through broadcasters, distributors and production companies, domestically and abroad, and will pitch the project on your behalf. Most agents or reps will work on a percentage basis, and some will work on more of a for-hire basis with fees to be paid upfront.

Attending industry markets and events (i.e. the IFP Market, the Sundance Film Festival) can provide essential access to production company executives and sales reps. Submitting your project to competitive opportunities (i.e. screenplay contests, director and producer labs, etc.) can also open a few more doors: you get to develop your project under the guidance of accomplished professionals, and the project gets some great publicity and validation.

Where to Find Them

Browse industry trades (Variety, Hollywood Reporter). Subscribe to indiewire.com, which provides daily online coverage of the business of independent film. Pay special attention to a film's credits: what companies have their name on films you admire? Visit company and agency websites, and rent the films they're attached to.

Internet Movie Database (imdb.com) lists films and key personnel. Like what one producer did with a particular film? Look them up on IMDB to see what else they've done.

The Hollywood Creative Directory (hcdonline.com) lists production and financing companies, including names of development executives. It's published three to four times per year, online and in print. The Blu Book is another one of their directories, listing production companies as well as service providers and vendors.

National membership organizations such as the IFP (ifp.org, also regional chapters), Film Independent, or FIND (filmindependent.org), the IDA (documentary.org) as well as regional organizations in major cities, such as Women in Film (various cities), Film Arts Foundation in San Francisco (filmarts.org) or Austin Film Society (austinfilm.org) are great resources and offer amazing programs and support systems for filmmakers.

Make the Most of "No"

Raising money is an unpredictable process. Even if you've gained the support of a foundation's program officer or you're a favorite of a wealthy relative, there's no guarantee. Funders and financiers have missions to fulfill and limited resources. They may well like your project but not have the means to support it. Try not to take rejection personally.

If your project is eventually rejected, try to get feedback from the review committee or donor: the decision may have been made due to lack of clarity in your proposal and you may be able to resubmit at a later date. Or the funder may not be willing to fund the actual production of your project, but you may be able to go back to them once you approach the distribution phase.

Sometimes "no" means "not yet." In the case of attempting to obtain funding from ITVS (the Independent Television Service), the average filmmaker has applied four times! But that was after numerous conversations with their program officers and carefully considering the review committee's comments.

That said, make the movie YOU want to make. But know that you may have to re-think some of the film's elements in order to secure significant funding—and that's not necessarily a bad thing, as some changes are for the better of the film. On the other hand, some filmmakers have turned down large sums of money because they felt that what the funder required would ultimately compromise their vision. (It is a business, after all.) That's why it's so important that you know your project inside and out, and are clear about your goals—both for your film and for your career.

Hopefully this attempt to give you a little information over a vast terrain has provided both insight and inspiration. Movies are being made every day, but well-executed stories with unique vision are hard to find. Your job now is to let those with deep pockets know that yours is one of the good ones.

Recommended Reading

Dealmaking in the Film and Television Industry, Mark Litwak

Film & Video Financing, Michael Wiese

Filmmakers and Financing: Business Plans for Independents, Louise Levison

Fiscal Sponsorship: 6 Ways to Do It Right, Gregory Colvin

43 Ways to Finance Your Film, John Cones

The Foundation Center's Guide to Proposal Writing

The Fundraising House Party: How to Get Charitable Donations from Individuals in a Houseparty Setting, Morrie Warshawski.

The Grassroots Fundraising Book: How to Raise Money in Your Community, Joan Flanagan

Risky Business: Financing and Distributing Independent Film, Mark Litwak

Shaking the Money Tree: How to Get Grants and Donations for Film and Video Projects, Morrie Warshawski.

Filmmaker Magazine, published by the Independent Feature Project

Michelle Coe has worked in the worlds of independent film and theatre for more than 12 years, including production, distribution, and artist support services. She has directed programs for national film organization AIVF, administered the McKnight Screenwriting Fellowship, presented numerous events at film festivals, including Sundance, served on funding review panels and screening committees (New York State Council on the Arts; Global Film Initiative; PBS' nonfiction showcase, P.O.V.), and has worked on various film and theatre productions. Until recently she managed the Production Assistance Program at Women Make Movies, and has now segued into the performing arts as an Artist Representative for dance and theatre companies at Pentacle in New York. She continues to consult on film projects. Contact her at: michellecoefundraise@gmail.com.

Budget Forms

One of the easiest ways to start a budget is by simply filling in the blanks on a pre-made film/video budget form (like the one you can download from the bonus website for this book). There are also a few film/video budgeting software programs available online as freeware or reasonably priced cloudware, such as Celtx.

Budgeting Software

Filmmakers have been budgeting movies without software for decades with no problem, but today's budgeting software gives you much greater flexibility to make quick changes, share, and examine different budget scenarios. However, it doesn't really matter whether you use comprehensive budget software like **Movie Magic Budgeting** or **Gorilla Scheduling and Budgeting** or just fill in the blanks of a previously existing budget that was used on another project–the important thing is that your budget form includes *every possible expense* that may occur in making your project. Use whatever works best for you. Just make sure you include everything.

Estimating Costs

Once you have your production plan in place you will be able to break down your shoot into production elements such as locations, travel, equipment, etc. You can *estimate* a good chunk of your budget just by researching online. Bookmark or otherwise compile the **rate cards** and contact info you find online so you can easily find them again when needed. The rest will require a few phone calls and e-mails to get specific vendor quotes. Anyone selling or renting equipment will be more than happy to send you a price list. Contact vendors directly and ask if you can't find it online.

Costs for equipment can vary widely depending on the source and region of the country. Shop around to get the best prices. Rate cards are not carved in stone. Almost always, you can negotiate better rates for longer rentals or rentals during off times such as the dead of winter or holiday weekends. Keep in mind, as with anything else, *price alone does not tell the whole story*. If you're dealing with rental houses you should take customer service, equipment condition, availability of latest equipment, convenience, and reputation all into consideration as well. Carefully scrutinize and ask questions about any price that seems too good to be true—it almost always is. The best source for rental house info is always other filmmakers.

✔ Make sure your budget form includes all expenses. You can estimate many items by researching online.

When it comes right down to it, budgeting is an exercise in guesswork. But there is a difference between blind guessing, as in the lottery, and educated guessing, as in the stock market. Nobody knows what lottery ball will pop up, but with stocks you can see certain things coming if you know what to look for. It's the same with guerrilla filmmaking. Here are some things to look out for when trying to balance your budget:

4 COMMON BUDGETING MISTAKES

1 EXCLUDING OR DISCOUNTING ITEMS YOU *HOPE* TO SECURE

Your roommate's boyfriend is a camera operator for a production house and while you're out for drinks he says he can get you a free HD Varicam for a weekend, but a week before production, he has no idea what you're talking about and says he can't do it . . . The principal of the elementary school said you can shoot there for free, but the day before the shoot the school board president calls you demanding a $500/day location fee . . .

These are what I call "phantom freebies" and they can easily send your production into a panicked tailspin. The bottom line is unless you are extremely positive that this is a sure thing, done deal, rock-solid agreement, you should leave that item in your budget at full price. Whenever possible, try to get things on paper or save a trail of e-mail conversations so there's no confusion about what you're getting, when you're getting it, and how much it will cost you. The closer you get to production without these great deals and favors fully secured, the harder it will be to change course and get another camera or school or whatever it was you planned on getting for free or at a discount. Don't let your budget be led astray by the siren call of "free" or "cheap" unless you're confident. Once it's secure, *then* you can move that money elsewhere in the budget.

2 NOT INCLUDING ENOUGH CONTINGENCY MONEY

Your contingency is your "what if" money. It's your all-purpose slush fund for unexpected things that happen during production or items that run over their estimated budget. Unexpected things will ALWAYS

15%

happen in filmmaking and it's a pretty sure bet that at least one category of your budget WILL run over. I can't overemphasize how important it is to keep some contingency money in the budget on standby. Don't make the amateur mistake of eliminating your contingency as a line item to balance your final budget. If you're truly desperate and the numbers still don't add up, you can cut that 15% figure down to as little as 10%, but anything less than that is opening the door to hasty compromises and a potential production shut down.

3 NOT CREATING ALTERNATE BUDGETS

Films rarely have one budget. There's the 35 mm film budget, the shooting on location in Paris and London budget, the DSLR camera budget, the budget with name actors, the budget with unknown actors, etc. Each of these budgets represents an alternate production scenario based on unfolding events and access to money and resources. Once you write out your initial budget, you should then save alternate versions with different sets of line items based on all the likely scenarios. The only thing these budgets need to have in common is the grand total. Making alternate budgets further forces you to consider the true production value of each resource. They are also invaluable to your decision making if you do suddenly have to change your production plan.

4 OVERLOOKING A HUNDRED "LITTLE THINGS"

Remember, the budgeting process is essentially brainstorming *every* cost you're going to incur to make your shoot happen. Every cost includes all those "little things" that new filmmakers often overlook, such as the cost of taxes, permits, cab fare, photocopies, cell phone charges, insurance, overtime meals, and on and on. All

these "little things" can add up quickly and eat away at your precious contingency if they're not in the original budget. You can find numerous examples of documentary budgets online at filmmaking sites like itvs.org, wmm.com, documentary.org and sundance.org. Just because it seems insignificant or you don't write it down, doesn't mean you don't have to pay for it. Estimate what it will cost and put it in there.

RAISING THE M-O-N-E-Y

ROSE ROSENBLATT & MARION LIPSCHUTZ PRODUCERS/ DIRECTORS

(The Education of Shelby Knox, The Abortion Pill)

Both: M-O-N-E-Y . . . That's by far the hardest thing.

Rose: Everything else is a piece of cake.

Marion: The only positive thing I can say about raising the money is that by the time you're making the film, it's been put through a real vetting process because somebody's decided to give you the money, usually a couple of people, and you've had to really prove that it's a good enough idea and planned it out, but . . . We'll launch things with a grant, or a couple of grants because everybody needs to see footage these days, like commercial [media outlets], and by that I mean cable or HBO or any of those places. They usually want to see footage before they'll commit money. And the trick is how do you get footage? And footage means, unless it's an amazingly compelling character or you've got great access, they want to see that *story*. So it's a tough thing to raise enough money to get the story far enough along to show it to people . . . 'Cause it's such an old Hollywood joke. How do you raise the money? Uh . . . persistence. That's one of the most critical things. It's practice, practice, practice. Persistence really is such a key ingredient. Also knowing when to give up, knowing when, "I've persisted with this idea, I've gone to every place I can think of, I've embedded myself in the network of people who care about this." That's very important because, certainly if you're raising money from foundations the people who are gonna give you money aren't filmmakers, but they're experts in the subject you're making your film on.

Rose: And I learned this, and I don't know if there's a short cut, but it's this idea of appropriateness. You think you have a great idea and you go to a person who couldn't possibly fund that because that's not what they're supposed to be funding. And you think, "It's such a great idea and it's a great movie, and you fund movies, you should fund this!" You take this rejection so to heart. But you have to really know who you're going to and what they're about and there's this thing called a mandate, which [means] they're supposed to fund films on this topic. Don't bring them films on another topic like disabilities if they're funding the environment. There's no way they're gonna fund you. You gotta do your homework.

10 WAYS TO LOWER YOUR BUDGET

1 ### GET FREE OR INEXPENSIVE EQUIPMENT

One of the easiest things you can do to shave some dollars off the bottom line is to beg, borrow, or maneuver your way into the equipment you need for your project.

Free or inexpensive equipment is all around you. You just have to sniff it out. If you find a DP, crew member, or friend with their own equipment or access to equipment, you can: (a) barter for their services, (b) borrow or offer to rent their equipment, (c) negotiate a good rate for them *and* their equipment. Some might even do it for cost if they like your project. The other route is to *maneuver* your way into a free equipment situation. Hands-on filmmaking programs are one way, but there are also multiple jobs at TV stations, film/video rental houses, colleges, production companies, and in corporate video departments where you (or a very close friend) may borrow equipment as a standard perk. Imagine that. You can actually get paid to borrow the equipment you need for your project. Now *that's* resourceful filmmaking! (Also see "Hot Tip: Educational Equipment Access" on page 79.)

2 ### GET FREE OR INEXPENSIVE CREW

Low-cost or free crews are pretty common for personal projects with tight budgets. Look for people who are serious and take a professional approach to their job, even if they are less experienced. Seek out the hungry boom operators looking to move up to sound mixer. Look for the Asst. Camera person with a gleam in her eye, who's ready to be a DP. If you have production skills, barter your services for those of a colleague. It's a fairly standard practice for small groups of indie filmmakers to just take turns cooperatively working on one another's films for free. (Just make sure this is mutually understood before you give up half your summer for your friend's film only to find out that he'll be vacationing in Cancun during *your* shoot.) If you enroll in a film school or workshop, there's a good chance you'll get a free crew. If you pay any of your crew (and you really should if you can), I recommend you start with the DP, Sound Person, and/or Editor as these are your make-or-break positions. (Also see "Assembling a Crew" on page 85.)

The best way to get good free crew members is to first BE one for your fellow filmmakers.

3 GET FREE OR INEXPENSIVE FOOD

Feeding your crew good food can get expensive, especially with larger crews and longer shoots. As any hungry college student knows, free or cheap food isn't too hard to come by if you know where to look and who to ask. (For specific food tips see "Hot Tip: 5 Down and Dirty Food Ideas" on page 92.)

4 BE CREATIVE WITH VISUALIZATIONS

Shooting original video is generally preferable, but it's not always practical or affordable to shoot all the material you may need. If a portion of your documentary really calls for some visuals of Carnival in Rio, a guerrilla war, aerial shots of towering skyscrapers or anything else that's a little too expensive, inaccessible or otherwise difficult to shoot within your means, you still have many creative (and cheaper) options to visualize the story for your audience: you could buy some stock footage, use animation, shoot a recreation, illustrate it with drawings, show newspaper clippings, license footage from another film . . . I can go on all day long—and so can your B-Roll with just a little more imagination.

5 | SHOOT AND TRAVEL OVER LESS DAYS WITH LESS PEOPLE

This is simple mathematics. The more you shoot and the longer you travel, the more your film will cost. With unfolding subject matter, knowing when to stop shooting and start editing is often difficult, but many projects such as historical docs or reality shows can be scheduled and planned ahead of time. Do the math for each shooting day and look for shoots that can be eliminated or combined. Travel is a necessary part of following a story, but you want to make sure your travel is cost-effective and adds value to your project. Traveling for six hours and feeding and putting up a five-person crew in a hotel just to shoot some B-roll for a montage of your subject's hometown is not a wise investment of your resources. Instead, you could just shoot it with your DP only. You could also make the most of the trip by interviewing your subject's family members and friends while there. Maybe instead of video of their hometown, a montage of still pictures will suffice . . . Make travel count. Take the minimum amount of crew, stay only as long as necessary, and shoot as much material as you can while you're there.

6 | GET CORPORATE/AGENCY SPONSORSHIPS OR PRODUCT PLACEMENT DEALS

Making a documentary about the history of video gaming? Why not see if the good people at EA Sports or Rockstar Games will support your project with grants or donations? Want to highlight the plight of teen mothers? Why not seek help from a national charity that

shares the same mission? Look for natural allies in your mission who have deeper pockets than you. While not appropriate for many docs, some subject matter or doc genres may seek a product placement deal to show a sponsor's product onscreen in exchange for value. Trying to line up product placement deals for the documentary, *Paper Chasers*, which is about hip-hop entrepreneurs, we did not get any cash (unlikely for indies). But we did convince sponsors to supply specific budget items such as food, drinks, wardrobe, and discounted hotel, car, and RV rentals, which freed up precious dollars in our micro-budget.

A product placement deal helped secure this crew RV for *Paper Chasers* at a nice discount.

7 | USE ORIGINAL MUSIC

Why pay an expensive fee to use a popular song or stock music from a library when there are thousands of independent musicians looking for exposure? Many of these fellow indie artists will gladly give you prerecorded tracks. Better yet, you can easily find talented musicians and composers who will even create original music for your project for a fraction of the cost of the average popular music license. Original music tailored to your project can be an inexpensive, but powerful storytelling element.

8 USE PUBLIC DOMAIN FOOTAGE

Did you know that there are hundreds of hours of footage and thousands of historical photos and musical recordings available for anyone to use free of charge? This is mostly historical material on which the copyright has expired. In other words, it is in the *public domain*. You'll nevertheless have to pay to download or have material transferred, but it's still a great bargain. In the same vein, you can also search sites like Wikimedia.org where there are stills and videos with various Creative Commons licenses that allow you to download and use media for free under many circumstances. (See "7 Commandments of Archival Footage" on page 305.)

9 USE NATURAL LIGHT AND CHINA LANTERNS

You can avoid the cost of rentals and the hassle and setup time needed for professional lighting instruments by using available lighting instead. Position your subject strategically to use the natural light on location. As illustrated in the lighting section of this book, you can get some beautiful lighting with a simple house lamp, inexpensive china lantern, or sunlit window and a reflector. Staging your shooting and interviews outdoors is also a common way to get around professional lighting.

Position subjects and compose shots to take advantage of natural light.

10 LOG AND TRANSCRIBE YOUR OWN FOOTAGE

Transcripts and logs are a doc necessity. However, professional video transcription is costly even on the *low end*. If you have 20 or so tapes to log and transcribe it could break your budget. Enlist an intern, a good friend, or just do it yourself if you're up to the task. You'll be much more familiar with your footage, plus you'll save hundreds or even thousands of dollars to boot! (See "Transcripts" on page 289.)

WHERE TO FIND PRICES

Producing guides such as "L.A. 411" and "N.Y. 411" are great for film vendor listings, but they often omit smaller vendors and only cover major cities. Here's some other sources to check for prices:

LINE ITEM	WHERE TO LOOK
Equipment Rental	■ Rental House Published Rates ■ Film Cooperatives Rental Rate Cards ■ Borrowlenses.com
Equipment Purchase	■ BandHPhotoVideo.com ■ Ebay.com/Amazon.com/Craigslist ■ Manufacturer Web Sites
Crew	■ Rate Quotes from Potential Crew Members ■ Consult Other Filmmakers with Similar Projects ■ Filmmaking Job Boards for Going Rates ■ Union Rate Cards (SAG/Aftra, ASC, etc.) ■ Crew for Hire Services
Transportation and Lodging	■ Car/Van/RV Rental Company Web Sites ■ Airline Web Sites ■ Hotel Web Sites ■ Travel Web Sites (i.e., Expedia, Travelocity)
Location	■ Offers to/Quotes from Potential Locations ■ Local Film Commission Location Books ■ Consult with a Location Manager ■ Consult Other Filmmakers who have shot at Similar Locations
Post-production	■ Individual Editor Quotes ■ Transcription Company Web Sites ■ Published Film Budgets
Music and Sound Licenses and Rights	■ Quotes from Musicians/Performers ■ Music and Sound Effects Library Sites ■ Music Supervisor/Sound Designer Quotes
Meals and Craft Services	■ Caterer Web Sites ■ Supermarket Web Sites ■ Local Restaurant Menus

(See the Resources section on the Crazy Phat Bonus Website for links to specific sites.)

Budgeting is truly an art form that improves with experience. The less experienced you are, the greater the contingency you should have. It's much better to err on the side of having an overinflated budget that takes into account all the possibilities, rather than an overly optimistic (i.e., unrealistic) budget that relies on unsecured contributions to the production and a perfectly smooth shoot. Like many other steps in preproduction, budgeting forces you to really examine and *think* through your production decisions.

Do you really need to hire that camera operator with a Movi stabilizer for an extra $1200.00? Or is it better to go just handheld and use that $1200.00 to license some more stock footage or music? Should you rent a high-end camera package? Or are you better off renting a less expensive camera package and using the money you saved to hire a more experienced documentary editor?

There isn't necessarily a right or wrong answer to these issues, just a long list of choices that will impact your final film and budget. Your job is to figure out what that impact will be and decide what *value* it brings to your finished film. Remember, every dollar you spend here is a dollar you can't spend there. Think through your budgetary decisions and try to get as many dollars on the screen as you can.

CRAFTING A SUCCESSFUL CROWD-FUNDING CAMPAIGN

MIKE ATTIE & MEGHAN O'HARA, CO-DIRECTORS

incountryfilm.com

(*In Country*, a documentary film about Vietnam War re-enactors)

Meghan: It takes forever to make a good Crowd-funding campaign. There's so many things to think through. You have to get your text just right. I think one of the things I see when I see people that don't have successful campaigns is that I don't think they thought through everything from the start.

Mike: You have to think a lot about sort of not just selling a big film but so much of the support you're going to get is from people you know and getting people excited about what you can do, I think, is really key about who you are and what you can do.

There's a lot about making a personal connection with the audience out there. I think that was a big thing. We talked to a lot of people who had done Kickstarter campaigns and we did quite a bit of research too. That all helped. (Kickstarter. com is a popular crowd-funding site.)

A lot of the effort was finessing the language to be very Kickstarter-specific. It's very different than writing a grant application.

Meghan: We had just won a pitch contest, so we could state that. We met a writer from IndieWire and he wrote an article about our film. All that happened precipitously and it gave us a lot of legitimacy that we didn't have at all before that.

We set our goal to $15,000. It was a big debate. We were too nervous to set it too high. We didn't want to fail. Then we reached it in six days . . . Part of that was from some friends that we didn't know were willing to give a lot of money and they just did right away . . . we got two mystery donations from people that found us on Kickstarter and just liked our project and they gave us $1,000 each.

Mike: A thing to remember in our case—and this is a big one too—is that we got picked as a Kickstarter project of the day.

Meghan: Someone from Kickstarter saw our pitch at Camden, and liked it. When we launched that put us on the front of the Kickstarter page for a long time. We had pretty much every donation level . . . we had a lot of people that were just giving a dollar, which was really great also, because it attracts more people, it elevates the status of the campaign.

We did a soft launch by announcing it on Facebook and that was where a lot of the money came from. I think the thing that Facebook allows you to do and the thing that is crucial about Kickstarter is you have to make it an event. You have to get people to feel like something's on the line and it's like they're participating in an event. We had people that were watching our page to see every new development. It was crazy.

Mike: The thing that I also like about it too is getting these random donations from people you've never met. You can e-mail with them and learn how and when they found out about the film and find out they had some really interesting connection to Vietnam or to the war. They were just really interested in the story. Actually, I found it to be really fun. I love the connections that you make when you're making a film and it's not just with the people in your film but with your audience too.

As sort of crazy as it is, it's also really exciting and invigorating to see, to have these interactions. I think initially when there's this avalanche of e-mails it was hard to keep up, but then later on you could actually get into real dialogs with people and it was just a great experience.

Meghan: We had my mom writing thank you notes back to people because we both had to teach and we just didn't expect the response. I got out of class and I opened up my laptop and I spent the next five hours writing thank you notes.

Meghan: You just have this manic feeling the whole time of where else can I post this, what else can I do to keep it going.

I think it's good to do a Kickstarter when you really need it, because then you're most passionate about asking, because you really believe.

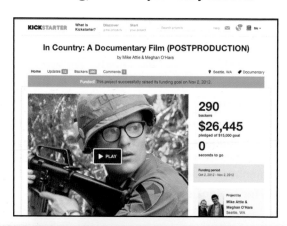

CHOOSING AN EQUIPMENT PACKAGE

Your choice of equipment is largely going to be determined by the budget and resources you have readily available. However, other factors such as approach, subject matter, crew size, and intended distribution will also affect this decision.

For example, if I wanted to shoot a segment on gang activity in the inner city, I probably wouldn't show up with an Arri Alexa camera and the larger crew that goes with it. By the same measure, if I was going to shoot a doc on active volcanoes of the South Pacific that is going to appear in IMAX movie theaters, I wouldn't shoot it with a with a $1500 DSLR camera. You want to make sure you get the right set of

tools to do the specific job at hand. Any less than that and you are screwing yourself out of the crucial resources you need to fully execute your vision. Any more than that and you're screwing yourself out of money that would otherwise go toward important production resources, such as pay for a more experienced crew or an extra few days of shooting. Think it through thoroughly.

It's generally best to travel light when shooting documentaries. Documentary filmmakers are like the Special Forces of the filmmaking army. They must be mobile, flexible, and prepared to deal with a variety of dynamic situations quickly and efficiently. The more equipment you have, the more crew and time it's going to take to prep, transport, and set it all up. Moreover, you will be a much more conspicuous presence with a lot of gear. Peep out the "Doc Equipment Packages" chart on page 80 for an overview of the basics required on just about any sized down and dirty doc shoot.

> ✔ Choose the equipment that's most appropriate for your subject matter, shooting conditions and intended distribution.

CHOOSING A CAMERA FOR YOUR PROJECT

CLIFF CHARLES, DIRECTOR OF PHOTOGRAPHY
thepeoplesdp.com
(*When the Levees Broke, Good Hair, Venus and Serena*, etc.)

What are the Project Mandates?

I would say that regardless of what the project is, whether it's a commercial documentary or whatever, you want to pick the right tool for the task at hand. When you start a project there are often certain mandates that are going to come from a TV network, a distributor, a director's preference, or any other "powers that be". So one of the things that I try to find out right off the bat is—What are the mandates? What aspect ratio, what delivery format do they need?

I eventually go through a process of elimination. Based on what they tell me, I can already rattle off in my brain . . . that excludes this camera and this camera. Okay, so let me think about *this* camera. Another thing that I try to find out as soon as possible is budget. What kind of money are they working with? It really just depends what the job calls for, what the budget is, what the mandate is on delivery specs, what the producer's and director's comfort levels are with formats.

When we did *If God is Willing and Da Creek Don't Rise*, there was a mandate that we had to shoot on tape, and the first Hurricane Katrina documentary that we did (*When the Levees Broke*) was shot on film. So I said, "I have to get the very best tape camera there is." So at the time Sony had just released the Sony SRW-9000, and that was a 4:4:4 HDcam SR camera. Working with Spike Lee we have the component of vérité, but we also had a heavy component of in-studio interviews. So I went with that camera studio style for the interviews, and then the camera also allowed me the opportunity to put on ENG zoom lenses when we did our vérité. So I had two configurations for that camera. The downside is that camera weighed a ton. It was the heaviest camera that I've used in the last 15 years, probably in 20 years. But the camera's quality was amazing. I've never shot with a tape camera that shot better than that. I pick and choose based on what the job calls for. You pick your brush based on what kind of painting you want to paint.

Third Party Accessories And Servo Zoom Lenses

Generally speaking, I like to have a camera that's pretty contained. I try not to have too many third party items attached to the camera. I like to be able to have a camera that records internally, because these are all things that have the potential of creating a problem when you're in a situation that you have to be moving quickly and dealing with situations that are not ideal. So I don't want to deal with a third party recorder that's connected with an HDMI cable, because when I'm running around, something gets bumped, and then the HDMI cable comes out and cuts recording in the middle of something that's really important. And now I'm forced to make everyone stop this vérité moment, as I reconfigure and secure my cable. It's nice to have a self-contained package.

The other thing that I really like to have is a zoom lens with a servo motor. When I was doing the documentary, *If God Is Willing and Da Creek Don't Rise*, it was great that I had a camera that allowed me the ability to put a zoom lens on with a servo when I was doing the ENG, because it's just an invaluable tool.

Servo is a documentarian's best friend, because with a servo lens, you're able to change the emotional content at the flick of a switch. If you're shooting a narrative film, you may want to cut. You can cut camera and then change lens. But when you're doing a documentary, you can't do that. You need to be able to keep moving. So when your interviewee subject begins talking about something very emotional, if you are on that servo lens with a wide shot, you can now zoom in. The other thing that I love to do is a very slow zoom-in, to give you that sense of movement and connecting you even closer to the subject. So, yeah, servo, I think, is a documentarian's best friend. Just the ability to zoom is a very important tool for the documentary filmmaker.

Physical Conditions And Camerawork

You also have to factor in the physical conditions—weather, terrain, how fast you'll have to move and set-up. Some cameras are more temperamental than others, especially when it comes to heat and humidity. You should take things into consideration like battery life. Some cameras have really high power needs. They really suck a lot of juice, which means that you need to carry big batteries and a lot of them. Now if you're doing a job where you're really on the move, that might not be your best option. You might want to go with something very lightweight, with low power consumption. So you have to factor in all the variables, and they make a camera for just about every scenario. So you'll figure out what works for you.

Pixels and Resolution

Pixels are the little dots of light that form a picture on video screen displays. The more pixels on a screen, the better the picture quality. The term resolution refers to the size of a video image in width and height of pixels, the little electronic dots that make up screen displays. If a video has a resolution of 1280 × 720 that means it is 1280 pixels wide by 720 pixels high.

Progressive vs. Interlaced

There are two different ways that video cameras create images: interlaced and progressive. Interlaced images are formed by combining two different fields, each representing half of the image, to make one video frame. Interlaced video has some distinct drawbacks; namely, when you freeze-frame or slow down interlaced video, you will often see jagged lines in the image as a result of this electronic combining of two different fields.

Interlaced Video

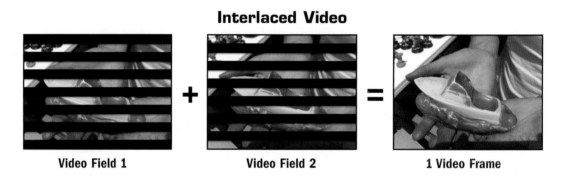

Video Field 1 + Video Field 2 = 1 Video Frame

A progressive video image, on the other hand, is formed more like film in that each frame is formed by a single image. This is why 24P (P is for progressive) video footage more resemble the look and feel of film, which is shot at 24 fps (frames per second). Progressive video looks and feels more cinematic. (Similarly, the European standard PAL video is recorded at 25 fps.) This is why 24P is heavily preferred by many filmmakers over standard NTSC video, which is recorded at 30 fps. Believe it or not, subtracting those six little frames of video per second helps make the difference between the more natural look and feel of film and the more artificial look of video.

Frame Rate

Frame rate refers to how many frames of video you are shooting per second. Frame rates are usually shown in camera specs followed by a designation of "p" for progressive or "i" for interlaced scanning as explained on the previous page. So typical frame rate specs are expressed in terms such as 24p, 30p, and 60i. Video frame rate accounts for a good deal of the aesthetic look and feel of the video. For example, film is shot at 24 frames per second (fps), so video that is shot at the same 24 frames per second looks more cinematic and film-like. Video shot at 30 fps looks more "broadcasty," like the local news.

HDV Image Size

High definition video can basically be put into two distinct categories based on resolution:

1280 × 720 or 1920 × 1080, which is also known as "full HD".

Resolution

Video resolution refers to the size of the image in pixels. In camera and TV specs resolution is listed as the number of horizontal pixels × vertical pixels. The most popularly used resolutions are 1920 × 1080 and 1280 × 720 for HD cameras and TVs. For some comparison, old school standard definition (SD) cameras have a resolution of 720 × 480. When listing HD resolution, most manufacturers simply state the vertical pixels: 1080 or 720 followed by the type of scanning (interlaced or progressive) as in 1080i, 1080p, or 720p. (See previous page.) In addition to good old HD, we now also have 2K (2048 × 1080) and 4K (3840 × 2160*) video. Although it sounds like much more, 2K video looks essentially the same as 1080 HD video, because 2K and 4K video formats prioritize the horizontal resolution of the image rather than the vertical resolution referred to in HD. Check it . . .

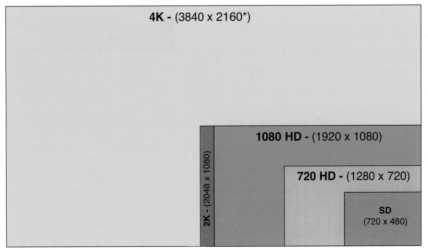

*There are actually several different "4K" resolutions.

A camera is a major investment, if you're thinking about a purchase you want to make sure you get something that's going to serve your needs at present and well into the future. (And for the last digital decade, the term "in the future" means about three to five years.) So there are some basic features that I recommend you seek out in any camera. You may not be able to get all of these things at your particular budget level, but the more you can find in the same camera, the better.

Manual Controls

The first criteria that I'd say is a must for any serious video shooting is **manual controls**. Most, if not all of the controls, on a typical *consumer* camera are full-auto, which means you can't manually control things like focus, exposure, white balance and shutter speed just to name a few. If you want to shoot good video, you've simply gotta be in full control of as many aspects of your image as possible.

XLR Audio Inputs

The next thing I think you really should have is XLR audio inputs. Video is literally only half the story . . . the other half of the story is audio. In order to get good audio, you are going to need good professional audio equipment. Good pro audio equipment all has one thing in common—all real-deal audio components for filmmaking have XLR inputs and outputs. Lower-quality consumer audio gear does not.

The one big exception I'd make to having XLR Inputs are DSLR cameras—which are now wildly popular—but *don't* have XLR Ports.

So it's okay that your DSLR camera does not have XLR ports, the image quality is very high and there are some dedicated workarounds to use XLR mics with DSLRs. But if you are getting a dedicated *video* camera for professional, serious indie or film school work—I think XLR audio ports are a definite must.

So with the exception of DSLR cameras, I think manual controls and XLR ports are the minimum bar to entry. Those are the basic things we need. Now let's talk about some of the other things that we really want if we can get them.

Big Sensors

So at the top of the list of things you don't 100% *need*, but may really *want* in a camera are big sensors or imaging chips.

Imaging chips are to video what negatives are to film. It's where the image is actually captured. There are two big advantages to large sensor cameras—better low light performance and more shallow depth of field. So the bigger the chip, the better your image just like a negative. And of course the bigger the imaging chip, the more expensive the camera, so a big sensor is a very good thing to have ... if you can afford it.

Peaking

The last important feature that I recommend you look for in a camera is **peaking**. Peaking is a feature that makes it much easier to judge focus when shooting HD video using a small monitor. This is particularly useful when shooting daylit exteriors. It's a feature that some, but not all cameras have. But I think it's a very useful tool to have when shooting HD in the field, especially if you don't have a big monitor. (See "Peaking," page 116.)

Interchangeable Lens

So those are the most important things and valuable features that I recommend you look for in a camera. Now let's talk about some of the more luxury features and conveniences you may also desire in a camera. starting with an interchangeable lens.

As I write this many dedicated entry and mid-level video cameras still have a fixed zoom lens. They have a zoom lens, so there are variable focal lengths from wide to telephoto, but the lens is permanently affixed to the camera, so those are the only focal lengths you can shoot at and the best optical image quality you'll ever get. However, if you get a camera that has an interchangeable lens, you can shoot at any focal length with any brand or type of lens—zoom or prime—that fits your camera. The creative possibilities are unlimited.

I should also mention that the *budgetary* possibilities may be a little more limited when it comes to interchangeable lens. Just because you have a camera that can take different lenses doesn't necessarily mean that you can afford the various lenses available. While video technology has advanced considerably and gotten cheaper year after year, the prices of optical lenses have not really gone down at all. "Good glass" is still expensive. It's actually not that uncommon now for people to have lenses that costs more than their *cameras*.

That being said, you can be well served by a single good fast zoom lens until you can acquire more. Plus, you can always rent a lens from your local rental house or an online rental business like **borrowlenses.com**, which will actually ship a rental lens to you. (I know! Crazy right?!) Renting lenses and borrowing them from friends is a good way to figure out what you like and what will work best for your project.

So a camera with interchangeable lenses is a nice option to have. It's an easy choice if you already own lenses that have mounts or mount adapters to fit the camera you want to use. With that in mind, I should also point out that if you *can* afford a dedicated video camera with an interchangeable lens, you can't really go too wrong with investing in "good glass".

The average useful (i.e. non-obsolete) period for a video camera these days is three to six years tops. But a good lens on the other hand, can serve you for life as you move from one digital camera to the next. Another note here is that as long you take good care of it and avoid scratches, top shelf lenses like those made by Zeiss and Canon tend to hold their value very well, so resale is always an option down the line.

One big thing I want to point out here is that while interchangeable lenses offer more creative choices and better optical image quality, most are lacking one big feature that is especially practical for documentaries, which brings me to the next feature I'd look for in a documentary camera . . .

Servo Zoom Lens

Servo zoom lens are zoom lenses that are motorized, so they can quickly and smoothly zoom in or out on a subject with the push of switch—a **rocker zoom control** marked with a "T" for telephoto and a "W" for wide. Giving up a servo motor is the one big sacrifice that you'll likely have to make if you go with a camera with interchangeable lenses, since hardly any interchangeable lenses on the market have servo zooms right now, except for much more expensive professional broadcast lenses like those made by Fujinon.

Because documentary can be unpredictable and you never know what you'll actually end up needing to use in the edit room, the ability to be able to make a smooth quick zoom move is very desirable. Many servo motors also allow you to adjust the speed, so you can make your zooms even smoother. It's much more difficult to make a smooth zoom move by hand. Many zoom moves you make on a non-servo lens will probably have to be edited out of your final project. All fixed lens video cameras have servo motors. Interchangeable lenses definitely have their benefits, but don't sleep on the benefits of having a servo zoom for docs.

Slow Motion

Another nice feature to have, but by no means a necessity for most documentary work, is slow motion. The ability to shoot at 60, 120 or 240 fps (frames per second) in addition to the more standard 24 fps or 30 fps, can come in handy for certain types of work more than others. If your projects routinely involve sports, action, fast motion, or glamour shots, in-camera slow motion is a nice plus. I honestly think many filmmakers give more value to the ability to shoot slo mo than is practical. It's more a matter of your style and content. I have rarely been in the middle of shooting and decided that now is the time for the slow motion shot. It's simply not something that many filmmakers need to call on that often and you can still make anything slo mo in post as long as you shoot it at a high shutter speed. (See "Shutter Speed Basics" on page 127.)

4K Sensor

Okay, here's where comparing cameras gets a little more complicated. Chip size only tells *half* the sensor story. The other half of figuring out the quality of a camera sensor is **resolution**. In other words, how *many* total pixels are squeezed onto a chip? This will determine the **sharpness and detail** of the image. This is best judged by total *active* pixel count. I say *active* pixel count, because depending on the camera model and type of lens it takes, not

all pixels on a sensor are actually used to form an image. (To add another layer of complications to the matter, there are also different types of pixels, but I'm not even gonna go there. It's complicated enough already!)

One of the newest luxury features to be offered in the world of video is 4K imaging sensors. In case you're not already familiar, to give some perspective: regular old HD is usually 720 × 1280 pixels or 1080 × 1920, however 4K imaging sensors can be as big as a whopping 4096 × 2160. (Similar to HD, there are also slight variations on pixel count between different 4K models, but all are approximately 4000 pixels wide. So 4K video is **4 times** better than **standard 1080 HD**.)

There is a growing field of (relatively) affordable cameras that can shoot spectacular 4K video. Among them are The Red One (the original 4K indie maverick), the Black Magic Design Production Camera 4K, the Sony F5 and Canon's EOS-1D just for starters. (See the "Camera Guide" on pages 45 to 58 for specs and prices.)

Time-lapse

Another nice bonus feature to have in a camera is the ability to do time-lapse (a.k.a. interval recording). Time-lapse allows you to **lock down** your camera and shoot a scene over two hours, but play it back with those two hours condensed down to 30 smooth seconds. The end result can be stunning shots of epic sunrises, a bank of storm clouds rolling in, a flower opening in the morning dew, concert stagehands converging on a field and setting up a massive stage from scratch, etc. It is by no means a necessity or even a commonly used doc camera feature, but when appropriate for the story at hand, time-lapse footage, like slow motion, can provide some nice stylized visuals that can enhance your film and raise production values.

So to sum it all up in a neat little chart . . .

WHAT TO LOOK FOR IN A CAMERA		
YOU NEED	**YOU WANT**	**YOU LIKE**
■ Manual Conrols	■ Big Sensor	■ Interchangeable Lens
■ XLR Audio Inputs*	■ Peaking	■ Servo Zoom Lens
		■ Slow Motion
		■ 4K Sensor
		■ Time-lapse

*DSLRs excepted.

There are a mind-boggling number of choices and even more specs to consider when picking a camera today. I have kept the focus mostly on the more affordable video cameras in the under $10,000 category since they are the most popular among indies, film schools and freelancers. The next few pages represent my best attempt at compiling all of this camera information in one convenient place.

Some of the real specs were more elusive than others depending on who was presenting the math. I tried to research and sort out confusing or fuzzy manufacturer's information and name prevailing prices as found at major camera dealers. Inevitably, most prices will lower and a new crop of cameras will come out in the not too distant future.

In the meantime, the next few pages chart my personal picks and commentary on some of the best affordable video cameras on the market today from entry-level starter cams to those loaded with professional features. (You can sign up to the free Down and Dirty DV Nation mailing list or visit my online Camera Buyers Guide at **DownAndDirtyDV.com** for more specs and links to the most recent cameras.)

DOCUMENTARY CAMERA GUIDE

MODEL	SPECS	NOTES
BLACK MAGIC Cinema Design Camera (2.5K) **$2,000.00 (body only)**	■ 2.5K image sensor ■ Active sensor size = 15.6 × 8.8 mm ■ 13 stops of latitude ■ Canon EF/Zeiss ZE mount *or* MFT mount ■ 23.98p, 24p, 25p, 29.97p, 30p ■ 5" touchscreen LED (800 × 480) ■ Electronic iris control ■ Weight = 1.7 kg / 3.75 lb	■ Raw 2.5K (uncompressed) ■ Apple ProRes and Avid DNxHD (compressed) ■ 2 × 1/4" audio jacks (unusual) ■ 10-bit HD-SDI 4 : 2 : 2 ■ Micro HDMI (Type D) output ■ Film or video dynamic range
BLACK MAGIC Pocket Camera—**$1,000.00**	■ Super 16 mm sensor ■ Sensor size = 12.48 × 7.028 mm ■ Active MFT mount??? ■ 23.98p, 24p, 25p, 29.97p, 30p ■ 3.5" LCD screen (800 × 480)	■ Apple ProRes 422 (HQ) ■ CinemaDNG RAW ■ 3.5 mm stereo audio input ■ Weight = 355 g / 0.8 lb ■ Micro HDMI (Type D) output

PANASONIC

- Records MPEG-4 AVC/H.264
- 49 mm filter size
- Weight = 3.9 lb incl. battery
- HDMI/AV ports
- Focus/zoom/iris rings
- 3 × 1/4.71" full HD MOS censors
- Each sensor = 2.19 MP
- AVCR format
- 1080-60p, 60i, 30p, 24p
- Optical image stabilization
- 3.5" LCD screen
- Fixed lens—f1.5 min. aperture
- 2.84-34.1 mm 12× zoom lens
- 35 mm equivalent = 30-358 mm

AG-AC90—$2,000.00

SONY

- Unique built-in projector
- 96 GB built-in Flash memory
- SD/SDHC/SDXC memory card
- 2 XLR audio inputs
- Memory stick PRO Duo/HG Duo, Duo HX
- 52 mm filter diameter
- Fixed lens—f1.5 min. aperture
- Weight = 1 lb 5 oz (615 g)
- RCA/HDMI 1.4/Mini USB
- 1/2.88" ExmoR CMOS censor
- Carl Zeiss Vario-Sonnar T*
- Aperture—f/1.8-3.4
- 3.8-38 mm 10× fixed zoom lens
- 35 mm equivalent = 26-260 mm

96GB HXR-NX30—$1,900.00

DOCUMENTARY CAMERA GUIDE—CONT'D

MODEL	SPECS	NOTES
SONY	■ APS-C sized Exmor CMOS sensor ■ Sensor = 23.5 × 15.6 mm ■ 1080—60p, 60i, 24p, 30p/720—60p ■ 18–200 mm Servo Zoom Lens—f/3.5–6.3 ■ Sony E-Mount ■ nterchangeable lens!!! ■ 1.6× crop factor ■ 3.5" LCD screen (1920 × 480)	■ Rare interchangeable servo lens ■ Kit lens poor in low light ■ Media = SD/SDHC/SDXC ■ Optional 128 GB flash memory unit ■ 2 XLR audio inputs ■ HDMI/component/RCA ports ■ Hot shoe for photo flash ■ Best suited for event videography ■ 67 mm filter diameter ■ Weight = 6 lbs. 15 oz. incl. battery

NEX-EA50UH—$3,300.00 (incl. lens)

MODEL	SPECS	NOTES
PANASONIC	■ 3.45" LCD screen (1920 × 480) ■ 1080—24p, 30p, 60p fps ■ 720—30p, 24p ■ Fixed 3.9–86 mm lens ■ 22× servo zoom ■ Aperture f/1.6–3.2 ■ 35 mm equivalent = 28–616 mm	■ Records to SD/SDHC/SDXC cards ■ 2 media card slots ■ 2 XLR audio inputs ■ HDMI/Firewire/RCA ports

AG-AC130A—$3,700.00 (w/o mic)

CANON

- Super 35 mm CMOS (24.6 × 13.8 mm) (28.2 mm diagonal)
- Canon EF mount
- 3.5" LCD screen
- ISO 320–20,000
- 24–105 mm f/4 lens (optional)
- 2 SDHC/SDXC card slots
- Built-in ND filters
- Great in low light
- HDMI
- 2 XLR Audio inputs/3.5 mm jack
- Very limited LCD movement
- Record directly from sensor to recorder for quality closer to C-300
- Ant uses Atmos Ninja 2 to shoot 10 bit/4 : 2 : 2 Pro Res with his C-100 rig

EOS C-100—$6,200.00 (with 24–105 mm lens)

$5,500.00 (body only)

CANON

- HD MPEG-4 AVCHD
- Super 35 mm CMOS (24.6 x 13.8 mm)
- 1080 60i–true 24p
- ISO 320–20,000
- 4" rotating LCD monitor
- Time-lapse and stop-motion
- Slow-motion and high-speed
- EF or PL mounts
- Built-in ND filters
- Records to CF Card (type 1)
- Dual CF card slots
- 4 : 2 : 2–50 Mb/s–MPEG-2
- HD-SDI port
- 2 XLR audio inputs
- Timecode and genlock in/out
- Lens not included
- Good run and gun doc cam

EOS C-300—$14,000.00 (body only)

DOCUMENTARY CAMERA GUIDE—CONT'D

MODEL	SPECS	NOTES
SONY NEX FS-700U—$7,800.00	■ 4K Exmor Super 35mm CMOS sensor ■ 1080/60p AVCHD video ■ 960 fps super slow motion ■ ISO 320 to 64,000 ■ 3.5" LCD screen with VF attachment	■ Optional Flash memory unit ■ Records to SD/SDHC/SDXC ■ HD-SDI/HDMI/RCA output ■ Built-in ND filters ■ Weight 6.75 lb (3,060 g) w/ full load
SONY HXR-MC2000U—$1,700.00	■ 1/4-inch Exmor R CMOS sensor ■ Sensor = 4.2 MP (2.65 MP effective) ■ AVC-HD 1080—60i ■ Built-in 64GB hard drive ■ 12× zoom G-lens—f/1.8-3.4 ■ 35 mm equivalent = 30–357 mm ■ 2.7" LCD touchscreen	■ Built-in mic, but NO XLR inputs! ■ 3.5 mm Mini-stereo audio port ■ Also records to SD/SDHC/SDXC cards ■ Shoulder-mounted ■ Optical steady-shot ■ Records MPEG-4 AVC/H.264 ■ HDMI/component/RCA ■ 37 mm filter diameter ■ Weight = 5.9 lbs
BLACK MAGIC DESIGN Production Camera 4K	■ 4K Super 35 mm sensor ■ Global shutter ■ Canon EF lens mount ■ 23.98, 24, 25, 29.97, 30 fps ■ 12 stops of dynamic range ■ 5" LCD touchscreen (800 × 480)	■ 4K (3840 × 2160) and HD (1920 × 1080) ■ Compressed Cinema DNG RAW ■ Apple ProRes 422 (HQ) ■ Media = SSD (solid state drives) ■ 2 × 1/4" audio jacks (unusual) ■ 6G-SDI output ■ Thunderbolt/USB 2.0 connectors ■ ships w DaVinci Resolve and UltraScope

SONY

- Super 35 mm CMOS image sensor
- 8.9 MP sensor
- Internal 2K and HD recording
- Highly modular design
- FZ-mount w/ PL-mount adapter

- Records to SxS media cards
- Dynamic range rated at 14 stops
- Built-in 10-bit 4 : 4 : 4 at 440 Mbps
- 4K/2K RAW recording to optional recorder
- 240 fps 2K w/ firmware upgrade

PMW-F5 CineAlta Digital Cinema Camera

$16,500.00 (body only)

CANON

- Full-Frame CMOS sensor
- Sensor 36 × 24 mm—22.3 MP
- Canon EF 24–105 mm f/4L lens
- 3.2" LCD screen
- 1080–30p, 25p, 24p
- 720–60p, 50p
- ISO 100–12800

- 2 CF and SD card Slots
- Records .MOV MPEG-4 AVC/H.264
- Compact Flash/SD/SDHC/SDXC
- HDMI/composite video/audio
- 3.5 mm audio jack
- HDMI C (Mini)/ AV Out/USB 2.0
- Wireless and GPS compatible

EOS 5D Mark III —$3,000.00 (body only)

$3,500.00 (w/ 24–105 mm lens)

CANON

- 18.0 MP CMOS (APS-C)
- 18–135 mm f/3.5-5.6
- 1080p : 30 fps, 25 fps, 24 fps
- 720p : 60 fps, 50 fps
- 3" tilting LCD screen
- Mount = Canon EF-S

- Records in H.264 (.mov) format
- Records to memory card SD/SDHC/SDXC
- ISO 100–12800, extended mode 25600
- 67 mm filter
- Optical image stabilizer
- Advance live view
- No XLR inputs
- Weight = 18.52 oz—body/ 16.93 oz—lens

EOS Rebel T5i DSLR–$1,000.00

(body only $700.00)

DOCUMENTARY CAMERA GUIDE—CONT'D

MODEL

NIKON

D90—$1,200.00

PANASONIC

Lumix DMC-GH3—$898.00

SPECS

NIKON
- CMOS
- DX
- 3" LCD screen
- 18 mm–105 mm
- Mount = Nikon F

PANASONIC
- AVCHD/MJPEG/H.264
- 4/3" type MOS
- 1080p @ 24 fps
- 720p @ 60/30 fps
- 16:9 & 4:3 capable
- 3" free angle LCD screen
- mirrorless system

NOTES

NIKON
- Record to SDHC/SD cards
- 5.8× zoom lens
- 67 mm filter size
- 12.3 megapixel stills
- ISO 100–6400
- Weight = 1.4 lbs

PANASONIC
- Records in H.264 (.mov) format
- Record to SD/SDHC/SDXC
- Micro 4/3" system
- 16 megapixel stills
- 62 mm filter size
- Continuous auto focusing capability
- 10× zoom
- Mini-HDMI output
- No XLR input
- Weight = 19.4 oz (*body-only)

CANON

- 3:2 Native
- 16:9 and 4:3 capable
- 3" LCD Screen
- 1080p @ 24/25/30 fps
- 720p @ 50/60 fps

- Video encoded in H.264 (.mov) format
- 60 fps slow motion capable in 720p mode
- Takes 18 megapixel stills
- No XLR inputs!
- Internal Mic/Mini-stereo mic input
- Separate audio recorder recommended
- Max video clip length = 12 min. in HD
- No autofocus in video mode!
- Follow-focus and support rig recommended

EOS 7D DSLR—$1,500.00 (*body-only)

PANASONIC

- AVCHD
- 1/4" 3MOS
- 1080p and 720p
- 4–48 mm
- 16:9, 4:3, and 3:2
- 1 lux minimum
- 2.7" LCD screen

- Optical image stabilizer
- 3.1 lbs (with battery)
- 12× zoom lens
- HDMI output
- Takes 10.6-megapixel stills
- Detachable handle
- Records directly to SD and SDHC memory cards
- 43 mm filter size

AG-HMC40—$1,800.00

DOCUMENTARY CAMERA GUIDE—CONT'D

MODEL	SPECS	NOTES
SONY	■ AVCHD	■ Detachable handle with Dual XLR inputs
	■ 1/2.88"	■ CMOS Records to memory stick or SD Cards
	■ 1080p	■ Weight = 2.85 lbs (+battery, mic, XLR unit)
	■ 3.8–38 mm	■ 37 mm filter size
	■ 16:9 native	■ 12.3 MP still images
	■ 3.5" LCD screen	■ Built-in GPS
	■ 3 lx (low LUX mode, 1/25 shutter)! Infrared NightShot	■ Rain and dust-proof
HXR-NX70U—$2,800.00	■ XLR adapter	
CANON	■ 1/3" CMOS	■ XF105 only–HD/SDI out, SMPTE timecode, Genlock
	■ 4.25–42.5 mm	■ Dual XLR inputs
	■ 16:9	■ Records to CF and SD cards
	■ 4.5 lux (full AUTO mode)	■ Built-in 3D assist features
	■ 1.6 lux (Manual mode)	■ 58mm filter size
	■ 0.24 Color viewfinder	■ Optical image stabilizer
	■ 1080p/720p mode	■ 10× zoom lens
		■ Small and lightweight
		■ 2.4 lbs
		■ Limited zoom
		■ Poor sound
XF100/XF105—$2,500.00/ $3,000.00		

PANASONIC

- AVC HD, 24p
- 3.9–51 m
- 1080p mode
- 3.5" LCD screen
- 0.44" color viewfinder
- 3 lux minimum
- 1080–60i, 30p, 24p/720–60p, 30p, 24p
- Records directly to SD and SDHC memory cards
- 72 mm filter size
- Weight = 3.7 lbs (4.3 lbs with battery)
- 2× XLR audio inputs

AG-HMC150—$3,500.00

SONY

- AVCHD
- 24p
- 4.1–82 mm
- 1/3" CMOS
- 1080p mode
- 3.2" LCD screen
- 0.45 color viewfinder
- 1.5 lux minimum
- Weight = 5 lbs
- Dual XLR ports
- Records to PRO Duo or SD/SDHC cards
- 3 built-in ND filters
- 72 mm filter size
- 20× G-lens

HDR-AX2000—$3,500.00

SONY

- 1/3" CMOS
- HDV/DV switchable
- 1080p/24p
- 4.1–82mm
- 1.5 lux minimum
- 3.2" LCD screen
- .45" color viewfinder
- 24p
- 72mm filter size
- Weight = 5 lbs
- 20x zoom lens
- 1.2MP still capture
- Records to MiniDV or Compact Flash or CF (with optional add-on)
- Good in low light

HVR-Z5U—$4,400.00

DOCUMENTARY CAMERA GUIDE—CONT'D

MODEL	SPECS	NOTES
SONY HXR-NX5U—$3,800.00	■ AVCHD ■ 3 1/3" CMOS sensors ■ 1080i/1080p/720p ■ 4.1–82 mm ■ .45" color viewfinder ■ 3.2 LCD screen ■ 1.5 lux minimum	■ HD-SDI and HDMI output ■ SMPTE timecode in/out ■ Dual XLR inputs ■ 20× zoom lens ■ 72 mm filter ■ Simultaneous HD/MPEG-2 SD capture ■ Memory stick Pro Do/SDHC cards (solid-state storage) ■ Built-in GPS ■ Active SteadyShot ■ Weight = 5 lbs
PANASONIC AG-AF100A—$4,200.00 (*camera body-only)	■ AVCHD ■ 4/3-type MOS fixed pickup ■ 1080p ■ 3.45" LCD color screen ■ .45" viewfinder	■ HD-SDI, HDMI output ■ Timecode, waveform ■ Uses still and cinema lenses ■ Records to SDXC, SDHC, and SD memory cards ■ Depth of field similar to 35 mm ■ Optical ND filter wheel ■ Interchangeable lenses ■ Excellent image quality ■ Record button awkwardly located where zoom rockerwould normally be ■ Handgrip gets bad reviews ■ Overall issues with design choices ■ Weight = 2.9 lbs

SONY

- HDV/DVCAM/DV
- 4.4–52.8 mm—12× zoom lens
- 1/3" CMOS sensor
- 1080i/24p mode
- 3.2" LCD screen
- 1.5 lux minimum
- Uses Compact Flash cards and Mini DV tapes
- 72 mm filter size
- Weight = 5.3 lbs

- Interchangeable lens
- HDMI output
- Dual XLR audio
- A bit front-heavy
- 1/3" bayonet mount

HVR-Z7U—$6,000.00

SONY

- AVCHD
- 1080p
- 3.5" lcd screen
- .28 lux minimum
- S35 CMOS
- Color viewfinder

- Slow & quick motion
- E-mount interchangeable lens system (most others via adaptor)
- Records to SD/SDHC/SDXC
- 67 mm filter size
- Geotagging with built-in GPS
- Dual XLR inputs
- HDMI output
- No built in ND filters
- Weight = 2.3 lbs (body only) 6.1 lbs (w/lens)

NEX-FS100—$4,00.00
(body only)

DOCUMENTARY CAMERA GUIDE—CONT'D

MODEL	SPECS	NOTES
CANON	■ 3 × 1/3" CMOS Sensors	■ XF305 model ONLY–HD/SDI out, SMPTE timecode, Genlock
	■ 4.1-73.8 mm 18× HD L Series zoom	■ Records to Compact Flash (CF) cards
	■ 1080p	■ Slow-motion and fast-motion modes
	■ 16:9 native	■ SuperRange Optical Image Stabilization system
	■ 82 mm filter size	■ MXF file format
	■ 4" LCD color screen	■ MPEG-2 50 Mbps codec
	■ .52" color viewfinder	■ Dual XLR inputs
XF300/XF305—$5,000.00/ $6,000.00	■ 4.5 lux minimum	
	■ Weight = 5.8 lbs	
JVC	■ 1/3" CCDs	■ Records to SDHC cards or optional SxS adapter
	■ 1080i/p 720p	■ HD/SD-SDI, FireWire output
	■ 4.4-61.6 mm	■ Variable frame rates
	■ 4.3" LCD screen	■ 82 mm filter size
	■ .45" viewfinder	■ 14× zoon lens
	■ 1.25 lux minimum	■ Shoulder Mount Form Factor
		■ Native MOV, MP4, AVI Capture
GY-HM750—$6,000.00		■ Weight = 7.5 lbs (includes lens, viewfinder, mic, battery)

PANASONIC

AG-HPX370—$7,200.00

- 1/3" 2.2MP 3-MOS
- 16:9 native
- AVC-Intra/DVCPRO HD
- DVCPRO 50/DVCPRO/DV
- 0.4 lux minimum
- 3.2" LCD screen
- .45" monocrome/color switchable viewfinder
- Interchangeable 17× Fujinon HD zoom lens
- Timecode, Genlock
- HS/SD-SDI
- Improved noise sensitivity
- Records to P2 and SD memory cards
- Scan reverse function for use with film lenses
- 4 channels of audio
- Camera can be remotely controlled
- Weight = 11 lbs

WHY DSLR CAMERAS ARE LAME

Intro

I think there are equally compelling arguments both for and against shooting video on DSLR cameras. (DSLR = Digital Single Lens Reflex) I'll try to share both arguments and let *you* decide whether it's a good choice for you. DSLR video cameras are essentially high-quality **still photo cameras** that now have added HD video functionality. As such, DSLR cameras are designed first and foremost with still photo shooting in mind–**NOT** video. This means they have some major limitations and require you to jump through a few more hoops than if you were to just shoot with a traditional video camera.

Here are some of the biggest DSLR issues as I see them . . .

1. Major Audio Limitations

One of the biggest drawbacks of DSLR cameras right out of the box is that they do not have XLR audio inputs. Instead, they come with a single mini-stereo audio input. This means you can't plug in any of your professional-quality mics if you only have a camera. Instead, you will need some type of audio adapter to feed sound into the camera, or you will need to record sound on a separate device. Not only that, but many popular DSLR models, such as the **Canon 7D** do not allow you to manually control the audio. They have **autogain** audio only, which is simply unacceptable (i.e., whack) for professional-quality work. Also, if you go the route of a separate audio recorder, you will also need to sync the sound with the picture in postproduction–film style, which is an extra step you don't have to take when shooting with a dedicated video camera. Most DSLRs do have a tiny built-in onboard mic, but it's not good enough for professional-quality audio capture. It's primarily useful for a "**dirty track**" for syncing or just recording personal home video. And to top it all off, as of the time I'm writing this, there are no on-screen audio meters to show you your audio levels. Lame!

2. You Need to Assemble a Franken-Camera

Because these are still cameras first and foremost, they are shaped and held like still cameras, which are normally way too shaky for motion-picture photography, so you need to assemble what my fellow author Kurt Lancaster refers to as a "Franken-Camera" in his book *DSLR Cinema: Crafting the Film Look with Video*. This means shooting with some type of third- party support system that usually involves some combination of a shoulder mount, grip handles, support rods, mounting rods, and often a counter weight. If you've only been shooting video with traditional prosumer video cameras, this is a whole other way of holding and operating a camera that will take some practice and getting used to. (It's actually much more like shooting with a film camera.)

3. Great Danger of Soft-Focused Shots

All the DSLR cameras have one chief asset that makes them extremely attractive: a big, beautiful video imaging chip. The size of the video chip is to a video camera what the size of a negative is to a film camera—so the bigger the chip, the better and more high resolution the image, also the greater the natural **shallow depth of field** (DOF). However, what comes along with high resolution and extremely shallow depth of field is hypercritical focus, meaning you've gotta get it right every time all the time, baby, or your clients will definitely notice. And unfortunately, the built-in LCD screens on the backs of these cameras are even smaller than those found on most prosumer video cameras, so you have no accurate way to judge this very critical element of focus on these super high-res HD images. Not to mention that on one of the most popular models, the Canon 7D, the focus assist, which magnifies the LCD screen image to help you focus, is disabled during recording ... Like I said, whack.

4. Overheating and 12-Minute Clip Limit

Another limitation of DSLR shooting is that you are limited to a maximum shot length of 12 minutes. The problem is that the camera automatically cuts itself off and stops recording after 12 minutes to avoid overheating that giant imaging chip. This probably isn't a big deal for narrative and scripted projects where the average take will probably run well below 12 minutes. However, in the world of freelance video where some of our easiest and lucrative gigs are event videos, a chief requirement is that we must shoot continuously for a long time, such as in the case of concerts, speeches, wedding ceremonies, etc. I don't care how dope it looks— your client is not gonna be happy if you missed part of the wedding vows or 10 seconds in the middle of their encore performance of their signature song, so this issue has to be carefully considered in the context of what you'll be shooting, especially when dealing with live events.

5. It's Really Not That Much Cheaper

I suspect that the biggest reason DSLR cameras have exploded onto the indie, student, and freelance scene is the price. At $1800–$2500 each, they are considerably cheaper than the average HD prosumer video cameras, which are more in the $3,000 to $7,000 range and don't offer nearly as much raw image quality as popular DSLR models such as Canon's 5D Mark II. However, here's the catch...if you want to routinely shoot with a DSLR camera in any professional capacity at all, you will ultimately want to add on a bunch of accessories to just to make it fully functional and more practical for video shooting, most typically:

a. Audio Recorder or Adapter ($300–$500)

b. Support Rig ($500–$1,800)

c. External Monitor ($200–$600)

d. Follow Focus ($200–$1,800)

e. Matte Box ($500–$1,100)

So by the time you complete your Franken-Camera rig, you've laid out about as much money or very possibly more than if you just had purchased a dedicated video camera to begin with.

6. Rolling Shutter Issues

The first few generations of prosumer video cameras were powered by CCD imaging chips. The new crop of DSLRs are powered by cheaper CMOS imaging chips that allow manufacturers to pack a lot more bang for the buck in chip size. However, like anything else that does the same thing for less, there's a drawback. In this case the drawback to CMOS technology is that it's more prone to an issue called **rolling shutter**. What this means in practical terms is that if you tilt, pan, or otherwise move the camera swiftly, there's a good chance that the resulting image will blur, distort, and/or appear "stuttery." So camera moves with DSLR cameras are best limited only to those that are slow and steady.

7. The Depth of Field Is Too Shallow

Sure, shallow depth of field looks more cinematic and film-like, but there's such a thing as too much of a good thing in my opinion. There are plenty of times when it works well for the genre and the story, but there are also plenty of times when it doesn't. A bride standing at the altar or a close-up of an ice-cold beverage on a table looks great in the super-shallow depth of field of DSLRs. However, seeing only one skier clearly out of a pack of 12 racing down a slope or watching a motivational speaker giving a speech at a podium are situations in which super-shallow depth of field can be awkward and impractical for the content. Not only that, but heavy use of shallow DOF is essentially an aesthetic style, and like all aesthetic preferences, it can also go *out of style*. (Remember the frenetic handheld style popular in indie films in the '90s like Laws of Gravity, Clerks, El Mariachi? Don't see so much of that style anymore, do you?) Any stylistic choice such as shallow depth of field, should be motivated by the content and story on screen and not done just because you could. Shallow depth of field is a powerful visual storytelling device that can be used to great effect to shift the audience's attention, give meaning to props and characters or visually create certain emotional states. So if you can't answer the crucial question as to *why* a given shot has extreme shallow depth of field in terms of **the story** you are telling, you are probably overusing it and diluting the real impact of the technique. As these cameras find their way into the hands of more and more clueless amateur shooters, heavy use of shallow depth of field may become real old real quick and ruin it for us all, that's all I'm saying.

. . . So those are all the main reasons I think DSLRs are whack. However, there are two sides to every issue. So in the interest of being fair and balanced, let's look at the flip side of shooting with DSLRs as I lay out all the reasons why DSLR cameras are da bomb on the next page.

Intro

So I just told you how whack and impractical DSLR cameras are, but now I'm gonna share all the genuine reasons I think DSLR cameras are the bombdiggity . . .

1. You Can't Beat the Image Quality for the Price

As of the moment I'm writing this, you simply cannot beat the superior image quality of DSLR cameras for the entry-level price of less than $3,000. For a fraction of the cost, you can shoot images on a chip that is more than 10 times the size of dedicated video cameras that cost triple the price.

2. Super-Duper Stealth Mode

When you're "borrowing" sensitive locations (i.e., NYC subway train, Beverly Hills Mall, etc.), shooting in a hostile environment (i.e., Middle East protest, inner-city 'hood, etc.), or are in any other situation that requires you to shoot covertly, DSLR cameras are a good choice because they draw considerably less attention and look just like still cameras. The lower-profile innocent appearance of a video-capable DSLR camera versus a full-fledged video camera could ultimately help you avoid being kicked out (the subway), captured (Syria), or punched in the mouth (inner-city 'hood). So if you regularly shoot in risky places, a DSLR is an ideal choice.

3. You Can Build the Rig as You Go

Yes, sooner or later, you will want to buy some accessories to make your camera fully video-friendly—such as an audio recorder or adapter, a monitor, a support system, and perhaps a follow-focus and all the little bells and whistles you'll need to make the camera actually do what it do. But the beauty of DSLR shooting for broke filmmakers is that you don't have to get everything all at once. You can save up for the initial camera purchase and then buy some "bells" one paycheck and maybe get some "whistles" for Christmas and slowly build your rig as your finances allow. The most important thing is that you just get into the game, and the low entry-level price of DSLR cameras offers easier access to filmmaking and the ability to slowly and steadily build a formidable "**Franken Camera**" with full video functionality and superior image quality.

4. More Practical Options for Multicamera Shoots

Again, the math is real simple here. It's a lot easier to buy or hustle up three affordable $2,000 cameras than it is to pull together three $6,000 cameras. The rental rates for DSLR cameras are considerably cheaper than their prosumer and professional video counterparts. Also, because these cameras have become so popular so fast, chances are if you are tied into any filmmaking community or group at all, there are probably at least two other people who have DSLR cameras, particularly

Canon 7D's, 5D's, or T2i's, which are the most popular models as I write this. So not only is it easier to gather three DSLR cameras, but you can also probably get three cameras of the exact same brand, so you won't have to worry as much about matching up the images. This popularity also means it's easier to find experienced operators if you rent or borrow the cameras from friends.

5. You Can More Easily Borrow the Lenses

Borrowing lenses is even easier than borrowing cameras. Because these are still camera lenses and not dedicated video lenses, they are much more affordable and in greater supply around you. For every one person you know who's a videographer, you probably know two who shoot still photos and have a few decent lenses that you can borrow. Some of my friends have even formed informal DSLR and lens co-ops. Each has invested in a different set of lenses, and they simply borrow and trade them back and forth whenever they shoot, as well as loaning and borrowing each other's cameras for multicamera shooting. (The stakes aren't as high with the costs of DSLR cameras, so in general I've noticed that people are a little more generous with a Canon 7D than, say, their $25,000 Red camera package.) And again, even if you don't have any friends with compatible still camera lenses you can borrow, these lenses are also much cheaper to rent and save up for as you go. So DSLRs offer you an affordable option to swap out and shoot with superior prime and zoom lens versus many popular prosumer video cameras which have fixed lenses that you can never change.

6. Great Low-Light Sensitivity

Another major advantage of having a big, beautiful imaging chip is that the big chip doesn't need nearly as much light as smaller prosumer video chips. This means it performs much better in low lighting conditions—a huge advantage for indie, low-budget, documentary, and international filmmakers who often have to rely more on natural lighting conditions and stealth shooting to pull off their projects. Fewer lights means less time, hassle, and money spent lighting and more time spent shooting your project.

7. Super-Duper Shallow Depth of Field

Apart from price, video-capable DSLR cameras offer extremely shallow depth of field. Shallow depth of field is the cinematic look that shows your subject in sharp, clear focus while the background behind them is completely soft-focused (or the opposite if you prefer). While you can achieve decent shallow depth of field from any prosumer camera under the right conditions (primarily long lens and open aperture), you can achieve an even greater shallow depth of field under almost any circumstances with a DSLR camera just by virtue of the larger chip size. This look is associated with the cinematic look of 35mm film, which also naturally has a much more shallow depth of field because it uses a big negative. DSLR cameras can achieve such an extreme depth of field that you could easily show someone's eyes in focus while their nose and ears are out focus . . . if you're into that sort of thing.

Conclusion

... So those are all my basic pros and cons of DSLR shooting. The extra hoops you have to jump through to make DSLR cameras truly video-friendly may not work for everyone, but make no mistake about it, DSLR cameras are a revolutionary game-changer in the world of indie film. They are the very definition of a "disruptive" technology. Suddenly, the entry bar was lowered, and the video quality bar was raised simultaneously, opening the flood gates for a new generation of Down and Dirty filmmakers to do what we do with better image quality than ever. The DSLR movement may be just an intermediary step to more affordable large-format prosumer video cameras. Time will tell, but for now, I think the long-term future of these powerful and awkward new filmmaking tools is still to be determined.

When it comes to video shooting, DSLR cameras have some "issues." But hey, don't we all? However, just as in life, "issues" are only a big problem when you don't deal with them (or bury them deep deep in your soul). So here's how to give your DSLR camera some much needed video therapy or at least hide its worst shortcomings . . .

ISSUE	PROBLEM	SOLUTION(S)
No manual audio control	■ You can't record professional-quality audio if you can't have 100% control over your levels. ■ Cameras autogain boosts hiss when it's quiet on set.	■ Use a preamp or adapter that has XLR inputs and manual control. ■ Record audio separately on a digital audio recorder. ■ Record audio separately on a digital video/audio recorder.
No XLR inputs	■ You can't use professional XLR mics and sound gear. ■ Unbalanced mini-stereo audio is more noisy.	■ Use a preamp, digital recorder with XLR, or external video/audio recorder. ■ Use and CLR to mini-stereo adapter cable.
No on-screen audio levels	■ It's impossible to accurately judge your audio levels. ■ You can't adjust tone from a mixer.	■ Use Magic Lantern firmware, which adds on-screen audio levels. ■ Use an external video/audio recorder with on-screen levels.
Depth of field is too shallow	■ You would actually like a person's nose and eyes to both be in focus at the same time. ■ You want the background and foreground to be in focus.	■ Shoot with wider lenses or wider zoom lens settings. ■ Shoot at a higher F-stop (F8 or above). ■ Avoid ND filters if you don't absolutely need them.
12-minute clip limit	■ You may need to record longer than 12 minutes at a time. ■ You may miss part of a wedding, speech, or performance.	■ Shoot with multiple cameras. ■ Stagger the start time when multicamera shooting so all cameras don't run out at the same time.
Hard to judge focus	■ Big picture—little LCD screen makes it hard to tell what's sharp. ■ There's a high risk of soft-focus shots.	■ Use an external monitor—the bigger and sharper, the better. ■ Use Magic Lantern firmware, which adds peaking functionality. same time.

VIEWFINDER

This little add-on magnifies the LCD viewfinder and can be used in lieu of a monitor.

ONBOARD MIC

You'll want something better than the camera's little built-in mic for better audio quality.

SUPPORT RIG

DSLRs are small and less steady when handheld, so you'll need a support rig—rods or some other type of handheld apparatus. You'll also need something sturdier than your camera body to mount all these accessories to—hence a support rig.

FOLLOW FOCUS

This is an expensive but useful tool to make focusing smoother and more accurate. You can mark exact focal points on a follow focus and have an A.C. pull focus for you.

Image courtesy of B&H Advertising

XLR AUDIO ADAPTER

Professional mics have XLR connections. DSLRs don't. So you'll need an adapter box to connect pro mics and mixers to your DSLR and help you manage the audio quality.

HD MONITOR

The most essential accessory in order to better judge your image quality and focus.

MATTE BOX

A matte box has two important functions: to hold filters and to shade the lens from sunlight.

ARM MOUNT

This an adjustable support arm that can be used to easily move your monitor to various viewing positions.

A QUICK LOOK AT LENSES

Shopping for a good lens can be almost as daunting as shopping for a camera. A typical lens description reads like this: **Canon EF 70–200mm f/2.8 L IS II USM.** So to clear up some of the confusion, here's a quick guide to some common lens features and terminology or—as I like to think of it—Lensology.

LENSOLOGY 101

Zoom = lens that can be adjusted to multiple focal lengths.

Prime Lens = lens with a single fixed focal length; 12 mm, 50 mm, 85 mm are prime lens standards.

Servo = lens with motorized zoom control.

L = luxury lens, maintains same f-stop regardless of focal length—a very good lens trait to have for documentary work. Non-L zoom lenses will lose light as you zoom in to telephoto forcing you to re-adjust exposure.

OIS = Optical Image Stabilization, a feature that helps steady handheld shots.

USM = Ultrasonic Motor—these Canon EF lenses have motors that are quieter than most and less likely to bust the mood, scare off wildlife or be heard on mic.

Cinema Lens = a general term that describes the very highest quality lens for film and video. These lenses tend to be faster, very well made and ideally suited to deal with issues specific to capturing a moving image as opposed to a still image. These are what the pros like to use and they are priced accordingly.

PL Mount = this type of mount is found on many expensive professional cameras. All the best lenses come in PL mount.

EF/EF-S Mount = The mount of many popular Canon cameras including the 5D line, the 7D, the 60D and the C100/C300, which also have optional mounts.

Tilt Shift = Lens with extreme shallow depth of field around the edges that make things look like toy models.

WORD TO THE WISE:

Don't even think about using a lens without a protective filter of some kind. A screw-on **clear UV filter** is standard issue to protect your lens from accidental scratches and impact. The filter cost $40–$80, but a busted lens is a tragedy.

Factoring In Crop Factors

In the world of film, the 35 mm format is the gold standard. With the rise of digital DSLR cameras, manufacturers enabled the masses of broke aspiring filmmakers like us to shoot with less expensive 35 mm still photo lenses. However, video chips that are as big as a 35 mm frame of film—called full-frame cameras—are still pretty expensive, so they started using image sensors that are actually smaller than 35 mm frames. So the full-frame image being projected onto the smaller sensor of that camera ends up being cropped or cut off by a certain amount depending on the size of the sensor. To understand how a given lens will look on a cropped camera vs. a full-frame camera you need to multiply the lens focal length by that particular camera's crop factor. Example: Using a 50 mm lens on a Canon 7D, which has a crop factor of 1.6, means you would multiply 50 mm × 1.6 to get the equivalent look of an 80 mm lens on a full-frame camera. This is very important to understand when shopping around for lenses.

COMPARATIVE SENSOR SIZES AND CROP FACTORS

35mm Full Frame	crop factor = 1	Canon 5D Mark ii, Sony NEX-VG900
APS-H	crop factor = 1.26	Canon D7000
Super 35	crop factor = 1.4	Sony FS-100/FS700, Kine-Raw Mini, Arri Alexa, Canon C100/C300, Sony F3, Red Scarlet
APS-C	crop factor = 1.6	Canon T4i, Canon 7D, Sony EA50UH
4/3"	crop factor = 2	Panasonic AF100
Black Magic Cinema	crop factor = 2.4	BMCC Camera
2/3"	crop factor = 4	Panasonic HPX500
1/2"	crop factor = 5.2	Sony EX3, Sony PMW-200, Go Pro Hero 3
1/3"	crop factor = 7	Panasonic HMC-150, iPhone 5*, Canon XF-100

●●● = 3 Chips
* close enough at 2.84"
** front camera = 1/6"

THE PROBLEM WITH 4K

I think the significance of 4K shooting has been somewhat over-hyped by many indie filmmakers. Don't get me wrong it's *very* cool and a *huge* leap in the state of the art that we can capture video at such an incredible resolution—4× that of standard HD video. So it *is* a big deal . . . just probably not that big a deal for *you*—at least not yet, because there are some very simple practical matters that seem to be overlooked in all the 4K hype:

1. There are very few places that you can actually SEE a 4K image.
2. 4K footage requires much more media storage, which gets expensive fast.
3. 4K footage requires much more computer power to edit and render.

At the time I'm writing this, the price of projectors that can actually show an image in 4K is still very expensive. So astronomical, that outside of a few high-end private post-production/screening facilities, there isn't any place you can actually see 4K resolution onscreen. Plenty of things are being shot in 4K alright, but most of them are being edited, screened and distributed at the same standard HD resolutions (1080p or 720p) as everything else. The theaters in the US are still in the process of converting to expensive HD digital projectors and I simply don't see them throwing out that technology for even more expensive 4K projectors in the immediate future.

Similarly, 4K televisions and monitors are still in their (expensive) infancy and I think 4K cable will happen later, rather than sooner. HD still hasn't saturated the US market and I doubt that the cable companies, Netflix or YouTube or anyone else will be broadcasting any significant amount of programming or videos in 4K anytime soon, so very few people will ever get see a film at 4K resolution for the time being.

The simple fact is 4K is *so good* that we don't have many practical means to actually see it in it's full glory. Beyond that, from a producing and technical standpoint, shooting 4K is also impractical because it requires much more (at least 4× more) digital storage space and processing power as working with 1080 or 720 HD footage.

Sure, the better the original acquisition format, the better the end product will look, but the difference in cost, hard drive space, computer power and editing workflow hassles may not be worth the modest improvements you'll get after "down-rezing" 4K to standard HD resolution. If you're shooting a very cinematic and visually beautiful subject matter or shooting a narrative feature that will likely be distributed theatrically, I'd give 4K a serious look. Otherwise, I think we're still a few more camera generations away from 4K being a practical acquisition format for most independent documentary projects.

A Quick Comparison

As digital technology improves and prices come down, it's becoming more popular for filmmakers to buy some or all of their own equipment. In fact, you could set yourself up with a pretty complete production package for less than $10,000. On the flip side, you could rent a high-end production package for three weeks for almost the same price and get much greater production value and variety of equipment for your dollar:

How to Decide

As with everything else in your budget, you will have to do the math for your particular situation. If you only need the equipment for a short time, it probably doesn't make much sense to buy. One advantage of renting is that you can always shoot with the latest and greatest equipment and customize the package to your particular shooting situations and budget.

However, if you will be shooting over a few months or producing several more projects over the next year, a purchase may be a better choice in the long run. Just be aware that regardless of what camera you buy, you can be sure that camera manufacturers will put out an even better (and probably less expensive) one within a year's time. It WILL happen. Just accept it. It is the blessing and curse of video equipment. Research and decide what's most practical for you. Remember your camera is just a tool. To keep things in perspective and avoid getting a case of camera-envy, read the Down and Dirty Camera Creed on page 74 put it on your wall and recite each morning when you wake up and every night before bed.

Buying a Used Video Camera

And a last word about video cameras, I don't think it's really worth it to purchase a used video camera that's more than say a year or two old. Just like computers, the technology keeps getting bigger and better and the prices keep getting cheaper, so I think you're better off getting the best camera that fits your budget and will grow with your needs and work well with the most recent technology. If you do buy a used camera, you want to find one that has as little wear and tear as possible.

Somewhere at the bottom of the "Others" or "Miscellaneous" menus of most video cameras, is usually a record hours meter. This meter is like an odometer for a camera, that tells you how many hours it's been used to shoot. When comparing used cameras, ask how many hours are on the camera to give you a relative idea of how much wear and tear the camera has been through. If you do go the route of buying a used camera, I'd also only consider those that had a single owner, rather than one from a rental house, film school or similar heavy-usage situation.

✔ Purchasing video equipment is practical for long or multiple projects. However, renting will allow you to shoot on more high-end equipment.

The Down and Dirty Camera Creed

This is my camera. There are many like it, but this one is <u>mine</u>.

My camera is just a tool. Without me and my knowledge and skills, my camera is useless. Without my camera, as a filmmaker, I am useless.

Some cameras may be bigger, some cameras may be better, but I don't have those cameras. I only have <u>this</u> camera and it's all I need to tell my visual story.

I will master it. I will learn all the buttons, settings and workflows I need to know. My shots must be properly exposed- neither over, nor underexposed - but just right every time. My focus must be sharp and clear. My white balance must be true.

I will strive to always get the shot, make every camera move smooth, every shot meaningful, and every composition a masterpiece. Even though I will not always be able to achieve all these things, I will still always <u>try</u>.

With this camera I will tell great visual stories. So be it, until there are no more audiences to watch and no more stories to tell . . . The end.

SMARTPHONE CAMERAS

Since I first published this book, smartphones have become ubiquitous filmmaking tools. From location scouting to research, director's viewfinders to visualization tools and slates—there's an app for that. However, if you wanna use your smart phone as a video camera, you're gonna have to raise the quality bar as high as you can get it. I've successfully slipped some HD iPhone B-Roll and 8 mm FX footage into a few projects and was very happy with the results.

Just because you're shooting on a smartphone doesn't mean you can throw the rules of production value out the window. In fact, you should do everything you can to raise the production values in every other area possible if you want your work to still look and feel professional. The most noticable weak point to address is audio. However, there are a number of things you can do to up your production value: check 'em out . . .

PROFESSIONAL MICS

With the right adapter or accessory, you can get just about any professional XLR mic to work with your smartphone. In order to make this a reality you'll need one or more of the following:

XLR-mini Adapter Cable

At the very least you'll need a cable that goes from the pro XLR connectors to the more consumer mini stereo jack.

XLR-mini Adapter

This is pretty much the same as the XLR-mini adapter cable, minus the actual cable.

Power Source

If your mic requires phantom power, you'll also need a power supply like this Beachtek PS-1 box, a Juiced Link box, or a mixer.

Wireless Lavs

Wireless lav mics don't need phantom power, so if you've got a mini stereo cable out of the receiver, you're good to go.

Wireless Shotgun

If you have a wireless mic unit with a buttplug, you can use any shotgun or handheld mic unit wirelessly with your smartphone.

Mini-Stereo Shotgun

There are little mini-stereo shotgun mics made just for phones. Not as good as pro XLR mics, but way better than no external mic at all.

Notice that I didn't list just using the built-in phone mic as an option . . . that's because it's **not** a option if you're *serious* about shooting a film project on your cellphone. The importance of good audio is a constant. (The one exception here would be if you were to mount a separate smartphone on a boom pole and get it in close as a boom mic.)

TRIPODS, MINI RIGS, AND STABILIZERS

The first thing you have to do if you decide to go the route of cellphone cinema is remember that the root word is still *cinema*. That is to say all the other principals of filmmaking don't change just because you're shooting on a cellphone. It still needs to be just as *cinematic*.

Like all equipment the cell phone is simply another tool to do the same job. And like any other camera it needs to remain steady. To that end there are a number of accesories that you can get to help you stabilize your little HD video camera that also happens to be able to make calls, send texts, and play Mine Craft.

There are simple adapters like the Glif adapter pictured here that will allow you to put a cell phone on a standard tripod.

The Gorillapod is also a popular and versatile choice that allows you to creatively attach a camera to a fence, branch, or pole.

For smooth moving shots, there are also steadying devices like the Woxom Sling Shot.

The Owle is a device that aids handheld work by adding more weight, easy grips and mounting points for accessories and a tripod.

Cinevate makes some nifty and relatively inexpensive iPhone/DSLR dollies like the one pictured here.

Whatever they make for the big cameras, they now also make for small cameras like the MobiSlyder, a little slider/jib for smartphones and very small cameras.

LENSES

One of the big limitations of cell phone video cameras is that they have fixed non-zoom lenses, so you are limited to a single field of view and have to move closer or farther away from your subject in order to change your frame. (And don't even think about using any type of digital zoom on your phone. It's a cheap artificial effect that looks like complete

digital pixelated garbage. End of discussion.) However, there are many different companies that sell little inexpensive lenses that you can mount onto your phone to get macro, wide-angle and telephoto shots. iPhone filmmaking has matured to the point that some higher end lens manufacturers now offer products—like the iPro Lens System by Century Optics that offers telephoto, macro, wide and fish eye lenses—for those more serious about getting the best images from their phone.

FILTERS

There are also a variety of color and special effects filters that you can get to enhance your image, but I think such effects are always best done in post-production. However, if you know you like the look of a certain filter and don't mind being "married" to it in post, then you can save yourself some time and go with that star filter or kaleidoscope effect.

APPS

The built in camera apps on many phones are have pretty basic functionalities such as manual touch to focus and set exposure. However, there are a number of apps that give you much greater manual control over your phone's video. These best of these apps allow you to set and lock in on a specific exposure, focus, audio level, and even adjust frame rates. The more manual control you have over your image, the more you can make your phone camera perform like a dedicated video camera.

FILMIC PRO

Filmic Pro is one of the most popular apps for iPhone filmmakers. It allows you to manually set white balance, exposure, frame rate, audio level, and video quality.

8MM

This is a brilliant and simple app that has a variety of vintage film looks that mimic 8 mm and other old film stocks by adding grain, flicker, and even frame jumps. While you probably wouldn't want to shoot an entire documentary project with this app, it's perfect for shooting short creative segments such as flashbacks, segues between scenes, and montages.

PCM RECORDER

The built-in recorder apps that come with your phone are okay for voice memos, but for video production you've gotta step it up. That's where a dedicated pro audio app like **PCM Recorder** by Tascam comes in. It allows full manual control over your audio levels, and even has a built-in equalizer, limiter, and other pro features.

EDUCATIONAL EQUIPMENT ACCESS

Renting and purchasing equipment are the most common and obvious means for filmmakers to shoot. But in the world of Down and Dirty, do-it-yourself, broke-as-a-joke filmmaking, we sometimes have to be more creative. So another practical means of obtaining cheap or reasonably priced access to equipment and editing facilities is to enroll in an independent film workshop, filmmaking cooperative such as Chicago Filmmakers in Chicago or Downtown Community Television (DCTV) in New York, or a filmmaking class at a local college or university. Virtually every major city has several filmmaking workshops/ programs that could serve you well.

Many an indie film began (or was entirely completed) as someone's class project. The acclaimed indie film *Raising Victor Vargas* began as director, Peter Sollet's, short class project at NYU. John Singleton developed the script for *Boyz in the Hood* while a student at USC. Not only will these programs give you access to equipment, but they will also give you access to crew members and instructors who can help guide your vision and solve problems as they crop up. I know of several people who signed up for programs simply to get access to equipment.

As an alumni and now a film instructor at a major film school (NYU), I can testify that there are many advantages to this approach, especially for the novice filmmaker. There are also a few distinct drawbacks, particularly for more independent-minded filmmakers. All film schools and workshops are *not* created equal. Some have the latest and greatest equipment, but strict controls on equipment access and the type of projects they support while others have more liberal access, but the equipment is abused by students and poorly kept. More reputable programs offer better instructors and more competent students (i.e., crew members). If you go with this means of getting equipment, you need to take time to research the workshop/school you are considering. Discuss your project with instructors before you enroll. Be honest. See if it's something they will support. Most important, talk to *students* that have actually attended the program. They will usually be brutally honest and tell you if the program or equipment is lacking in any way.

ADVANTAGES	DISADVANTAGES
Access to full equipment package	Equipment may be in poor condition
Access to editing facilities	Project may be limited by assignment
Instruction and feedback	Must attend classes
Access to crew members	Program may end before you're done
Ongoing technical instruction	You may be assigned to a lame crew

DOC EQUIPMENT PACKAGES

	SMALL	MEDIUM	LARGE
Camera	■ DSLR Camera ■ Prosumer HD Camera	■ Pro HD Camera ■ DSLR Cam Full Rig ■ Compact Big Chip	■ 4K Cinema Camera ■ HD Cinema Camera ■ Pro Broadcast HD Cam
Camera Extras	■ Tripod ■ Screw-on Filters	■ Tripod ■ Viewfinder (DSLR) ■ Field Monitor ■ Monopod	■ Tripod ■ Matte Box/Rods/Filters ■ Large Field Monitor ■ Follow Focus
Sound Gear	■ Shotgun Mic ■ Boom Pole ■ Shockmount ■ Windscreen ■ Headphones	■ Shotgun Mic ■ Boom Pole ■ Shockmount ■ Headphones ■ 1 Lav Mic ■ Windjammer ■ Zeppelin ■ Wireless Lav Mic	■ Shotgun Mic ■ Boom Pole ■ Shockmount ■ Headphones ■ 2+ Lav Mics ■ Zeppelin ■ Windjammer ■ Handheld Mic ■ Wireless Lav Mic ■ Field Mixer
Lighting Gear	■ 3 Light Kit ■ Reflector ■ Gels and Blackwrap	■ 3 Light Kit ■ Camera Light ■ Reflector ■ China Lantern ■ Small Grip Package ■ Gels and Blackwrap	■ 3 Light Kit ■ Camera Light ■ Reflector ■ China Lantern ■ Fluorescent or LED Light(s) ■ Soft Box ■ Medium Grip Package ■ Gels and Blackwrap
Other Gear	■ Cloth Backdrop	■ Dimmer ■ Cloth Backdrop	■ Dimmer ■ Cloth Backdrop ■ Camera Stabilizer ■ Slider or Dolly ■ Jib

See the Glossary for detailed descriptions.

Be Practical

You will also have to take some practical matters into consideration when researching documentary subject matter, talent, and locations. In many cases, these practical considerations will present significant barriers to production. When faced with barriers, you must train, think, and plan harder. You must hear *The Eye of the Tiger* in your head . . . "Dunt! Dunt-Dunt-Dunt!" Always think R-O-C-K-Y before shooting . . .

THINK R-O-C-K-Y BEFORE YOU SHOOT

Relevance: If you make it, will anybody care? Is the timing right?
Originality: Are there six other docs on Tupac? How will yours differ?
Commitment: How long/hard will this shoot be? Can you commit to that?
Kash: How much will it cost? Can you afford to travel there or stay? *(Author freely admits that using K is a reach here.)*
Your Access: Can you gain entry into the world you want to show?

There's no magic formula here, but you should have satisfactory answers to these questions before you start shooting. Think of everything that could possibly stop you. Then think of solutions and workarounds for each. Get creative. Ask yourself *how else* can you tell this story. Your time, money, and energy are all limited resources. Don't be scared of the challenge, but also be realistic about what you can accomplish within your time frame, filmmaking resources, and level of experience.

> ✔ *Be realistic about what You can and can't do. Always think "R-O-C-K-Y" before shooting.*

Okay, you've got your equipment package figured out, but who's going to actually use all this stuff? You still need a crew. Generally speaking, documentary crews tend to be smaller than narrative film crews since they don't require as much equipment and usually benefit from being more mobile and low-key. I like to work with as few people as necessary to keep my subjects

relaxed and to maintain my focus on the subject matter rather than directing crew. Here's a basic breakdown of typical production duties for three different sized doc crews.

TWO-MAN CREW	MICRO CREW	FULL CREW
Producer/Director	**Producer/Director**	**Producer**
■ Supervise setup	■ Supervise setup	■ Supervise crew needs
■ Assist with setup	■ Warm up subject	■ Quality control
■ Warm up subject	■ Brief subject	■ Secure releases
■ Brief subject	■ Conduct interview	
■ Conduct interview	■ Quality control	**Director**
■ Quality control	■ Secure releases	■ Supervise setupt
■ Secure releases		■ Brief subject
	Camera Operator	■ Conduct interviews
Camera/Sound Operator	■ Light scene	
■ Light scene	■ Set up and run camera	**Camera Operator**
■ Set up and run camera		■ Supervise lighting
■ Set up and mix sound	**Sound Operator**	■ Set up and run camera
	■ Set up and mix sound	
	■ Boom (if necessary)	**Gaffer**
		■ Light scene
		Sound Operator
		■ Set up and run sound
		Boom Operator
		■ Boom
		Production Assistants
		■ Assist with all of the above

Introduction

One of the most important tasks of producing any film or video is hiring crew. Your choices of people to work with are more important than just about any other decisions you will make outside of choosing subjects. It's more important than your format, your equipment, or your budget. Apart from your concept, 50% of the success or failure of your project will be directly related to the *quality* of the crew you hire.

Good Crew Members

Good crew members will take your vision and run with it. They will use their expertise and creativity to add new layers and ideas to your project. They will put their experience and knowledge to work for you, instantly coming up with clever solutions to problems that have kept you awake for nights. They will push you and everyone else to hang in there during the trying times and keep making the project better. They will tactfully help you avoid common mistakes. They will help bring your project in under budget and on time. They will literally give up weeks of their life, completely forgo sleep, and even *bleed* for your project.

Bad Crew Members

On the flip side, bad crew members will take your vision and squash it. They are inflexible. They will whine and complain about the most mundane or obviously uncontrollable things. They will break your concentration at every turn. They will show up on location late and leave early. They will slowly drag down the morale of the entire set. In short, a bad crew member is a life-sucking, paralyzing ball and chain around your ankles that will stifle your every step, criticize every decision, and ultimately become your biggest obstacle to a successful production. Here's how to tell if you've got a good or bad potential crew member.

✔ *Whether you're paying them or not, choose your crew members wisely. They may make or break your project.*

LOOK FOR CREW MEMBERS WHO:	BEWARE CREW MEMBERS WHO:
■ Come recommended from another filmmaker	■ Don't understand the limitations of your budget
■ Are excited about your project	■ Are more concerned about the equipment than the content
■ Have positive "can-do" attitudes	■ Look down on your video format
■ Are eager and hungry	■ Show up late on set or miss meetings
■ Want to get more experience	■ Have unrealistic expectations
■ Have something to gain	■ Seem overly concerned about the pay rate
■ Have access to equipment	■ Are routinely argumentative or negative

THE PRODUCER—DIRECTOR RELATIONSHIP

CHRISTINA DEHAVEN, PRODUCER
(My Uncle Berns, The Apple Song—Black Eyed Peas, The Cut Man, 761st)

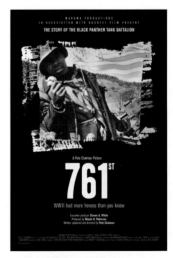

It is a marriage because these are literally the "parents" of a film. These are the two people that carry from start to finish the creative aspects and the practical aspects . . . financial, legal, administrative, everything else that you need to power the creative goals of a film or power a project of this size. I've encountered a lot of directors who try to do everything themselves just because they don't quite understand how important it is to have a producer. They say, "Oh, I'll just direct and produce it myself. Maybe I'll shoot it, too."

It's a collaborative process. You *can* make a film by yourself. It has been done before. But, it's not going to be nearly as good as it could be with the help of a collaborative team, a collaborative team effort, and at the forefront of that team is a producer.

Everybody has to have a producer and the communication between these two people is the most important thing because they are the central heart of communication for every single major department, both technical and creative, from production design to the editor to the sound mix to everything, these are the people that keep it together.

And people will constantly look to the producer and director to be on the same page, to answer questions and to do everything, solve problems when they arise. Keep everyone posted. Keep everyone in the loop. And follow the project along to completion. So, that relationship—I can't emphasis it enough—is probably the most important one on any kind of project.

761st—Maroma Productions/Double 7 Film

ASSEMBLING A CREW

Okay, so you've developed your idea, you've scraped together the cash, and you're ready to make a movie, but you still need the people who are going to help you make it happen. There are several routes you could go. Some may be more effective for you than others depending on your budget, level of experience, and unique situation. Wherever you get your crew, it's important that you understand their expectations, scope of knowledge, and how to best use their talents.

CREW SOURCE	ADVANTAGES	DISADVANTAGES
Film Schools and College Campuses	■ Usually eager to learn and work on a "real" project ■ May bring additional equipment ■ May recruit other crew members ■ Already have some training ■ Open to new approaches ■ More tolerant of low-budget conditions	■ Limited experience ■ May think they know more than they really do ■ May require more supervision ■ May be afraid to admit they don't know something ■ May be preoccupied with their own film projects
Word of Mouth/ Recommendations	■ You already know what you're getting ■ You have advance knowledge of how to get the best from them ■ You can view previous projects	■ There are NO disadvantages to word-of-mouth referrals, they should be taken into account whenever you can get them
Friends and Family	■ Eager and excited ■ More tolerant of low-budget conditions ■ You already know what you're getting	■ Completely inexperienced ■ Must be carefully trained ■ Risky for key crew roles ■ Must be carefully supervised
Film Classified Web Sites	■ Can reach a lot of people at once ■ Brings professionals to you ■ Most ads are free ■ Only people attracted to project and pay rate will apply	■ You really don't know who these people are ■ Must do *extensive* interviews ■ Must sift through many applicants ■ Must plan ahead to meet publishing deadlines

> ✔ *Word of mouth is best when it comes to hiring crew. Learn how to get the best out of crew members.*

BEFORE YOU HIRE A PROFESSIONAL CREW

CYBEL MARTIN, DIRECTOR OF PHOTOGRAPHY
CybelDP.com

Reprinted with permission from Shadow and Act on the IndieWire Network of film sites: blogs.indiewire.com/shadowandact

I believe documentaries change minds and make this a better world. It is (the majority of) film crews' nature to give you 110%. However, it is unfortunate to see a film crew retaliate if certain basic expectations are not met. When this happens, you might perceive a decline in enthusiasm or your crew may only execute the bare minimum of their duties. The worse case scenario is just plain awful.

The "problem" is really a very simple one. If you are new to the film industry you likely have no idea what a professional crew's basic expectations are in film production. And often, they don't want to tell you for fear of offending and losing the job.

I will speak from my experiences and use the term DP, but you could easily substitute sound mixer, gaffer, driver, etc. I will not address the needs of a professional editor as I am clueless, but their contribution is HUGE. **Make sure your editor is happy.**

The first meeting or phone conversation is key. **Show us you're serious.** If you are producing the project yourself or working with a first time doc producer, here are some actions you can take to demonstrate your intentions and your commitment to the project. You might be thinking "I'm the one hiring. Why should I show my commitment to MY project?". It's only because we know from experience how challenging making a documentary is and how frequently people give up in the struggle, especially when they have a "real job" to attend to. **Your commitment gets ours.**

Website—You should have a professional looking website. Flashy graphics aren't necessary. You should have bios of key people, a film synopsis, photos and contact info. In the future, you can add video clips, screening dates and press. If you want to be inspired by some sexy documentary websites, look at HBO or Brick City for Sundance Channel.

Social Media Component—Facebook, Tumblr, Twitter, etc. The ways social media has impacted documentary filmmaking are numerous. Make sure to create new accounts specifically for your film persona. Film crews love to keep friends, family and potential clients informed of what we are working on.

We will drive people to your social media sites and continue to promote your project even in a "downtime". You can show us appreciation in simple yet effective ways. A simple tweet thanking your crew members publicly or posting a set picture commenting on how good the shoot went that day or any other form of social media acknowledgment is always appreciated.

Please tell us upfront if there is anything confidential about your documentary idea. Otherwise, with the best of intentions, we might mention it online.

Video footage—The second you have a documentary idea, you should start shooting. Get your feet wet. That footage is an easy way for you to explain to us what you hope to achieve. If it looks great, we'll be thrilled to build on that aesthetic. If it looks awful, we'll be thrilled to take over and show off what we can add to your project. One of the most engaging documentaries I've ever seen looked terrible. I can tell different camera operators were brought in later. My relief that those moments were captured and this story told far outweighed my desire for pristine footage.

Shooting Schedule—When are we shooting? How many hours per day? How many interviews, important events, potential travel dates, etc. Do you need a crew who can shoot with less than 24 hours notice? Does your project require living in Bali for the month? (If so, call me.) Discussing the schedule during that first meeting will support you in finding the best crew.

If at all possible, I recommend keeping the same crew for the duration of a documentary (assuming you're proud of the results). It's just much easier for the same crew to maintain a consistent look, gain knowledge of the subject matter and trust with key people. Don't worry if, because of timing and budgeting constraints, you have to hire different DPs. Just follow the rest of the basics in this post and you'll do great.

Budget to Pay Crew—If your desire is to work with a professional crew, then you must pay them. Many first time director/producers make their livelihood in a different industry and see this foray into filmmaking as fun. A "labor of love". It is fun for us as well, but it is also our job. You must remember this is our means to paying mortgages and health insurance. It's what allows us to attend seminars to brush up our skills and buy new equipment.

You will need *to create a budget for your film* and know what you can pay per day. You can offer to increase that amount when more funding becomes available. We know documentaries work on tight budgets and will be flexible. I've made concessions for when the project involved costly international travel or the director was also a filmmaker/artist. You can hire a student (there are many talented ones) or shoot the footage yourself until you are financially able to hire a professional crew. The money you save can be used to pay a competitive rate for a DP to film pivotal scenes.

(Originally published on IndieWire.com)

THE CREW MEETING

The week before any big shoot, you should sit down with your crew and go over everything that will happen during production. This meeting should include the producer, director, camera department, sound department, production coordinator, and anyone else who will have an active role on the shoot. You can do this in a formal office setting or over dinner or drinks—whatever floats your boat. It doesn't matter. What matters is that you clearly communicate your vision, everyone understands their individual roles, and that all logistical issues and crew concerns are worked out *before* your shoot day. Some topics you'll want to cover are listed below.

Crew Meeting Agenda

✔ Call Time
✔ Plan Changes
✔ Topic Briefing
✔ Shooting Schedule
✔ Equipment Package
✔ Transportation and Travel
✔ Directions
✔ Crew Member Roles
✔ Location Logistics and Concerns
✔ Handling Talent and Location Owners
✔ Shot List/Storyboards
✔ Difficult Scenes
✔ Estimated Wrap Time

✔ *Meet with your crew members beforehand to go over logistics and to get everyone on the same page.*

Meals

Food is one of the great secrets of the pros. It has a tremendous psychological effect on the crew. When the big studios and production companies do a show there is always a "spread" of delicious food and a continuous supply of snacks, drinks, and coffee. Crew members often speak of three things when describing a particular project they've worked on: the quality of the project, the organization of the shoot, and the food. Good food is a *standard* part of the deal for all professional film and TV crews. It is (and should be) expected at every level from pro to amateur. I wish I could lean into the ear of every new filmmaker and shout this through a bullhorn:

DO NOT SKIMP ON FOOD FOR YOUR CREW!!!

This is one of those critical "little details" that so many new filmmakers overlook or save as an afterthought. Feeding your crew good food is extremely important, especially if they are working for free. In the long run you will not save a dime by being cheap when it comes to food for your crew. (Oh, you'll save on the food itself, but you will lose immeasurable amounts in crew morale, energy level, pacing, and attitude toward the shoot.) As a general rule, the more hell you put your crew through, the better your meals and snacks should be. The crew is the machine that creates your project. Food is the fuel that runs the machine. The better the food, the better your machine will run, the better your project will turn out. It's that simple.

Food Strategies

Because doc crews tend to be so small, catering usually isn't a practical (or affordable) option. You will mostly be dependent upon local restaurants for meals. It is a vital part of preproduction to scout out and have menus from all the local restaurants. The Yelp! phone app and website is an excellent tool to research local restaurants. You can get restaurant phone numbers, addresses, maps, customer reviews, and menus with a few keystrokes. Also, most restaurants now make their menu available online or would be happy to e-mail or fax it to you if not. You can let the crew pick from the menu by setting a dollar amount per person. Or, a more simple solution is to just order a variety of different dishes and serve them up family buffet style.

✔ *Never skimp on food for your crew. The better you feed your crew the better they will perform.*

If you're feeding a large number of people, make sure you place your order a few hours or a day or two ahead of time and tell them when you need it delivered or will be picking it up. Whenever possible, picking up your order is the best option because delivery will always take longer and it's easier to check and correct the accuracy of the order at the restaurant. Always try to get plates, cups, ice, napkins, and utensils when possible to save a little cash. Also, don't forget to get receipts for your records!

Craft Services

The term **craft services** is just a Hollywood name for the snacks and drinks department. (Yes, craft services is a department.) You should have a craft services table (or box if you're on the road) stocked at all times with a variety of high-energy and sugary foods, spring water, and drinks. Try to find out your crew's favorite snacks ahead of time and have plenty on hand.

I know you may be tempted to save a few bucks, but stay away from generic food items. Name brand snacks and drinks are always better, even if it's only psychological. Instead of giving them "the very best," a table full of *Chumps Ahoy* chocolate chips and *Tropican't* orange juice tells your crew that you care about them enough to get "the absolute cheapest" thing you can get away with, and they may in turn give you the absolute cheapest effort *they* can get away with.

Apart from snacks and cold drinks, it is absolutely essential that you try to make coffee available on set at all times, morning, noon, and night. If food is the fuel of the filmmaking machine, then caffeine is the lubricant that keeps the parts moving. Keep your filmmaking machine gassed up and lubricated and you will get noticeable results in performance and morale—and a reputation as someone who takes care of their crew people.

If you have a sizeable crew, really try to find a dedicated craft services person. This is a perfect position for those eager friends and relatives that want to help out, but have no filmmaking experience. Their job is simply to keep the food and snacks flowing, help coordinate meals, and help clean up the mess afterward. It's a great position for someone who just wants to be a fly on the wall and observe. If the job's done well, the craft services person is often the most popular person on set.

Taking Care of the Vegetarians

Personally, I'm a carnivore, but these days I have rarely done a shoot that didn't involve at least one vegetarian or vegan (no meat, dairy, or egg products) crew member. Make sure you survey the crew members ahead of time for vegetarians or other special dietary needs, so you'll know how many veggie or special meals you'll need daily. To make life even easier, find out what types of common dishes they like and which local restaurants they prefer.

Vegetarians, and especially vegans, are sometimes treated like second-class citizens when it comes to meal time on a film crew. However, do not ignore these crew members' dietary needs. I can tell you from experience that vegetarians will not want a salad or a simple side dish for *every* meal. It's definitely harder to find menus that accommodate vegetarians, but you've gotta put in the leg work to make it happen or else you will have some miserable souls on your crew and it will be reflected on the shoot. Take care of these people and they'll take care of you.

> ✔ Keep snacks, water, and caffeine flowing at all times. Take care of the vegetarians on set.

5 DOWN AND DIRTY FOOD IDEAS

1 GET LOCAL RESTAURANTS TO DONATE FREE FOOD

This is a common practice that many indie filmmakers use to supplement their food budgets. With a little *advance* leg work and salesmanship, any producer should be able to talk at least one or two local restaurants into providing a free or greatly discounted meal or two for the crew, in exchange for a film credit or a shot of their business in the film (as B-Roll or an actual location). Although we know the ugly truth, filmmaking is still sexy to a lot of people who will be glad just to be a part of your project. Find these people and ask them to help you.

2 HAVE FRIENDS OR RELATIVES COOK FOR THE CREW

If your mom or friend is a great cook, have them hook up a hot home-cooked meal for the crew. Do not underestimate the power of a good home-cooked meal. For some crew members it will be their first in weeks.

3 TREAT THE CREW TO A LOCAL DELICACY

Okay, this isn't really a money-saving suggestion, but if you occasionally arrange for a shrimp cocktail, premium ice cream, or some other little rare or gourmet treat to be on set, it will provide a nice boost to crew morale and energy before you tell them it's going to be another 16-hour day.

4 BREAK OUT THE GRILL

Designate a Grill Master and cook up some steaks, burgers, and vegetables and turn it into a cookout. This is a good idea for remote locations. It can be messy, but it's a fun and cheap way to serve hot food cooked to order.

5 GET ALL THE FREEBIES AND EXTRAS YOU CAN

Whenever possible, get free extras from the restaurants you order from. Many will offer these standard, but if they don't, make sure you ask. Nothing makes a restaurant manager happier than a large order from a potential repeat customer. So I recommend that you always dangle out the possibility of ordering more meals during your shoot to encourage them to provide any or all of the following items for free: utensils, plates, cups, napkins, ice, condiments, tablecloths, tea bags, sugar, creamer, etc. (I've even been allowed to borrow an industrial coffee maker for the day!) If you work it right, you can get any or all of these items and sometimes even barter for a few free appetizers, drinks, or desserts. The bigger the order the more leverage you have. Remember, every free item is money back in your budget.

CHAPTER 2
LOCATIONS AND LOGISTICS

Making Arrangements with Your Subjects

Documentary filmmakers often have to be flexible and "on call" as their story develops. Be mindful of the fact that your subject is accommodating you into their personal/professional life and you will often have to shoot *at their convenience*. Try to schedule shooting or interview times and locations that are most convenient for your subject, as this will allow them to be the most relaxed.

Interview Locations

Choose a location with characteristics that help tell your story. Don't just choose a spot at random. Just like all other elements of filmmaking–lighting, camerawork, music, etc.–your choice of location is yet another aspect of your storytelling that helps reveal character and theme.

Scouting a location in advance is always your best bet. For interviews it's preferable to find a controlled environment. The less control you have over an interview environment, the more headaches you will have trying to make it look and sound right. *Sound* should also be a primary consideration when location scouting. (See also "5 Sound Rules to Live By" and "Location Sound Hazards" on pages 206 and 210, respectively.)

Generally, the best location for interviews will be a room in your subject's home or place of occupation. First off, this is where they will be most comfortable and it's probably the place where the themes and subject of your documentary are most *visual*. For example, you could interview a race car driver in his living room, but in his racing garage or next to his car would be more visually interesting. You could interview a former boxing champion on a bench in a public park, but wouldn't a boxing gym or locker room communicate more about your subject's world? . . . *The correct answer is, "Yes!"*

Another practical consideration is lighting. Is there ample sunlight or indoor lighting in the room? Is there ample electricity if you need to add lights? Is there enough room to shoot? Comfortable temperature? Does the room portray the character of your subject accurately? How long will it take to prep the room? If you are stuck with a barren, ugly, or inappropriate location, some alternatives are to use a neutral background such as a brick wall or cloth backdrop, shoot outside, or use shallow depth of field to keep the background out of focus. (See also "Hot Tip: Easy Do-It-Yourself Backdrops" and "Hot Tip: Shallow Depth of Field" on pages 252 and 240, respectively.)

✔ Choose a location that will help tell your story visually.

Introduction

Although documentary is a different animal than narrative production, you still must manage your locations with the same (if not more) deft social skills to ensure the complete success of your shoot. Do not make the common mistake of thinking that just because your subject works, frequents, or has access to a location, that you, your crew and camera will be automatically welcomed there. Often that will be the case, but many

times it will not. Even if your subject assures you that everything's cool and you trust them, make sure that they have *asked* the owner and explained the subject and scope of the shoot.

Your subject may be a doctor at General Hospital, but the hospital administration may have very strict policies about cameras in the building. Often subjects will be completely oblivious to such matters. If permission hasn't been secured from the proper people beforehand you may find yourself in a situation where you and your subject are embarrassed or even reprimanded. Worst of all, your big planned interview in that great location will be a total bust.

Corporate-owned locations, franchises, entertainment venues, government offices, military sites, schools, and places housing adult or illegal activity are all locations that must be researched and secured properly before you ever show up with a camera. Many of these institutions will have a public relations (PR) person whose main function is to act as a liaison between the institution and the media. That's you.

If your story will show the institution in a favorable light, help educate people about their business, or is in line with the political goals of the organization or individuals in charge, you are much more likely to get a "yes." If your story involves a controversial topic, you can almost definitely expect to get a "no." (I'll get into how to combat this later.) Either way, you need to communicate with these institutions as far in advance as possible. The following chart will help you determine who to contact and some of the issues you will likely confront.

> ✔ *Make sure you have permission to shoot from the location owners and not just your subject.*

LOCATION	LIKELY CONTACT(S)	COMMON OBSTACLES
Hospital	■ PR/Media Rep. ■ Administration	■ Policies against shooting ■ Patient privacy ■ Pending legal issues ■ Employee privacy ■ Internal politics
School	■ Principal/VP ■ Superintendent ■ District Spokesperson	■ Student privacy ■ Policies against shooting ■ Internal politics
Government Office (i.e., military, welfare, housing dept.)	■ PR/Media Rep. ■ Agency Head	■ Policies against shooting ■ Touchy political situations ■ Employee privacy ■ Internal politics
Entertainment Venue (i.e., nightclubs, concert halls, arenas)	■ Venue Manager ■ Venue Owner	■ Union rules governing film crews ■ Contractual obligations to talent that restrict shooting ■ Contractual obligations to other media that restrict shooting
Corporate/ Franchise Office (i.e., Microsoft, Subway, Sony)	■ PR Rep. ■ CEOs Office ■ Business Affairs	■ Bureaucratic shooting policies ■ Slow response to requests ■ Internal politics ■ Pending legal issues
*Adult Business (i.e., strip club, casino, bar)	■ Owner ■ Manager	■ Customer privacy ■ Pending legal issues ■ Desire for low profile
*Illegal Location (i.e., gambling house, brothel, crystal meth lab)	■ Organization Leader ■ Operation Manager	■ Fear of arrest ■ Desire for low profile ■ Customer privacy

*Adult and illegal locations always require extra special care, research, and safety precautions. Don't get assaulted, arrested, or shot at for the sake of a film. It will **never** be worth it. (But if you ever do, make sure you get it on camera!)

Dealing with PR Reps and Other Media Liaisons

Once you have sold them on your idea, the PR/media liaisons person will be your ambassador to the institution. They will usually arrange everything and instruct you as to who, when, and where you may shoot. They will often inform you of the best visual locations on the property and suggest great interview subjects that you may not have considered. I have found PR people to be helpful allies on many documentary shoots.

Be honest with a PR person or location owner when pitching your story. (For example, don't say your story is about the hospital's new cancer ward if it's really about assisted suicide, and don't agree to not shoot patients, then sneak in some quick shots.) I say this not just because it's ethically wrong, but because you will risk getting kicked out mid-shoot. And from a strictly personal standpoint, you will screw it up for all the rest of us who may want to shoot there in the future.

Doc Location Ethics

You can get into slippery ethical territory when you're trying to convince a skeptical location owner (or subject for that matter) who is reluctant to participate in your documentary, but there are ways to do it and still be honest: Empathize, relate, listen, address their concerns. Be passionate.

But most of all, focus on everything your documentary has to offer that will appeal to the location owner's best interest and sensibilities—a chance to be heard, a chance to correct a misperception, positive publicity, educating the public, expanding their audience, etc. Always put yourself in their shoes. Would you let someone shoot story X in your business? Think ahead about their likely concerns and come up with ways to address them one by one, beforehand. Be fair. And be honest. You will sleep well at night and be more respected as a documentary filmmaker.

> ✔ Be upfront about the subject of your project and stick to agreements with location owners.

The Exception to the Rule

Now having said all that, I should also say that there is a notable *exception* to the above advice. And that is the investigative doc. By it's very nature, the investigative doc often calls for filmmakers to gain access to secret, dark, and restricted places to uncover critical social and political situations that usually don't want to be uncovered. Penetrating these places to get at the truth will, more likely than not, require some deception along the way. Shooting under false pretenses, ambush interviews, and hidden cameras are all common tricks of the investigative doc trade. At its very best, the investigative documentary can serve as the catalyst to free people from Death Row, change laws, and help right longstanding wrongs. But at its very worst, it can easily ruin people's lives and livelihoods unfairly. There is a big difference between creating profound, hard-hitting video journalism that uncovers serious wrongdoing and taking sleazy, manipulative video sucker punches that deliberately twist the truth.

If you're in the doc game, you need to also be in the truth game, because along with the title "documentary filmmaker" comes great power and responsibility. Use it wisely, young Grasshopper.

> *A camera can do more damage than a gun. Be responsible about what you point yours at.*

TRAVELING WITH EQUIPMENT INTERNATIONALLY

STJEPAN ALAUPOVIC, PRODUCER, DP, EDITOR
www.stjepanmedia.com

Traveling internationally for a video project is a lot of fun but it can also be nerve-wracking. Not only have you invested thousands of dollars into your gear, but you most likely have only one shot to pull off the project. Things can go downhill quickly if you're not prepared, so I'm sharing some tips from my personal experience to help make your filmmaking abroad run smoothly.

Packing Like a Pro
We've all seen the disgruntled airport employee who likes to body slam our luggage like a pro wrestler. Now multiply that by 20 and imagine the baggage handlers doing that to a piece of gear that wasn't packed properly. It's not pretty. Packing right is the first step to smooth shooting while traveling.

Investing in some hard-shell cases will not only get your gear through airport carousels, but also all of the other transportation methods you may encounter on your trip. (Trust me—New York City cab drivers have nothing on some of the foreign taxis I've taken.)

When it comes to travel cases for gear, wheels are your best friends. While wheeled cases may be the more expensive option, you'll save yourself a lot of sweat and aches when transiting between airports, hotels and shoot locations.

The size and weight of the cases also are important factors. Research your airlines and find out what the specific restrictions are for checking in your items. Not all international airlines allow you to have a 50-pound bag. I recommend you do this when initially budgeting your project so you can factor in all the travel costs.

Now that you've purchased your cases, it's time to start packing your gear. Cameras, small monitors, lights, microphones, media, hard drives, laptops and other fragile items should go into your carry-on bag. This way, you can keep them close and have access during your flights. Foam customized carry-on cases are ideal because they prevent your gear from shifting during transit. B&H has a great selection of carry-on approved luggage for video equipment.

Stands, tripods, tape and cables can usually survive in your checked baggage, but it's wise to bubble wrap or pack these items in the middle of your clothes for extra protection. Golf-style cases can be checked and are a good option for holding larger items. The Transportation Security Administration (TSA) makes approved locks that you can use on your cases. You can even get your cases shrink-wrapped and pre-inspected for customs at some airports for a small fee if you want to prevent scratches, wear and tear and theft by baggage handlers.

Important Documentation: Carnets

To bring video equipment into many countries you may need a carnet. No, that's not a made-up foreign word. According to the United States Council for International Business, carnets are "international business documents that simplify customs procedures for the temporary importation of various types of goods." Basically, it's a list of the gear and corresponding serial numbers printed on an official document saying that you won't sell your gear on the black market in said country.

Carnets get stamped when you leave and return to the United States as well as at the airport's customs office when entering and leaving each country. They are accepted by most countries and allow you to pass through with ease. Unfortunately, carnets are not free but they will save you the cost of paying taxes in countries and even bogus fees in some places. The price of the carnet is based upon the cost of the gear you will be bringing and the number of countries you are visiting.

You could try to play the tourist card and say that your gear is for personal use, but why risk having to deal with customs? Chances are that you will be pressed for time, so I highly recommend using a carnet that is accepted by most countries. For a couple of hundred dollars, you can have a broker prepare the documents, which allows you to concentrate on the actual production. Check out Roanoke Trade (www.carnetsonline.com) for help on preparing a carnet.

Working with Foreign Power

It sounds obvious, but it's easy to forget when you're focused on all of the production details: some of your gear may not work with foreign country power sources. Nothing starts a trip out on a bad note like getting shocked or shorting out an important piece of recording equipment on the first day of shooting.

If your equipment is dual-voltage and has 110v/220v printed on it, then all you need are some travel adaptors. These will adapt your North American plug so that it fits the foreign outlet. Most modern day laptops and battery chargers are dual-voltage.

A travel converter or inverter is needed if your gear is not dual-voltage. This means that your piece of equipment does not have the same power cycle as the foreign country you're in. Believe me, the stench of burnt electronics is the last thing your client is going to want to smell. You'll have to do some math and figure out what type of converter or inverter you need to make it work. Take your gear to a local electronics store if you're not sure.

Things You're Forgetting

Again, traveling internationally takes a lot of coordination and it's all too easy to let some things slip between the cracks—like visas! Some countries are going to require that you have a visa to enter the country. Researching your destination is critical here.

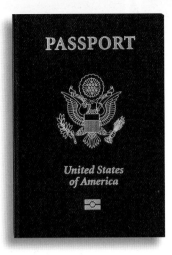

You'll also want to make sure your passport is current as some countries do not accept them if they expire within six months of your visit. Make sure you build in time for these items before you buy a ticket and do extensive research on entry and exit requirements for all of the countries that you're visiting. If you have to travel abroad last minute, for a premium fee, many companies offer expedited passport services.

Staying Healthy

While this is probably the last thing we think about as video professionals, it can make or break the project. This trip may be a once-in-a-lifetime event and the last thing you want is to be stuck in your hotel room because you're not feeling well.

Take a few days to relax and rest up before you depart. Drink a lot of water on the plane and, if you can, request an aisle seat so that you can get up, walk around, and stretch your legs throughout the long flight.

Before you leave, find out if your destination requires any vaccinations. Consider getting some sleep aids to help you sleep on the plane and adapt to time zone changes. It's also a good idea to travel with a general first aid kit. You never know when you may need a Band-Aid or some antacids. (Lots of great foreign food out there!)

Have a Backup Plan

The tips here will help you be more prepared, but remember—things can change at the drop of a hat when you're on the road. Have a conversation with your client and crew about backup plans in the event of delays, broken equipment, or even sickness.

Scheduling a few extra shooting days is wise, too, as there will no doubt be things you have no control over like travel delays and bad weather. Consider bringing along crewmembers that can act as backup videographers, too.

We're Not in Kansas Anymore!

Keep in mind that things don't always work abroad like they do in the United States. Have some patience with customs officers and locals. Remember that English is most likely not their first language.

Research the local culture and always be polite. Establishing a good relationship with the local crew and clients can lead to some incredible footage and get you access to things you would never otherwise know about.

Take a moment and enjoy each place and the people that you meet there. And remember, traveling abroad to shoot a documentary is almost always an amazing opportunity—as long as you plan it out properly.

STJEPAN ALAUPOVIC has produced award-winning videos and coordinated successful projects in Italy, England, Hungary, Romania, Switzerland, Thailand, Hong Kong, China, India, Taiwan, and Singapore.

HOW <u>NOT</u> TO GET YOUR CAMERA JACKED

One of the things that lower budget productions sometimes overlook is security. This is unfortunate because they are the people who can least afford to lose a few thousand dollars worth of equipment. Here are some things you can do to avoid being ripped off in the big city, or anywhere else for that matter:

1 **NEVER LEAVE EQUIPMENT UNATTENDED . . . EVER**

The number one thing you can do to protect your gear is not leave it unattended in vehicles, *especially* overnight, *especially* in cities. (Studies have shown that it only takes a crackhead with a crowbar about 30 seconds to break into *any* locked vehicle.) If you have so much gear that it's not practical to unload your vehicle, make sure you park it in a bonded (i.e., insured) garage or reputable lot with 24-hour attendants. You should be aware that many garages will likely charge more for large vehicles or not accept them at all. Never store valuables where they will be visible (and accessible) through windows. Use a cargo van over a passenger van for storing gear. Even during shooting someone should always be with the equipment if it is in, or just outside of, a vehicle.

2 **ALWAYS KEEP YOUR MASTER MEDIA SECURE**

Nothing on set is more valuable than the precious footage that you have spent days gathering, because you usually won't have the option to go back and capture those moments again. Once they're gone, they're gone. Master media, tapes, hard drives, etc. should always be downloaded, verified, and backed up as soon as possible.

3 **TAKE INVENTORY OF EQUIPMENT REGULARLY**

It's very easy for a busy and tired crew to leave some gear behind as you dash from shoot to shoot. Every single time you wrap at a location, you and the crew should double- and triple-check to make sure that you have all of your equipment. Keep a written checklist. Make sure you especially check for easily overlooked parts such as adapters, filters, cables, and especially anything small.

4 **BE WATCHFUL LOADING AND UNLOADING GEAR IN PUBLIC**

Apart from leaving it alone overnight, loading is the most vulnerable time for your equipment because the crew is busy moving gear back and forth or organizing in the back of the vehicle. It's very easy for someone with quick hands to lift an item sitting on the sidewalk and never even be noticed. Always have a dedicated set of eyeballs watching the gear during load in and load out.

BEING PREPARED FOR REMOTE LOCATIONS

ALRICK BROWN, PRODUCER & MICAH SCHAFFER, PRODUCER/ DIRECTOR

deathoftwosons.com

(Death of Two Sons)

Alrick: Aside from the physical challenges of being in Africa, there were technical challenges even with our small equipment package. I actually produced getting all the equipment together. We made sure we had backup everything, because when you're out there, you don't know what's gonna happen, so we had two  cameras. One was our main camera, one was our backup just in case anything happened we'd have an extra camera.

We had two cameras. We had our lav mics and we had our mixer, which we didn't have backups for. So if any of those went, we would've ended up just going straight into the camera. We anticipated the kind of scenarios that would come up. We took a crazy amount of batteries . . . enough batteries that would, literally, if we had to run the camera straight, run the lavs straight, we'd have enough batteries to cover the entire three weeks that we were shooting. We made sure we had adaptors so we could charge the batteries any chance we could, we even bought a charger for the car . . . Some of the villages are very remote—no running water, sometimes no electricity, and we just made sure that we had that stuff under lock.

Micah: It didn't take a huge amount of money to have this sort of preparation. We bought used equipment. We got deals on the rental stuff. We had people loan us things, we had a camera loaned to us. It's not like this anal, intensive preparation necessarily has to be expensive. It just has to be **thorough**. So we did the production phase on a very, very small budget, relative to the production value of the film, and it was just our hours that went into it, rather than dollars. Hours making sure everything was straight.

TRANSPORTATION CONSIDERATIONS

Okay, so your locations are all set, you've got a crew, equipment, and a shooting schedule. Now the only question is: "How are you gonna get these people and this stuff to where it's gotta go?" The answer depends primarily on the size of your budget, the size of your crew, and the distance you have to travel. Let's look at a couple of options.

VEHICLE	CAPACITY	RENTAL	COMMENTS
Car	■ 4–5 people ■ Sm./med. package*	$60–100/day	■ Best means for stealth shooting ■ Easiest to drive and park ■ You own or can borrow a car for free ■ Limited trunk space for gear ■ Least comfortable ■ Personal luggage requires a second car
SUV/Mini-Van	■ 6–8 people ■ Sm./med. package*	$80–150/day	■ Good for stealth shooting ■ Larger capacity for people and gear ■ No hidden storage for equipment
Cargo Van	■ 2 people in front ■ Med./lg. equipment package	$100–150/day	■ Can carry all gear plus luggage ■ More difficult to find parking ■ Only 2 passenger seats ■ Cannot double as crew vehicle
Passenger Van	■ 12–15 people ■ Medium equipment package*	$100–200/day	■ Can carry all gear plus luggage and crew ■ More difficult to find parking ■ 8 gas guzzling cylinders ■ No hidden storage for equipment

If you're carrying fewer people, you can fit a larger equipment package in these vehicles.

VEHICLE	CAPACITY	RENTAL	COMMENTS
Cube Truck	■ 2 people in front ■ Large equipment package	$150–250/day	■ May come with equipment package ■ More difficult and expensive to park ■ Very conspicuous/high profile
RV (Camper)	■ 6–12 people ■ Medium to large equipment package	$150-$300/day	■ Rolling office/interview location ■ Most comfortable crew travel option ■ Plan/edit while traveling ■ Overnight sleeping space ■ Gas guzzling behemoth ■ Very conspicuous/high profile ■ More difficult/expensive to park/drive ■ More prone to damage/accidents

5 TIPS FOR TRAVELING WITH EQUIPMENT

1 CARRY ON SENSITIVE EQUIPMENT

If you can at all avoid it, DO NOT check in or put cameras, mics, or other sensitive and valuable equipment in your check-in luggage. Doing so greatly increases the risk of theft or damage from rough luggage handling. A much safer option is to check in your personal luggage and keep all cameras, laptops, mics, and other sensitive equipment with you as carry-on luggage that will never leave your side. (Even if you go to the bathroom, take it in the stall with you!)

2 PROTECT YOUR EQUIPMENT

If necessary to minimize baggage, remove the equipment from it's case and wrap carefully in towels, clothing, or other protective material before placing in your check-in luggage.

3 TAG AND BE PREPARED TO OPEN ALL CASES

Put your name, phone number, address, and *destination* contact info on separate tags on all equipment and bags. Airport security will likely inspect all equipment. Don't put non-TSA-approved locks on check-in luggage as these will be cut off by security.

4 KEEP A MASTER LIST ON YOU AT ALL TIMES

Before your trip take a few minutes to type up a complete inventory list that includes all items, their exact quantities, and, most important, serial numbers for all equipment. This list may be needed in case of loss or theft while traveling.

5 TRAVELING WITH MASTER FOOTAGE

It's always best to keep your master footage in your carry-on luggage. After a long and successful shoot this is now your most valuable possession. Try to always make back-up copies before you travel and guard them at all cost. And *never* put hard drives containing valuable media in with your checked luggage. Hard drives and media cards are not affected by airport X-ray machines.

Using a small luggage cart makes carrying gear simple and fast when shooting solo.

STEALTH SHOOTING TACTICS 101

It's always less hassle to do things by the book when possible, but as many broke documentary filmmakers will tell you . . . it ain't always possible. At the end of the day, there's only one golden rule when making a Down and Dirty documentary—get the shot. Here are some of my stealth strategies for overcoming common shooting obstacles.

1 NO PERMITS, NO PROBLEM

Scout the location for security, the best shooting angles, and spots where you are most likely to go unnoticed. Talk and walk through your shots in a nearby location, out of sight, then go to the crucial location ready to roll. Save riskier shots for last. You don't want to get kicked out before you shoot what you came for. Keep a producer on lookout nearby to talk and run interference with authorities if you get busted. (Ultimately, this probably won't get you an okay to shoot, but it will buy you more time to finish getting your shot.) Never get into a big ruckus with a cop, security guard, or other authority figure when you don't have permits or permission. You have nothing to gain but unnecessary trouble once you've been busted. Just pretend you're a clueless film student or hobbyist, apologize, and leave quietly. Find an alternate location or come back another time, when the coast is clear.

2 TRAVEL AND SHOOT LOW PROFILE

This means roll with a skeleton crew of two or three people max: a camera operator, a director/producer, and/or a sound recordist or PA. DSLR's and smaller video cameras are obviously a better choice than full-sized cameras. Wrap the camera up in a large towel for cushioning and use backpacks or gym bags instead of camera bags. Don't take out the camera until you need it. Use **breakaway cables** if you have a separate sound person. Dress and act like the rest of the crowd. Depending on what you want to shoot and how stealth you have to be, a very small and less-obvious HD camera like a Go Pro Hero Cam or smartphone might be just the trick for a quick bit of inconspicuous shooting.

3 RECORD STEALTH SOUND

Nothing attracts attention like an 8-foot pole with a mic waving around on the end. If you're using a shotgun mic, try mounting it on the camera or on a pistol grip instead. Avoid wearing over the ear headphones which will attract too much attention. Instead, use low profile earbud headphones or rely on the camera's **auto gain control** (AGC). Wireless lavs can also be hidden beneath the clothing to pick up the audio of the wearer.

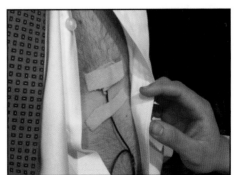

Dr. Scholl's MoleSkin Plus used to hide a lav mic on a subject..

4 USE STEALTH CAMERAWORK

Set your camera menu, record color bars, and do a test recording *before* you even get out of the car. (Make sure you disable or tape over the red recording light and turn off the recording beep in the menu.) Either, preset or use auto functions for white balance, iris, and sound. In this instance, you may also want to use autofocus if there is sufficient lighting. Keep the camera on and at the ready. Cradle the camera or hold it down low when walking. Avoid using tripods. Instead, use a **monopod** or whatever you have to work with to steady your shots. You can set your camera on a flat surface or nestle it in a towel or coat on top of a trashcan, mailbox, or car. If you must use a tripod, it's best to use a portable lightweight model that can be quickly set up and moved.

5 ADD PRODUCTION VALUE WITH LOCAL RESOURCES

The greatest asset a Down and Dirty filmmaker has is imagination. Where others see a Ferris wheel, we see a crane shot. Where others see a guy behind the wheel of a taxi, we see a location scout and production vehicle for B-roll. Anything that rolls, moves, lifts, flies, or has a great view that you can sneak onto with a camera could serve to add some free or inexpensive production value to your shoot. For the price of admission (and

This dramatic aerial view is courtesy of a Ferris wheel. Total cost: $3.50.

perhaps a generous tip for a cooperative driver or operator), you can shoot compelling footage, narration, and even interviews from double-decker sightseeing buses, cabs, tourist boat rides, Ferris wheels, rickshaw rides, observation decks, raised subway lines, horse-drawn carriages, helicopter tours, cable cars, public balconies, or even glass elevators. With a little imagination and creativity, the cranes, dollies, and jibs you need to add some movement and production value are all around you. If it has a dramatic viewpoint, you just need to get on it, bust out your camera, shut up, and shoot!

6 ALWAYS HAVE A "PLAN B"

Even if you do all of the above, you still have a good chance of being shut down by "the man" if you don't have permits or permission to shoot at your location. When this happens, make sure you're ready with **Plan B**—an alternative location or something else you can shoot instead. Don't let the whole day's shoot go to crap because of a single setback. There will always be unexpected setbacks. Don't just roll with punches . . . be ready to duck and punch back.

Location Releases

You should try to get signed **location releases** (also called "location agreements") as soon as possible after a location owner has agreed to let you shoot. This can be done in-person, by fax, e-mail, or standard mail. If you are unable to secure a location agreement before shoot day, it should be at the top of your list *before* you shoot. Location agreements vary, but almost all include:

❏ Name of location owner
❏ Location address
❏ Filmmakers, title of project, and production company
❏ Dates and times needed
❏ Permission and cost (if any) to use location
❏ How any damage or legal claims will be handled
❏ Signatures of location owner and filmmaker

✔ *Get a signed location release <u>before</u> you shoot.*

Location Insurance

A primary requirement of most locations, particularly commercial and corporate, will be that your production has insurance that covers the location by naming them as "additional insured." It is reasonable and advisable for them to cover their butts in case your lights set the curtains on fire or a customer trips over your tripod and breaks their ankle. They won't want to be held legally liable for any damages to their property or injury to others that result from your production.

Your policy should cover property damage up to $1,000,000.00 (standard). Covering specific locations is usually a simple affair. Basically you notify your insurance company of the name and address of the location(s) you want covered and they will fax and/or mail out the certificates of insurance for you to give to the location owner. You should plan on 24–48 hours for the insurance company to process your request, but I've also worked with companies that would process certificates the same day. Make sure you check with your insurance company for the turn-around time on certificates.

✔ *Many locations will require that you have insurance.*

Do You Really Need Insurance?

I know that many filmmakers strapped for cash ask this question, especially after they get that first insurance quote. They have a small crew and their location owners haven't asked about an **insurance certificate**, so they ask themselves if they really need production insurance.

The short answer is "No, if you're *sure* that nothing will go wrong." The problem with that answer is that you're never *sure* when or if something is going to go wrong. Having production insurance is like using a seatbelt or having airbags in your car. You don't actually *need* either one 99.9% of the time, but on those unavoidable tragic .1% of occasions when you really do need them . . . seatbelts, airbags, and *production insurance* are all invaluable. You or your production may not survive without them. I think there is a technical term for what happens when a filmmaker doesn't have insurance and a rare, but all too real catastrophe actually does happen. I believe the term is "totally screwed."

Shooting Without Insurance

Even so, I understand that many documentary makers don't have the luxury of putting their money anywhere else, but on the screen. (I have gotten insurance quotes that actually exceeded my entire project budget!) So they shoot without insurance. This is a common reality. It's also a gamble. Film shoots are magnets for improbable disasters—car wrecks, grand theft, injury—you name it.

Make sure that you fully understand the risks and consequences if there is a catastrophe, and do everything you can to minimize the chance of damage or injury. Consult other filmmakers for their candid advice about your circumstances. My advice is that if you can afford insurance, get it. The very nature of indie filmmaking is risky and sooner or later everyone's luck runs out. With a micro-crew shooting a documentary, you probably won't be dealing with as much risk as a narrative film crew, which usually has more people, equipment, and activity. But you're still dealing with risk, the unpredictable, and the ever-present Murphy's Law: "Anything that can go wrong, will."

Keep in mind, something as simple as a passerby tripping over a cable on the ground could lead to years of messy legal and financial headaches. Insurance is peace of mind, albeit a costly peace. If you genuinely can't afford insurance, you're certainly not alone in the world of indie filmmaking, but you really have to weigh the risks carefully before shooting without insurance. Remember, accepting risks is also accepting *consequences*.

> ✔ If you shoot without insurance, you risk liability for property damage, injury, etc. Do what you gotta do to make your film, but understand the risks you are taking.

SHOOTING IN DA 'HOOD

Standard documentary subject matter such as poverty, social justice, underground culture, etc., will almost always involve at least some shooting in rough areas, euphemistically known as "da 'hood." Documentary filmmaking can be a foolhardy or even dangerous endeavor if you ignore the real-world issues of class, race, and culture. Over the years I've shot extensively in various 'hoods throughout the country. In almost all cases, the crew I was part of was well-received and got the footage we needed without incident. Here are some tips for shooting in 'hoods from Baltimore, Maryland to Kabul, Afghanistan.

1 RESEARCH THE AREA

Before you even think about shooting in a rough or unfamiliar area, you need to find out as much as you can about that neighborhood. Try to get a sense of the cultural and economic make-up of that area, as well as how historical and recent events have affected the neighborhood. Talking to key people from the neighborhood ahead of time could be the difference between you and your crew being greeted with warm smiles or hurling bottles.

2 GET A 'HOOD AMBASSADOR

This is the best move you can make. In Beverly Hills you need a permit. In the 'hood you need an ambassador. The ideal person may be a long-time resident, civic leader, a gang member, a beat cop, an outreach worker, a local business owner, etc., anyone that has roots and respect in the neighborhood. Look for a go-between who may carry influence with the people you want on camera. Talk to them in advance (without your camera) and explain what you're doing and why. Really try to connect with them. If they get it and they trust you, they will ultimately become de facto producers on your shoot. They will make introductions, set up interviews, point out significant visuals, alert you to dangers, or even help provide security. They will advise you on how to handle yourself and give you tips on dealing with the people you really seek. If you're down with them, the neighborhood will be much more likely to trust you and open up. In a word, they will give you the Holy Grail of documentary—*access*. If you don't know the culture, the next best thing to an ambassador is an "interpreter." Think of this person as an cultural consultant. This is someone who is not necessarily from the area, but who can read the scene and is more familiar with the prevailing customs and norms than you may be.

3 STREET SMARTS

Bodily harm is usually not as likely as someone ripping off your equipment. Instruct all crewmembers to make sure that *nothing* of value is left visible in their cars. Video equipment, phones, laptops, clothing, and anything else that could command a dollar on the street is fair game for opportunistic criminals. If the equipment is not locked up at home base or with you, *someone* should be with the equipment. (See also "Hot Tip: How Not to Get Your Camera Jacked" on page 102.)

4 RACE MATTERS

While you may personally be open-minded and racially color-blind as a filmmaker, don't kid yourself for a minute—if you want *real* access to certain places and cultures, race matters. In many areas, the unusual presence of people of other races is often greeted with lingering suspicion at best, and flying insults and debris at worst. It's always better to roll with at least one or preferably several people who are of the same race as your subjects. The more of your crew members who look like, act like, and can directly relate to the people that live in the area, the better. It's just a fact of life in many cultures that people are more trusting of familiar faces. Hiring some locals when possible can be a good move. Of course, you can still win people's trust regardless of race, but plan on it being a longer, slower process—perhaps longer than you have to shoot.

5 TRAVEL AND SHOOT ON THE DL

Travel **on the DL** with a small crew in low-key vehicles. Use pistol grips over boom poles for sound. If you mostly need exterior shots, even the roughest areas are usually quiet and relatively safe in the morning hours between 5 a.m. and 10 a.m. You may wish to shoot out of a traveling vehicle or employ a guerrilla stop and shoot strategy using a driver and DP. Using this "Hop Off and Pop Off" method, by the time most people take notice, I'm already back in the car or pulling away.

Minivan's are the perfect stealth vehicle. Get it. Got it. Gone.

6 SHOW RESPECT

Make it a habit to ask before you start shooting anyone or their property. Take the time to explain what you are doing and answer questions as much as practically possible. If you fail to do your research and earn people's trust, you may have to negotiate shooting terms with hostile residents or even slip someone a few bucks or some other tribute to "protect" your crew and equipment. Sometimes coughing up a $20 bill or two is a small price to pay for a few hours of harassment-free shooting.

CHAPTER 3
IMAGE CONTROL AND CAMERA WORK

Introduction

Understand this: a camera is just *a tool*. Nothing more, nothing less. Simply having the latest greatest technology in your hands is worthless if you don't have the knowledge and skills to make it consistently perform at its best. If I gave you Jay Z's mic or Floyd Mayweather, Jr.'s boxing gloves do you think you could suddenly go out and cut a platinum album or become the welterweight Champion of the World? (The answer is no.) Well that notion is just as ridiculous as the notion that by merely having the best camera, you can shoot the best film. Don't worry about getting the best camera . . . worry about getting the best *camera work*.

Your *camera* is your tool. Your *camera work* is the culmination of your knowledge and skills. Reading books, studying DVDs and taking classes can build your knowledge. Experience shooting will build your skills and expand your knowledge. The camera, lights, and mics are nothing but *tools* you use to apply your knowledge and execute. Many great docs have been shot on cameras that were less than state-of-the-art and the audience never batted an eye, because they had strong content and used the camera they *did* have to great effect.

Technology is great, but don't get blinded by the hype. If you learn as much as you can about using cameras, the language of filmmaking, and image control you will ultimately be able to kick butt with any camera at any budget at any time. That's one of the key secrets to low-budget guerrilla filmmaking–focus on filmmaking craft over filmmaking tools. The doc, *Searching for Sugarman*, was shot mostly on Super 8 mm film, but was finished on an iPhone. It won an Academy Award for Best Documentary . . . The film magic isn't in the camera, it's in *you*, young grasshopper.

> *You don't need a great camera to get good images, you need a great understanding of image control.*

PRIMARY ASPECTS OF DV IMAGE CONTROL		
ASPECT	**AFFECTS**	**CONTROLLED BY**
Focus	■ Sharpness and clarity of picture	Focus ring
Exposure	■ Brightness/darkness of picture	Aperture and gain/iso
Color Temperature	■ Warmness/coolness of picture	White-balance control
Shutter Speed	■ How motion appears	Shutter control

Hallmark of the Pros

A clear and sharp picture is the hallmark of a professional shooter. Pay constant attention to your focus whenever you're shooting. Regardless of whether you're using a camera that cost $2000 or $20,000, or whether you're shooting stills, video, or film, there is only one way to do it right.

How to Focus

1. **Zoom fully into the subject's eyes or the object**
2. **Adjust focus until sharp**
3. **Pull back out to desired frame**

Once you do this, you are now free to zoom and readjust your shot without fear of losing focus. As long as both you and your subject stay in the same position every shot you compose will be nice and sharp. If you focus without first zooming all the way in, your shot may go back out of focus as soon as you try to zoom to readjust your composition.

Overcoming Common Focus Hazards

There is a simple, but HUGE problem facing just about everyone shooting HD on a budget—you have a camera that can create great big beautiful HD, 2K and 4K images on giant tv and movie screens, however, the only thing you have to judge focus by is that little teeny tiny 3" LCD screen on your camera. The end result is often finished footage with one soft-focused shot after another when you were so sure that everything looked in-focus when you were on location. There are two in-camera tools you can use to help avoid this common problem.

Focus Assist

The first focus aid is commonly called "focus-assist", "magnify", or "expanded focus", depending on which camera model you are using. However, they all do the same thing—blow up the image on your LCD screen to 2–4× normal, so you can better judge your focus by eye.

✔ *Always zoom into your subject's eyes to focus. It is much harder to focus in low lighting.*

This button is often found right near the record button. *This feature only affects the image on the LCD screen of camera.* Your recorded image or any image fed to an external monitor is not actually blown up or otherwise affected.

Even with focus assist on many cameras, you may find it tricky to work with, since it requires you to punch-in closer on a scene and temporarily lose reference for your real frame. This can be problematic for handheld work when you're trying to keep certain subjects or details just inside or outside of your frame. It's also easy to forget that you just hit the focus

Familiarize yourself with your camera's focus magnification indicator, so you don't get burned.

assist button and start recording what you think is a close up when it's really a much wider shot.

Peaking

I think one of the most useful tools available to help you judge focus on today's new crop of cameras with big imaging chips and little LCD screens is relatively recent feature called **peaking**. When you turn on the **peaking** feature on your camera, it will put a colored outline around all the sharply focused edges in the frame. I find that red peaking is easiest to see in most cases, but you can usually select the color of peaking in the menu, so you can always choose something that will easily contrast with your scene. Peaking will likely be found under the LCD settings menu. Just like other camera features, such as auto-focus, the peaking feature performs better on some camera models than others, so it's worth researching and doing some of your own testing. Also note that just like focus assist, peaking is never recorded to camera or sent out to an external monitor. However, if your camera doesn't have peaking, you'll also want to note that many external monitors now have a peaking feature as well.

Peaking can help you judge focus better, especially in bright sunlight and wide shots.

Some filmmakers aren't very fond of the peaking feature, because they find it annoying to look at all this "red crap" on their screen. I think this is just a matter of perspective. When *I* see all those red outlines on my LCD screen I see crystal clear images, I see my footage in focus on the big screen, I see happy backers, I see myself smiling in the edit room at all my super sharp-focused shots. I only see the **end result**.

So yes, looking at a bunch of red crap all over your image is indeed annoying, but you'll probably find it considerably more annoying to discover a few hours or days after the fact that you completely blew a golden moment by shooting it out of focus. Which is perhaps even worse than not getting the shot at all.

Sunlight and LCD Screens

Another issue you'll have to contend with is shooting in sunlight. When you're indoors looking at that little LCD screen, it's all good. But when you're outside in the sunlight, the average LCD screen is much harder to see clearly, so focus, exposure and other image aspects are much harder to judge. A simple solution here is to use an LCD screen shade or hood like the ones made by Hoodman. You can also just as easily, fashion your own lens hood with a little cardboard and

It's MUCH easier to see your LCD screen when you shield it from the sun.

tape. Similarly, for the DSLR camera crowd, Zacuto and other companies make viewfinders that you can attach to the back of your camera that not only keep out the sunlight, but also magnify the image on your LCD screen.

Low Light

It's much harder to focus in low lighting. Your chances of shooting something soft-focus increase exponentially when a scene is too dark. Like most auto-functions, the peaking feature does not work well in low light and your autofocus function will likely be all but useless in dimly lit environments. So in low lighting you're on your own, baby! The only effective tools you'll have will be focus assist and using your naked eye–*Uuumm! In low light, use The Force to focus you must, young Jedi!*

When you're behind the camera shooting documentary footage, you have one simple but critical prime objective–get the #!%&* shot! If it ain't in focus, you didn't *get* it. So whether it's focus assist, a viewfinder, peaking, or whatever else they come out with in the future–you need to use any and all features and tools available to help you accurately focus. It's crucial.

> ✔ When you're behind the camera on a doc, you have one prime objective: get the #%&* shot! . . . If it ain't in <u>focus</u>, you didn't "get" it.

EXPOSURE

Light Is Good

Even though today's video cameras are more capable than ever of shooting decent images in low light, the simple rule still applies that the more light you have to work with, the better the image you can capture on video. More light gives you more control over your exposure, focus, and **depth of field**, and the flexibility to shoot with more filters. A good exposure is absolutely essential to controlling your images. A properly exposed image should clearly show visual details in the scene. Notice how the details of the trees, the model's face, and fountain below are lost to bad exposure.

Underexposed

Good Exposure

Overexposed

Aperture and F-Stops

Apart from the amount of light in the scene, your image's exposure is controlled by turning the camera's **aperture ring,** which controls the amount of light coming into the camera lens. This determines the brightness or darkness of the image. (Some prosumer cameras use a dial wheel instead of an aperture ring, but the rules of exposure apply the same.)

The lens exposure is measured in units called **f-stops**. F-stops go in increments ranging from F1.2 to F22 with most video cameras covering roughly the F2 to F16 range. Here's all I've ever *really* needed to know about f-stops: Adjusting to lower f-stops is called **opening up the lens** and adjusting the lens to higher f-stops is called **stopping down or closing down the lens**. The lower the f-stop the brighter the picture. The higher the f-stop the darker the image. That's it. (See also "Hot Tip: Shallow Depth of Field" on page 240.)

Shallow Depth of Field" on page 240.

F-STOPS & EXPOSURE IN A NUTSHELL

1.2 - 2 - 2.8 - 3.5 - 4 - 5.6 - 8 - 11- 16 - 22

more light   **less light**

F-Stops & Exposure in a Nutshell

ZEBRA STRIPES AND GAIN

Your Friend the Zebra Stripes

Zebra Stripes (like Anthony Artis) are your friend. We are both here to tell you when you're doing something wrong and help you correct it–before it's too late. Zebra stripes is a camera function that helps you with exposure by superimposing vibrating diagonal stripes on the overexposed parts of the image. *These stripes are only seen on your camera's viewfinder or LCD screen.* Zebra stripes are *not* recorded to camera. Look for a switch or check your camera's menu for a "zebra" function. Set the zebra stripes function to "100%".

Now, whenever you point the camera at something that's *more* than 100% of the acceptable video level (i.e., overexposed), you'll know without guessing. These blown out areas of the video will not show any image details, just bright white. Once the details of the overexposed area are lost, they can't be "tweaked back in" during post-production. You don't want to close down the lens to get rid of all of the zebra stripes in the image. There should usually be *some* zebra stripes on the natural highlights in the image such as lamps, jewelry, the sun, shiny objects, etc. Where you *don't* want to have a significant number of zebra stripes is on your subject's face or

important details in the frame. If there are zebra stripes on your subject's face or on important details of the image, try these any combination of these remedies: (1) stop down your lens, (2) use an ND filter (or a graduated filter for an overexposed sky), (3) recompose the shot to include less of the overexposed area, or (4) apply powder make-up on shiny faces. (See "Hot Tip: Easy Powder Makeup," page 257).

✔ *Use zebra stripes to help judge exposure. Use gain if you need more light, but beware of video noise.*

IMAGE CONTROL AND CAMERA WORK | 119

Histogram

Another tool your camera may have to help you judge exposure is a **histogram**. A histogram is a dynamic graph that shows you where all the brightness levels are in a given scene at a given moment. As you adjust exposure or change composition, the histogram changes accordingly. The far left represents the dark areas of the image and the far right represents the brightest areas of the image. Spikes on the far left end the histogram indicate that parts of the image are underexposed. Spikes on the far right indicate parts of your scene that are overexposed.

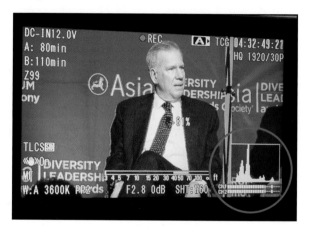

So *generally* speaking you're looking to adjust your exposure to avoid spikes at either end of the histogram, but of course only YOU know what your naked eye sees and what you want a given shot to look like. There are plenty of occasions, such as a snowy field or subject next to a campfire at night, that may spike on the far end of a histogram and still look perfectly natural or appropriate.

Using Gain to Boost Exposure

There are two types of **gain** in digital video: sound and video. Gain just refers to digitally boosting the light or sound levels. Both are measured in units called decibels or **dB**. If your image is still too dark after fully opening up your lens, you should turn on your camera's gain function. This will electronically brighten the image, often dramatically. The unfortunate side effect of using gain is video **noise** or static. *The higher you turn up the gain, the grainier your picture will appear.* Your image quality begins to look more like a VHS dub than DV. This is especially noticeable in the blacks and darker colors in the image. In situations such as shooting night exteriors, night clubs or **surveillance video**, you really won't have much choice. Remember, it's always better to get a grainy image than *no* image at all. It's best to add more light if possible, before using the camera's gain. However, this is not always desirable when doing doc work as it may make people more self-conscious and guarded than the low-key natural lighting. Use your own judgment.

When in doubt, always get a good exposure on a subject's *face*.

COLOR TEMPERATURE

Color Temperature in a Nutshell

All light has a color temperature. Color temperature affects what color that light will look like on video. Sunlight, fluorescent lights, and light from **incandescent** bulbs (a.k.a. **tungsten**), all appear as different colors on camera, because they all have different color temperatures.

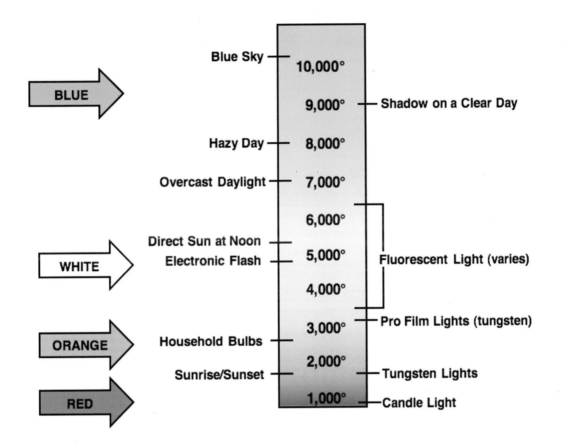

 Bad

 Good

Your camera's white balance function compensates for the variations in color temperature by making the dominant colored light appear as normal white light regardless of its true color. When a camera has not been properly white-balanced, sunlit scenes look hideously blue or indoor scenes look horribly orange. Most cameras have built-in preset functions for daylight and indoor white balance and fairly

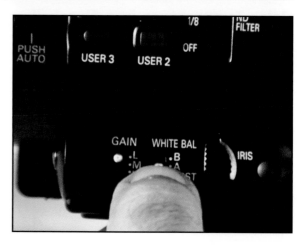

reliable auto-white balance (AWB) functions. Use these presets or auto if you like the look, but if you want to shoot like the pros, there's only one way to go baby . . . manual.

When to White Balance

You should always white balance anytime the lighting condition changes, such as the sun is lower in the sky or you turned on some overhead florescent lights. If you even *think* the lighting conditions may have changed, you should re-white-balance just to be sure. Remember to white balance *before* adding gels to your lights or your white balance will not be correct. You should use pure **white cards** or standard bright white paper for normal white balancing. (A crisp white T-shirt will also do in a pinch.) Avoid using off-white and cream-colored paper to white balance.

WB Menu Symbols

◢ = Manual

◯ = Indoor

☀ = Outdoor

White Balance Special Effects

White-balancing on colored cards will produce different looks. The cooler the color you white-balance to, the warmer the look and vice versa. Using a very pale blue or pale green card, known as a **warm card**, is a common technique to warm up an image. Unless you're sure you like the look, it's better to do color effects in *editing*, because you're pretty much stuck with that look once you white balance and it's nearly impossible to restore a normal white balance after the fact.

Mixed Sun and Indoor Lighting

When shooting in mixed lighting sources you can white-balance normally to split the difference or you can gel either light source to match the other. Color temperature orange (CTO) gels are used to make daylight appear as indoor (tungsten) light. Color temperature blue (CTB) gels are used to make indoor light appear the same color temperature as daylight. (See "Down and Dirty DV Gel Guide" on page 168.)

Working with the Sun

Clear and Sunny

Light Quality:
- hard and bright

Tips:
- beware of dark "racoon eyes" from subjects lit over-head midday
- use soft white reflectors in bright sun
- shoot early or late in the day when the sun is lower in the sky
- shoot in a shaded area
- use an ND filter

Partly Cloudy

Light Quality:
- inconsistent alternating hard and soft

Tips:
- try to time shorter shots with movement of the clouds so you have consistent lighting
- try using auto-exposure if light keeps changing
- shoot early or late in the day when the sun is lower in the sky
- shoot in the shade for more consistent and less harsh lighting conditions

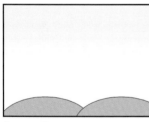

Overcast

Light Quality:
- soft, even and consistent

Tips:
- great conditions for shooting
- looks better on-camera than in real-life
- use soft silver or white reflectors
- try hard silver reflectors if very overcast

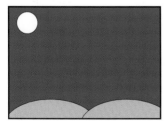

Clear Sky Moonlight

Light Quality:
- hard, cool, pale blue

Tips:
- shoot with a fast lens (f 2.8 or lower)
- use a little bit of gain to boost exposure
- try lowering your shutter speed a little
- large sensor cameras are preferable

SUN AS A HAIRLIGHT

I think this is arguably the easiest and most attractive way to utilize sunlight. The sun forming a glowing rim of light through people's hair always looks nice. When appropriate, add in a reflector or artificial light as a key light and you'll have a well-exposed subject that stands out from the background.

No Reflector
Hair, fields of wheat, foliage, water or almost anything else that lets some light pass thru looks good backlit.

With Soft Silver Reflector Fill
A reflector will help fill in the shadows in a subject's face and eyes.

With Soft Gold Reflector Fill
A gold reflector warms up the skin tone and mimics the look of **golden hour** sunlight.

✔ *Let God be your Gaffer! Learn how to control natural sunlight.*

SUN AS (FRONTAL) KEY LIGHT

You can also use the sun as your key light. This generally looks best during golden hour when the sun is lower in the sky in the early morning and late evening hours or on overcast days when shadows are less harsh and daylight is diffused and even.

Midday Full Sun (no Reflector)

The sun is a great keylight all by itself a lot of the time, but you have to look out for "raccoon eyes"

Midday Full Sun with Reflector

Here I used a reflector to fill in the dark shadows of my subjects eyes.

Sun as Side Key (no Reflector)

You can also use the sun as a key on one side coming from the left or right.

Sun as Side Key with Reflector

The sun as side key will usually look best with a reflector or other fill light on the dark side of the face.

The Secret to Silhouettes

To get a good silhouette, your background must be **bright** and the light on the camera-side of your subject must be considerably **darker** than the background. Exposing for the bright background will usually render unlit subjects as well-defined black silhouettes. The sunlit sky makes this easy outdoors, but indoors it's trickier to find a background bright enough to actually create a good silhouette.

SUPPLEMENTING SUNLIGHT WITH ARTIFICIAL LIGHTING

Artificial lights can be used to supplement any exterior scene, but an overcast sky is the easiest daylight scenario to work with because you don't have issues of harsh shadows, high contrast, raccoon eyes or the inconsistent lighting conditions that come with shooting on a partly cloudy day . . . Instead the cloud cover acts like a giant piece of diffusion giving you soft even consistent light.

No Reflector
Using the sun as a hairlight helps avoid "raccoon eyes" and separates the subject from the background.

With Artificial Light and CTB Gel
If you add an artificial light and gel it with a CTB (color temperature blue) gel it will match the sunlight.

With Tungsten Light and No Gel
If you use a standard tungsten light without a daylight-balancing CTB gel, it will give you a warmer look that contrasts the rest of the scene.

SHUTTER SPEED BASICS

Shutter speed is another reference that comes from the world of still photography where cameras actually have a little shutter or door that opens and closes in a fraction of a second to expose each frame of film to light. A shutter speed of 1/48 means the shutter is open for one forty-eighth of a second. Slower shutter speeds keep the shutter open longer. Faster shutter speeds keep the shutter open for less time. Most normal video shooting is done at a shutter speed that is **double your frame rate**, so if you were shooting at 24 frames per second (ex. 24P) you would shoot at a frame rate of 1/48 to achieve a natural look and feel to your video. (However, it's also common for 24P shooters to use "normal" shutter speeds of 1/32 and 1/24 as well for low-light situations.) In video "shutters" are electronic, but the principles of the concept all operate the same.

FRAME RATE	NORMAL SHUTTER SPEEDS
24 fps	1/48
25 fps	1/50
30 fps	1/60
60 fps	1/120

> **PRINCIPLE #1**
> The longer the shutter stays open, the more motion is captured in the frame, the more an object moving on-screen will be *blurred*.

> **PRINCIPLE #2**
> The longer the shutter stays open, the more light the frame is exposed to, which means the *brighter* the picture will be.

Motion and Shutter Speed

Remember to adjust your exposure after changing shutter speeds since your exposure will be noticeably different. Although shutter speed also affects exposure and depth of field, its *primary* use is to control how motion is portrayed in each frame of video . . . sharp or blurry. This comes into play if you intend to freeze-frame or slow down a shot later.

Fast-action sports such as hockey and tennis are frequently captured at higher shutter speeds so that slow motion and freeze-frames of the action look sharp and clear. The downside of using higher shutter speeds is that they can also cause a flickering strobe-like effect on the moving video. Sometimes filmmakers intentionally use a high shutter speed to portray a comic, surreal, or horror scene. Similarly, using slower shutter speeds such as 1/4 is useful for creating a surreal, flashback, or hallucinogenic effect. With a very slow shutter speed all of your motion and colors will trail and swirl across the screen when you move the camera . . . Groovy, man!

✔ *Normal video is usually shot at double your frame rate.*

SHUTTER SPEED AND MOVEMENT

Normal Shutter Speed — 1/48

- Used for most normal shooting at 24 fps
- Appears the way human eye sees
- Slightly blurred movement
- 24P DSLR cameras may only have "1/50"

High Shutter Speed — 1/1000

- Used for slow mo and freeze FX in post
- Used for fast action sports
- Gives normal footage a surreal feel
- Moving object sharp on paused footage
- Let's less light in lens

Slow Shutter Speed — 1/15

- Creates a dream or hallucinogenic feel
- At a speed of 1/4, motion creates long trails
- Considerable blurring of movement
- Lets more light in lens

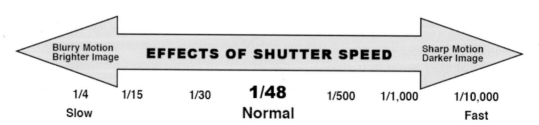

Blurry Motion
Brighter Image

EFFECTS OF SHUTTER SPEED

Sharp Motion
Darker Image

1/4	1/15	1/30	**1/48**	1/500	1/1,000	1/10,000
Slow			Normal			Fast

*1/48 is normal shutter speed when shooting 24 fps.

CREATING A "FILM LOOK"

1 SHOOT WITH A 24P CAMERA

This is probably the single easiest thing you could do to get that elusive film look. Basically these cameras shoot video at 24 frames per second (fps) or electronically mimic 24 fps, which is the same speed that film runs. (Traditionally, video has been shot at 30 fps.) Those few extra frames can make all the difference in the world. 24P video cameras are very capable of delivering a great film look right out of the box when set in their 24P modes.

2 USE FILM LOOK SOFTWARE IN POST

If you want to kick it up a notch and go beyond a generic "film look", there are a slew of editing program plug-ins such as **Film Convert** and the **Magic Bullet** software suite that actually mimic various film stocks and development processes used by big budget features.

3 LIGHT IT LIKE FILM

Just because a camera is capable of shooting in low light does not mean that it shoots the *best images* in low light. A BIG part of the reason film looks better than video is the lighting. Avoid low-light situations when possible and use professional lighting gear for controlled setups. When it comes to the professional look of your project, apart from a good D.P., hiring a good gaffer (lighting person) is a great investment.

4 USE FILTERS

Here is another cinematographer's secret: There is an entire arsenal of filters that can enhance the look of your footage to appear more like those beautiful frames of film. The most common are 1/4 and 1/2 Black Pro Mist Filters, Warming/Enhancing Filters, Graduated Filters, and Fog FX Filters. (You can find more info on filters and their use at Tiffen.com.)

5 USE SHALLOW DEPTH OF FIELD

A big part of a film look is shallow depth of field (d.o.f.). You can achieve this look by shooting with your lens in full telephoto for fixed and zoom lens cameras, shooting on a camera with a big imaging chip, or shooting with a long (85 mm or more) lens. Beautiful crisp professional lens and more shallow d.o.f. translates into a more filmic look. (See "Shallow Depth of Field" on page 240.)

Use Manual Controls

A primary difference between pro and amateur shooters is that the pros know how to *manually* control their camera image and many amateurs simply let the camera decide how the shot should look and sound by relying heavily on the camera's auto controls. The hectic and unpredictable nature of documentary shooting makes it tempting to just shoot everything in full auto mode.

The problem is that many of the auto functions on video cameras are unreliable. Think of it as driving a long road trip with your car's cruise control turned on . . . it's great until you zip past a police car above the speed limit. The cruise control doesn't know (or care) that you're going to get a speeding ticket. It only works well in the most *ideal* setting–open road with no traffic lights or change in traffic or speed limit. The same is true with most camera auto functions. As soon as anything outside of the ideal recording conditions happens, they become much less reliable.

Your camera isn't nearly as competent as you are. (Or will become by the end of this book.) Don't get punked by blindly relying on autofocus, auto-sound levels, or auto-iris. Take the time to learn and understand how to manually control the most important aspects of your video. The buttons and features will vary from camera to camera, but the principles of focus, exposure, and sound will always operate the same.

> ✔ For *professional results, use* <u>manual</u> *controls. Camera auto functions are often unreliable.*

AUTO FUNCTION DYSFUNCTIONS		
AUTO FUNCTION	**MOST LIKELY TO FAIL WHEN**	**MOST USEFUL WHEN**
Autofocus	■ A person, car, or object crosses in front of your subject ■ Lighting is low ■ Objects are in the foreground (leaves, mic stand, crowd, etc.)	■ You are VERY inexperienced ■ Doing tricky camera moves ■ You are having difficulty seeing the viewfinder ■ You are legally blind
Auto-iris	■ A bright object is in frame ■ A scene is backlit ■ There is snow on the ground	■ You are shooting "run and gun" ■ Lighting conditions change frequently or unpredictably
Auto Gain Control (AGC) Sound	■ An audience claps or laughs ■ Naturally sharp/loud sounds (gunshot, subway, scream, etc.) ■ There are silent gaps in sound	■ The sound level does not fluctuate much ■ You are solo in a "run and gun" situation ■ You don't have headphones

Auto Zoom vs. Manual Zoom

One thing I particularly like about shooting with fixed lens cameras is that they all have servo (motorized) zoom lens. This is the one auto-function that I think is generally better than manual. This is practical for docs, because it allows you to *smoothly* zoom and manually adjust your focus at the same time, so you don't miss any of the action while readjusting your shot. I'm also a fan of using servo if you've got it, because it allows you to get a variety of shots aka "good coverage" in a shorter amount of time.

Surprises and Panics

At some point in production a fleeting moment may come that you need to capture right that second. A protester in the crowd behind you may unfurl a controversial banner. The elusive and rare white leopard is about to pounce on his prey from a tree . . . whatever. Do whatever you gotta do to grab that image. Don't waste time screwing around with menu screens and white-balancing. Just get the #%*& shot, man! Your sharp manual focus and perfect white balance mean *nothing* if the protester has already been dragged away by police or the white leopard has already killed the antelope and made off with the carcass. (In that case, you may as well *be* the protester or the antelope because you blew it!)

Photo: *In Country.*

If you totally panic or have a brain fart in the moment, it's okay. Just quickly switch the camera into auto-lock or full auto mode. (That's auto-*everything*.) You will most likely still get a pretty decent image and sound. It will be just like using a consumer camcorder. Better to go full auto and sacrifice some image and sound control than to have unusable footage because you forgot to adjust the sound level or re-white-balance the camera in the chaos of the moment. Don't sweat it. Using manual controls will become second nature with practice. Just remember, after safety– getting the shot is always numero uno.

Run-and-Gun Shooting

Run-and-gun shooting is when you are on the go and things are happening so quickly or under such confusion that there isn't ample time or calm to concentrate on all the technical details you need to consider. This includes situations such as shooting in the crowd of a loud rowdy nightclub or a political protest that turns into a riot. Similarly, it may be wise to go with auto functions when covering a short or sudden event where a lot of action is happening all at once and you need to get full coverage before it all ends. Lastly, anytime you are shooting with unfamiliar equipment, pulling off a tricky camera move, or all by yourself as director, cameraperson, sound recordist, and/or interviewer is also an acceptable time to farm out some of those duties to the auto functions.

Rely on auto-functions when executing tricky camera moves.

✔ *Getting* _usable_ *shots is numero uno. Use auto functions if necessary to simplify run-and-gun shooting.*

CAPTURING TRUTH

ALBERT MAYSLES, DIRECTOR/DP
mayslesfilms.com
(Grey Gardens, Gimme Shelter, Salesman, Lalee's Kin, etc.)

As I see it, and many a documentary filmmaker doesn't live by this creed, I think that we have a great deal of responsibility to set the record straight. To end up with something that's totally authentic, and we turn away from that responsibility when we prejudge people, when we start out with a particular point of view, which we are determined to support even though it may not be supportable with reality, with fact.

We have a responsibility to tell the truth, and we have the means to do so with a video camera that doesn't run out of tape after ten minutes as with film, a video camera that is not so big and bulky as to scare people. We can do a very decent job of getting the viewer to feel that they are there themselves, even though they weren't present when all of this stuff was going on.

The responsibility is an ethical one: Tell the truth. And sometimes that truth can be extremely hurtful, and you don't want to do that. But at the same time, you don't want to be so protective that what is in the heart and mind of that person that you're filming doesn't get a chance to express itself because you were so overly protective. So the course in the middle is, with a feeling of responsibility, to get material that may be even somewhat embarrassing, but nevertheless, it's something that the person being filmed would feel, "Well, it's embarrassing but I want it to be recorded. I want people to know the tough part of my life as well as some of the better, more satisfying elements."

People would much rather open their minds and hearts to the camera than to keep a secret, that's just human nature. And I think we have an enormous advantage in filming people when we consider that they would prefer to connect in an open fashion with the camera. Now, that doesn't work if the person doesn't trust [the person] who is filming . . . The person filming must be of the kind who takes the responsibility to tell the truth, to care for the person that they're filming through a process of empathy. Without that empathy, there's no poetry. There's no beauty. There's no emotion that is going to come out on the screen.

Introduction: Who's Zooming Who?

The primary reason you should use the zoom control on your camera is to readjust your frame from wide to medium to close-up. I say that's all it should be used for 90% of the time. More seasoned event and documentary camera people learn to resist the newbie temptation to constantly push in and pull out of shots for no **story-driven** rhyme or reason. If you're zooming for any reason other than adjusting your shot, you should be clear what that reason is.

> ✔ Any zoom move should be motivated by the action and unfolding story.

Pushing In

We generally push in to draw the audience's attention to something specific in a larger scene. Every time you zoom in or out, your camera is "talking" to the audience to communicate some piece of visual information. Here's what your camera's saying in various situations.

PUSH IN TO	WHAT YOUR CAMERA'S SAYING
A particular person in the room	■ Hey, look! There's Mike Tyson in the front row of the ballet. ■ This scowling congressman does not like what his colleague just said. ■ This happy hippie is really into this band.
A particular detail in the large shot	■ Wow, check out the size of that "rock" on her finger! Is that from Tiffany's? ■ That is a very nice statue in the corner. This must be a classy joint. ■ Who would've guessed she had a tattoo *there*? Now, you don't see that every day.
Get more intimate during an interview	■ This is the climax of a dramatic story. ■ It's getting emotional now. Here come the tears. ■ Come a little closer; I want to tell you something important now.
Show a close-up of some action	■ Now she's adjusting the engine bolt clockwise with a #12 Rawley's wrench. ■ Notice how he's holding the peeler to create those cute little decorative lemon peel flowers. ■ Check out what he's doing to those piano strings with his teeth. That's crazy, man!

Forget the Tripod and Go Handheld

Handheld shots can add some real energy and a more subjective point of view to a scene when tripods aren't practical or desirable. The basic techniques are simple, but take practice to master. You can also use a camera stabilizer such as a Steadicam or Glidecam, which takes even more practice. There are several important things to consider if you want to shoot handheld like the big dawgs . . .

How to Shoot Handheld

1. Brace your camera elbow against your body. Use your free hand to steady your camera hand or to steady the camera by gripping the lens.
2. Keep your lens zoomed out to it's widest setting or use a wide prime lens.
3. Assume comfortable footing and lower your center of gravity slightly as you twist left or right to follow the action.
4. Avoid zooming. Move in closer or farther away to adjust your frame.

Handheld Editing Considerations

Handheld shots often won't intercut well with tripod shots *in the same scene*–it's like stepping on a boat, then back on the dock, then back in a boat–the audience will accept either shot, but the two may not cut smoothly together. The steadier the camerawork, the more likely you can juxtapose shots in editing.

Motivation and Style

Handheld footage should be a *motivated* stylistic choice that fits with the subject matter. Look at other documentaries and try to analyze when and why they go handheld and what effect it has on the viewer. Is it all handheld or just some scenes? Is the camera movement helping to tell the story? How does it affect viewpoint? Ask yourself these important questions *before* you go handheld.

Standard

- Elbows braced against body
- Slightly bent knees
- Best all-purpose handheld position

High Angle

- Arms extended overhead
- LCD screen angled down 45°
- Use to shoot over crowds/obstacles

Low Angle

- Hold camera near ground
- Walk smoothly with bent knees
- Mostly for POV and following shots

Cradle

- Cam at waist level with braced elbows
- Ideal for long handheld takes
- Good for "roving" high-energy shots

USING TRIPODS

Introduction

When you need a steady image such as zooming in to shoot something far away or shooting an interview, put that camera on some "**sticks**" and join the Rock Steady Crew. Smooth pans and tilts and nice even zooms are best accomplished with a good professional video tripod. Be warned if you're serious about this video thing and you're buying a tripod: Cheap consumer-level tripods are far more trouble than

they're worth. They simply won't do the job and you'll eventually end up spending more to buy a professional-quality fluid-head tripod or suffer through one botched camera move after another. (Believe me, anytime I can tell you how to save a buck, I will . . . but a tripod is not the place to be cheap.

What to Look for in a Tripod

1. **Weight Capacity:** Make sure your tripod is rated to handle your camera's weight.
2. **Fluid Head:** Any tripod that you shoot with should have a "fluid head." Fluid head tripods are made just for motion picture work. They are more expensive, but necessary and worth it to pull off smooth professional-quality camerawork. (If you *prefer* whack amateur moves just stick with the rickety plastic consumer models.)
3. **Pan and Tilt Tension Knobs:** Another feature to look for in a professional-quality tripod are knobs to adjust the pan and tilt tension, which will allow you to adjust the tripod to move as fast or slow as you like up and down and left and right.
4. **Quick Release Plate:** A good tripod head will have a quick release plate that will stay attached to the camera during shooting. This will allow you to easily remove and replace the camera on the tripod whenever you need to quickly go handheld or move the camera. This item is a *must* for unpredictable documentary production.

General Tripod Tips

When performing camera moves, be careful not to end up in an awkward yoga-like position. Always start in the least comfortable position, then end in the most comfortable position. Also, don't use your pan or tilt tension knobs to **lock down** shots. Don't use your pan or tilt locks to adjust tripod tension. Doing either will eventually shorten the life of your tripod. If your tripod has one, use the spirit bubble (a.k.a. "level bubble") to make sure you are even with the horizon, but still always check your frame line against the horizontal lines in your shot.

Filmmaking has its own language and scripts. Film crews have a dialogue to get each new camera **take** up and running. This little script allows filmmakers to ensure that everyone and everything is ready and rolling when the action starts.

PRODUCER/DIRECTOR	TRANSLATION	CREW ACTION	CREW SAYS
1. "LIGHTS!"	Turn on lights	**Gaffer:** Turns on all set lights.	**Gaffer:** "Striking!"
2. "ROLL SOUND!" (when using *separate* sound recording system, otherwise just check that sound op is ready—"Ready sound?")	Start recording sound.	**Sound:** Starts recording and waits for pre-roll. **Sound:** When the sound device indicates full recording speed.	**Sound:** "Rolling!" or "Ready!" **Sound:** "Speed!"
3. "ROLL CAMERA!"	Start recording picture.	**Camera:** Starts recording. **Camera:** Waits for record light to finish blinking to indicate full speed.	**Camera:** "Rolling!" **Camera:** "Speed!"
4. "SLATE!"	Put the slate in front of the camera.	**P.A.:** Holds the slate open with shot information. **Camera:** Focuses on slate, if necessary.	**Camera:** "Focused" or "Got it."
5. "MARK IT!" (Most necessary when using separate sound recording system *or* multiple cameras)	Record the slate text and clap.	**P.A.:** Claps slate, then pulls it out when cued. **Camera:** Resets or refocuses the shot.	**Camera:** "Clear Slate." **Camera:** "Set" or "Camera Ready"
6. "ACTION!"	We're starting.	**Prod./Dir:** Cues talent to start.	

COLOR BARS

Why You Should Use Color Bars

It's a good practice, and especially important if you are shooting for broadcast, to try to record a minute of color bars at the beginning of each media card or tape. Color bars are the multicolored patterns generated by video equipment that help ensure that your video colors are accurate from one monitor to the next. By recording the color bar pattern at the top of your footage you now have a *standard reference point* that will allow you to more accurately adjust the color on various monitors to look exactly as you intended it to when you recorded it.

Although some cameras don't have true professional **SMPTE** color bars (pictured below) which are the most accurate and useful, the simple straight-lined color bars found on these cameras are still better than none and will help you judge hue, brightness, and saturation. If you forget to record color bars during production, it's no big deal. Just record them at the end of the shoot.

How to Adjust NTSC Color Bars

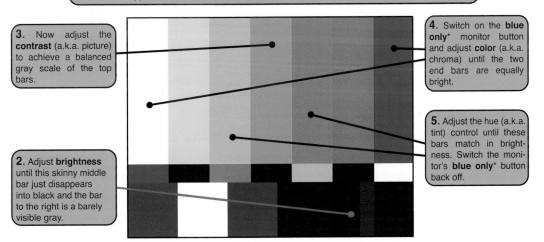

1. Let your monitor **warm-up** for 5–10 minutes and turn the **color** (a.k.a. chroma) all the way down until the bars appear in black and white.

3. Now adjust the **contrast** (a.k.a. picture) to achieve a balanced gray scale of the top bars.

4. Switch on the **blue only*** monitor button and adjust **color** (a.k.a. chroma) until the two end bars are equally bright.

5. Adjust the hue (a.k.a. tint) control until these bars match in brightness. Switch the monitor's **blue only*** button back off.

2. Adjust **brightness** until this skinny middle bar just disappears into black and the bar to the right is a barely visible gray.

If you are using a TV or a monitor without a "blue only" feature another alternative is to (A) cover your screen with a blue gel or (B) adjust the color (chroma) level until the colors no longer "bleed" into each other, then adjust the hue (tint) level until the yellow bar is lemon yellow, not orange or green, and the magenta bar looks correct, not red or purple.

> ✔ *Record a minute of color bars at the top of each tape. Use color bars to adjust monitors when screening footage.*

THE TECHNICAL VS. THE CREATIVE AND IN-CAMERA VS. POST

CLIFF CHARLES, DIRECTOR OF PHOTOGRAPHY

cliffcharles.com

(When the Levees Broke, Good Hair, Venus and Serena, etc.)

The technical is there just to support the creative at the end of the day. So I'm picking the tools that are going to achieve whatever the image is supposed to be. But one thing that I always try to do is figure out how am I going to properly represent whatever the main idea is. I'm always thinking about how I am pushing the narrative forward, through shots, through lighting. Should this be close up? Should this be wide? Some of it becomes intuitive, and then some of it you have to think a little bit more about what decisions you have to make. But you're basically relying on your own experiences, the years of work that you do. You rely on that to call upon things that worked, things that did not work. It's a jigsaw puzzle. You're constantly puzzle making.

On Doing It In-Camera

I think what happens with any technology that makes something easier is that you also have the potential to be less disciplined. So I think that people become a little lazy when they have 13 stops of latitude. They become a little sloppy when you can shoot it raw, and you've got 13 stops of latitude. I think the notion of fixing it in post is a flawed one. I think that it's fantastic that we have all of these new opportunities, but I think those new opportunities should serve to only *enhance* what you're already doing, not to replace it. And that might sound old school to some people, but I think there really is something to be said about pre-planning and visualizing what you're going to do, making that happen, and then utilizing these wonderful tools to just enhance it and to take it even further.

You have the ability now to really build upon your look, and I think it's very short-sighted to be sloppy, just run out there and shoot, and then just sit in a suite, putting on a whole bunch of power windows to try to fix it or to try to create something that you had no clue as to what you were trying to create before. I think it's very short-sighted, and I think that you're not serving your project, or even your career, in the best way when you do it that way. So I think that's the thing, is being sloppy, because of the fact you have these tools that make things a lot easier for you.

Let's be real, anybody and their Mama can make a film now. And sometimes it feels like anybody and their Mama *are* making films these days—mostly bad ones. Wannabe filmmakers that shoot soft-focused, shaky camera, poorly-edited, bad-sounding, cheesy-looking lame, lackluster low-quality amateur productions really do bring our craft down to lowest common denominator . . . But it doesn't have to be like that.

Too many people think merely having the best filmmaking tools makes them a good filmmaker. Let me clear that up right now—it doesn't. *Making good films makes you a good filmmaker.* And if you want to make good films, the number one thing you want to infuse into your productions beyond a good *story* is **production value**.

Just cause you have the latest sports car, doesn't make you a good driver. Just ask comedian Eddie Griffin who infamously crashed a $1.2 Million Ferrari Enzo after just a few practice laps for a celebrity race. (Look it up on YouTube.) Great tools are useless without the hard-won skills and knowledge you need to master them and make them perform their best. In my best Al Pacino *Scarface* impression: "First chu get da knowledge. Den chu get da skills. Deeeen chu get da *tools*, my amigo!"

So production value is just a fancy way to say filmmaking "professionalism". It's adding as many elements as possible that are the hallmark of careful attention to storytelling detail and big-budget films. In other words, you want to try to do as many things as possible to make your no-crew, no-budget production look more like a big-crew, big-budget Hollywood production.

Any good film—doc, narrative, or otherwise—starts with good solid content and story, but even that will only go so far if you botch your great story with whack execution. The gap between amateur and professional work can be greatly lesened if you know the specific details to pay attention to that will give you the most storytelling bang for your buck. Here are some of the tools, tips and techniques that if mastered will help make all of your work look better and **BE** much more profesional. Some cost more money and require specialty tools, but many can be faked or substituted with a little Down and Dirty imagination and all offer a great return on the the extra time, money, and effort they take to get. Here's ten tips to help you "put your money on the screen" and take your videos from "newbie to groovy" in 10 minutes flat:

#1 – SHALLOW DEPTH OF FIELD

Having everything in the frame be in full focus is fine for your Dad's video of the school play, but if we wanna get cinematic with our video storytelling, we need to selectively choose what things in our frame we put in focus and when.

When just one subject or object is in focus and everything else in the background or foreground is out of focus it's called **shallow depth of field**. It looks much more interesting, artistic, and professional. For many many years, this was a cinematic look only achievable with big-budget 35 mm film cameras. Now the popularity of affordable DSLRs, big-chip video cameras, and interchangaeble prime lenses has made this professional cinematic look more available than ever.

The art of directing a film is not just directing the people and events in the frame, it's also directing your audience's attention by taking the time to selectively choose what they see, and when and how they see it. It literally can be used to focus your audience's attention onto and away from any given thing in your shot at the exact moment you choose. You are *directing* their attention to what you want them to notice at a particular moment, rather than letting their eye wander all over the frame.

Apart from just artistry, shallow depth of field can be used to add suspense, humor, irony, and meaning to a shot. It's also an excellent technique to mask ugly, undesirable or inappropriate things in the background of any location. Most importantly, it's an effective way to further engage your audience's attention.

Keep in mind though, that any tool or technique loses it's effectiveness and can get stale fast and in a hurry if it's over-used. So don't make every dang shot of your feature doc a shallow d.o.f. shot. Instead, apply it only to the specific scenes and moments where it's truly going to aid your visual storytelling and your investment in the added production value of shallow d.o.f. shots will *keep* paying off until the credits roll. (See also "Hot Tip: Shallow Depth of Field" on page 240 for specific techniques to achieve shallow depth of field with any camera.)

| Sure the first one is an OK shot of this Jack-o-lantern, but the second shot with shallow d.o.f. makes it *art*, baby! | This shot takes on new meaning for the audience when the camera shifts from the building in the background to the sign in the foreground. | Background too busy, boring, or bad? Focus your camera only on the good stuff and make all the other crap disappear in a fuzzy blur. |

#2 – GREAT AUDIO AND SOUND DESIGN

I know I already have entire chapters, videos, and agitated tirades on the extreme importance of capturing good audio in my previous books, blog posts, lynda.com courses and elsewhere, but it's a point that I don't think can be over-emphasized for aspiring filmmakers. The easiest way to spot an amateur filmmaker from an experienced one from a mile away is by the attention given to audio. Nothing will cause festival screeners, potential distributors, grant foundations, an audience or even your own family members to hit he stop button and dismiss your project faster than bad audio. You simply can't easily disguise it, work around it or ignore it. There is a popular cliché saying among doc filmmakers. The only difference between a documentary and a home movie is good *audio*.

And like some cliches, it's often repeated, because it also happens to be 100% true. If I could, I would go around film schools and indie film sets and taser any aspiring young filmmakers I observed ignoring the importance of capturing good location audio. (Fortunately for many of you, recent restraining orders have barred me from doing that anymore.) I'm joking of course–mostly–but I really do think it's *that* important.

> ✔ *The only difference between a documentary and a home movie is good AUDIO.*

Bad sound is probably the number one thing that sabatoges otherwise potentially good video projects. And it really is completely heartbreaking for professionals and teachers like myself to watch a project that a lot more people would get to see and enjoy if only the filmmakers had paid the same careful attention to audio that they give to image. Instead the harddrives and closets of the world are littered with great video footage with horrible sound that no one will ever bear to sit through, let alone take seriously.

Photo: Cruce Grammatico.

So the exact same effort and time you take to carefully select a camera, D.P. and editor is the exact same time you need to take to select your audio equipment, audio person and sound designer. Audio is literally half the story, baby! If you ain't got good *sound*, you ain't got good *production value*, no matter how good it looks or how good your story is . . . Got it? Or do I need to take out my taser again?

#3 – LOCK IT DOWN

Another sure thing that will rob your production of any hope of looking professional is the repeated failure to use a tripod, which often results in shaky motion-sickness-inducing footage that's hard to watch, especially on a big screen. This common problem in amateur footage is even more noticeable any time you're zoomed in or shooting on a telephoto lens. Similarly, the popularity of DSLR cameras has led to more "shaki-cam" footage, because the cameras are so small and light, that they are actually harder to hold steady. Heavier cameras are just easier to hold steady.

If you just have a simple shot such as an establishing shot of a sign, subject sitting at their desk, close up of a prop, etc. you really should use a tripod. Yes, even if it's just a two- or three-second B-Roll shot. Don't misunderstand what I'm saying here: There's nothing at all wrong with doing **handheld camerawork**. However, bad handheld camerawork will mark your forehead with a big scarlet "A" for amateur. Handheld camerawork is very appropriate and practical for many doc projects. It can add a nice sense of energy, movement and subjective point of view to your footage when done well, but it needs to be fully respected and developed as a genuine filmmaking *skill*. Good handheld camerawork truly takes some knowledge of good technique, plenty of practice and often some additional camera accesories to actually do it right and have it still look professional.

But in everyday practice, I see a lot of footage that filmmakers—who actually had tripods with them—were just too lazy, hurried or inexperienced to set up and use the tripod for shots that really needed one. If a tripod is really not practical for whatever you're shooting at the moment, then you should consider using a lighter and more portable monopod, hiring a D.P. experienced in handheld doc camerawork or using one of the many camera stabilizing devices and rigs such as a shoulder mount rig, steadicam or glidecam. And of course, make sure your camera's optical image stabilization (often listed as "O.I.S." or "Steadyshot") is turned on when handheld shooting. The bottom line is that if you're not using a tripod for a shot, it still needs to be steady. The festival judges and audience don't care that the tripod is too heavy to carry up those steps, or too much hassle to set up for that quick B-Roll shot . . . they only care that it doesn't make them dizzy and distract from the story onscreen. (See also "Handheld Secrets of the Pros" on page 135.)

Photo: Cruce Grammatico.

#4 – KEEP IT MOVING, BABY!

One of the most effective things you can do to make your film shine like the big dawgs of filmmaking is to incorporate some smooth, steady, and artful moving footage. I'm talking about using higher-end filmmaking tools like sliders, dollies, and jibs. The operative word here is smooth. Using any of these fancy filmmaking tools will cost you considerable more time, effort, and likely money, but if you pull it off smoothly, it's easily some of the greatest production value bang for your buck you can get. These are the type of slick moves the pros make all day every day, because they have the budget, time, tools and experienced crew to do it.

However, the list of affordable filmmaking tools available to indie filmmakers to keep the camera moving has grown considerably in recent years, especially for those shooting on today's smaller and more portable DSLR and video cameras. So there's no real excuse not to add some major production value with a few smooth professional camera moves. In many cases, what you can't buy you can still rent, make yourself, or substitute cheaply. The one big investment that any fluid camera move will definitely require is time and patience. These moves are often a real time-suck on-set to get right. But every time you do get it right, it's more than worth it for the added production value. (See "Dolly Shots" and "Slider Moves" on pages 229 and 230.)

Sliders like this Kessler Phillip Bloom Pocket Dolly can add a huge leap in your production value.

#5 – LOCATION, LOCATION, LOCATION

Shooting in great locations has always been one of the easiest ways to make your production look a lot more big budget and professional. All over the world in every city, town, and countryside there are local landmarks, buildings, neighborhoods, and other stunning and impressive visual settings that are already fully art-directed and production-designed, because they are the real deal.

When I produced the gritty narrative feature, *Shelter* directed by Benno Schoberth, we had very little budget for locations or production design. However, with a lot of imaginative scouting (and a little charm and luck along the way), we were able to cheaply secure or "borrow" a bunch

Striking visual locations like this dilapidated city pool helped sell the gritty story and boost production value on *Shelter*.

Photo: Susan Chen

of compelling visual locations that were perfect for the grimy urban story, theme, and characters we wanted to portray. So perfect in fact that *Shelter* went on to win the coveted top prize at the very competitive I.F.P. Market amongst other festival awards.

Another big resource I recommend you try to take advantage of is any place with a great view. Great views are free. You just have to be a little creative about finding one you can frame in your background. The view of L.A. from the quiet top of the Burbank mountains, shooting the N.Y. cityscape from the Staten Island Ferry or the deck of a tour boat, the passing New England or West Coast seascape from the window of a moving train, early morning fog on a quiet country lake, the first-person perspective from the front car of a New York Subway system, the awesome view from your rich friend's top floor apartment . . . I could go on all day long if I thought on it a little longer. Look for the most beautiful and visually interesting things around you that fit the theme and mood of your doc and shoot them, baby.

Some locations may be more difficult to borrow than others, but with a little pre-planning, stealth (and Chutzpah) you can often score some great images to up the production value of your doc (see "Stealth Shooting Tactics 101" on page 107). Even if you can only pop off a few well-composed establishing shots and some artistic B-Roll in that stunning location or from that stunning viewpoint, it can go a long way to really opening up the look of your doc. Break out the slider and you could open every scene with a compelling camera move before we cut back to a more routine interior location.

The waiter likely won't notice that DSLR camera poking out of your oversized purse, but the *audience* will definitely notice this jaw-dropping shot.

#6 – CLEVER (AND APPROPRIATE) TITLES AND FX

Another element you can use to great effect to help your work look considerably more professional is well-composed and topic-appropriate titles and visual effects. Good titles don't necessarily cost money, but they do take some skill to create from scratch. If you develop some skills using a program like Adobe After Effects or Apple Motion, there is no end to how clever you can get with titles. When I say, "clever", I mean the ability to come up with titles concepts and transitional FX that are **topic-, story-, character- or theme-appropriate**.

There are plenty of built in titles and FX that look cool in and of themselves. Your titles have to be cool *and* visually tie into the themes and topics of your project. That means the colors, fonts, graphics and FX should fit the rest of the project. If you're doing a documentary on organic farming, slick metallic letters on your lower thirds and flaming screen wipes for scene transitions would be pretty ridiculous. If the same flashy titles and firey transitions are used on a project about a shop that makes futuristic custom motorcycles, it could be just the ticket to make your project look more polished and professional.

There are tons of plug-ins and high-quality pre-made title templates you can buy to make your titles look more professional.

Photo: Double 7 Images

Visual FX don't have to be expensive or complex. They just have to work. I shot this 1920s B&W recreation using the Vintage 8mm Camera iPhone app.

#7 – MAKE EVERY SHOT A MASTERPIECE

Let me be clear—it's normally hard enough to shoot documentary footage and just capture the scene with a decent exposure and focus. Things are happening in the moment, your subject moves and now the light's not good, you can't see the image on your little monitor in the bright sunlight . . . So in my book, if you just "get the shot" you've done your job. But if you get the shot and make it *visual poetry*–you've done your job *well*. And consistently doing the job of camera person well can be the difference between being a festival selection or a festival winner.

This is an area that obviously requires mastery of your camera. But it's also an area that requires that you continually deepen your knowledge and understanding of composition, light, and visual storytelling.

Read articles in *American Cinematographer*, watch the behind the scenes of your favorite shows and movies, take workshops in lighting, composition, and cinematography . . . Learn to not only visualize the coverage you'll need, but also learn how to frame it, choose the right focal lengths, select the best camera height, background, type of move . . . Learn how to control and manipulate all of the visual elements at your command as real life scenes unfold before you.

CLEANING YOUR LENS

Lens Cleaning Kit:

1. Lens tissue
2. Liquid lens cleaner
3. Blow bulb/brush
4. Optical lens cleaning cloth (optional for dry wiping)

If the hallmark of a pro shooter is a sharp focused picture, the first hallmark of a crisp picture is a clean lens. This is one of those lessons that might still escape you well after you've learned and adopted many of the other professional practices in this book. It will escape you that is, until the day it comes roaring back to bite you on the butt. (Do I sound like a man with experience here?) It's very easy to get caught up in the heat of the moment and not notice or completely forget about regularly checking and cleaning the camera lens, especially when shooting solo.

The dangerous thing about not developing a lens cleaning habit early is that often a dirty lens won't really show up in your footage depending on your lighting, camera angle, and focal length. But whenever the sun or a light shines in the lens, from the right angle—at just the right focal length—a thousand little specks of lint, fiber, fingerprints, and smudges will magically appear in front of your image then disappear again as soon as you change the camera angle or focal length.

So, even if you're looking for dirt, 90% of the time it won't be visible on the LCD screen. Your viewfinder and flip-out LCD screen are just too small and have too low a resolution to catch these tiny details. You have to check the *surface of the lens* itself. (**Note**: Avoid using Windex, tissues, toilet paper, paper towels, shirt sleeves, etc., to clean a camera lens unless you're actually *trying* to scratch your lens.)

Remove dust using a lens brush/blow bulb.

Lightly moisten wad of lens tissue with lens fluid.

Wipe gently in small circular motions.

Follow with a dry lens tissue to wipe smears.

CHAPTER 4
LIGHTING

10 WAYS TO PRACTICE SAFE SETS

Hey, clearly, I am Mr. Down and Dirty when it comes to production. I believe in doing whatever you gotta do to get the shot and finish the project, but I draw a clear and distinct line when it comes to safety on set. Stealing a location or risking arrest is one thing, but risking your (or anyone else's) personal safety for the sake of a film—yes, even a film as important as yours—is just plain stupid. And when serious accidents happen, it's never worth the shot. Read on for my tips to stay clear of this scenario and always practice "safe sets."

> ✔ *Risking safety for the sake of a shot is NOT "Down and Dirty." It's just plain dumb!*

1 DON'T BE STUPID

A reader once sent me a picture of some guerrilla filmmakers she saw on the side of the road that are the very essence of what I *don't* believe in. These filmmaking fools were 100 feet off the ground; on the wrong side of a highway overpass; and completely unsecured by a tether, safety chain, and apparently, also by common sense. Let me be clear here: This type of stuff is **NOT** "Down and Dirty." It's just sheer "dumbassery." I really can't put it any other way. Your camera and brain should always be fully engaged—at the same time—when it comes to filmmaking.

Photo courtesy of Linda Maxwell.

Witness two filmmaking idiots risking their lives to get a shot from the open ledge of a highway bridge 100+ feet off the ground. This ain't Down and Dirty filmmaking; it's just dumb.

2 SLOW IT DOWN

The pressure on a film set can be tremendous when the dollars are ticking away on a piece of equipment due back at the rental house, you're about to lose that last bit of golden sunlight, or the lead actor has to leave in two hours to catch a plane. These are the panic times. Bad things are more likely to happen when everyone is tense and rushing to get things done. Remember, the best filmmakers panic only on the *inside*, so take a deep breath and mentally (if not physically) slow down the pace long enough to make sure that everyone is still safe, because if they aren't, you still won't get the shot; plus you'll have a whole new set of problems to deal with. As Kanye West put it, "Drive slow, Homey. You never know, Homey."

3   ALWAYS KEEP A FIRST-AID KIT ON SET

Even in the safest of environments, little accidents can and will happen—cuts, bruises, burns, and such. When these things do happen, be prepared with the basic supplies to take care of the people who take care of you: your talent and crew. When a gaffer slices his palm trying to set up a light for your scene, it's so much classier and caring to have a large bandage and some Neosporin on hand than to have the poor guy walking around the rest of the shoot with a blood-soaked paper towel held on by a piece of gaffer's tape. Apart from bandages and

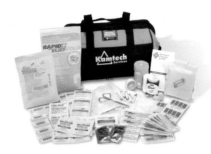

standard medical supplies like rubbing alcohol to clean and treat basic wounds, you also want to stock things like instant hot and cold packs, BenGay, tweezers, gauze, aspirin, or ibuprofen (lots of it), cold and allergy medicine, and relief for upset stomachs . . . whatever you keep in your medicine cabinet. You can get a fully stocked first-aid kit at any drugstore or pharmacy.

4   PUT UP SIGNS, ROPE IT OFF, AND MARK THE DANGER SPOTS

Another simple thing you can do is put up signs in big, bold print on bright-colored paper on and around everything on set that is of potential danger: "WARNING—Do not plug lights in this outlet!!!" "WATCH YOUR STEP," "PLEASE STAY OFF BALCONY," "DO NOT COVER GENERATOR WITH *ANYTHING*!!!" etc. (A safety sign cannot be big and obnoxious enough in my opinion.) Similarly, from any big-box hardware store you can purchase some iconic

yellow caution tape that has the word "caution" printed on every inch to rope off areas of the set that you want to keep people away from. If a potentially dangerous area does need to be accessed, limit access to only those crew members who need to deal with it directly, such as the grips or gaffers. And although they went out fashion in the '80's, neon colors are always in fashion when it comes to safety. Use bright, obnoxious neon pink, yellow, and green tape and paper signs to clearly note areas of caution and catch people's eyes.

Bright neon colors are always fashionable when it comes to safety. People can't help but see this light stand on the floor now.

5 KNOW WHERE THE NEAREST HOSPITAL IS

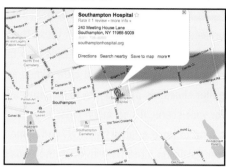

The producer or A.D. on set is normally responsible for this standard precaution. Knowing how to get to the nearest hospital emergency room is as simple as doing a Google Map search. Equally important is knowing the fastest route to get there. For a serious emergency, you may have to decide which is faster: driving versus calling an ambulance. Having the hospital's address already punched into your production vehicle's GPS unit will save you those extra excruciating minutes of trying to punch in the address and make navigation decisions while someone in your passenger seat needs urgent medical care.

6 GOT PHONE SERVICE?

While we're speaking of hospitals and ambulances, you should be very wary and extra cautious of shooting at any remote location with no phone service at all. The ability to be able to call 9-1-1 and get emergency medical help on set within minutes is not one that you want to be without. In the very worst-case accident scenarios, the inability to make a quick phone call can become a life-or-death situation. You need to have a full medical emergency plan and know all the nearest emergency healthcare providers and their hours of operation when you are shooting in remote and isolated places. It would also be wise to let those emergency care providers (i.e., paramedics, fire dept., etc.) know exactly where you will be shooting beforehand, so they can quickly get to your remote location if there is an unexpected emergency . . . and all film set emergencies are always "unexpected," but they should never be *unprepared* for.

7 SECURE EVERYTHING

Wherever possible, all heavy equipment should be safely secured in place so that it does not fall over or onto someone. Securing things is not only a safety issue, but also an equipment issue. Equipment that's not held in place is more prone to getting dropped, broken, or knocked over accidentally. By secure *everything*, I mean

- Put sandbags on lights and C-stands.
- Use extra sandbags outdoors in windy conditions.
- Make sure any overhead lights are securely fastened down and have safety chains or wires as well.
- Double check that the camera is secure on the tripod. If your tripod has spreader legs, sand bag those too.
- If someone needs to climb a ladder, the ladder should be secured in place by another crew member.

In other words, secure *everythang*.

8 HAVE A SAFETY BRIEFING

Whenever you shoot whatever you shoot, you should take a few minutes to make sure that the entire crew—from the bottom to the top—has been briefed on basic safety concerns for the day. This doesn't have to be a special safety meeting per se. You can just set aside a few minutes during your normal preshoot briefing with the talent and crew. (You do normally have a preshoot briefing with your talent and crew, *right*?) The A.D., producer, or director needs to brief everyone on safety concerns with any specific props, scenes, or vehicles; how to navigate (or avoid) any dangerous areas on location; and any dangerous equipment, lights, or rigging on set.

9 MAKE SURE EVERYBODY KNOWS WHAT'S UP

If you are doing a stunt or dealing with any unusual scenario, prop, or vehicle, such as using a helicopter; staging a Samurai sword fight or a gun battle; shooting on a boat; or rigging a camera car or anything else out of the norm with potential safety implications, make sure that everyone on set—from the production assistants to the talent to the craft services people—knows exactly what the scene is going to entail, who will be involved, when it will happen, and how everyone else can stay out of harm's way.

10 AVOID THE UNTRAINED, INEXPERIENCED, AND INCOMPETENT

When it comes to dangerous equipment and activities on set, there should always be an experienced professional who routinely deals with any of those types of props, equipment, vehicles, or stunts on set whenever these riskier scenes are scheduled. People who are untrained, inexperienced, and incompetent with specialty props, equipment, vehicles, or physical stunts are a big potential liability for injury and even lawsuits when all the dust clears.

If you feel like you have no choice but to have someone with little to no experience handle something on set that is potentially dangerous, I strongly recommend that you both do as much homework as possible on the subject matter and try to get some sort of training session with a professional beforehand. If you can't arrange for some one-on-one guidance by a professional, at least make sure you've taken the time to consult someone with previous experience in the issues at hand. Even a 20-minute phone consultation with someone who's already been there and done that successfully could save you immeasurable amounts of unforeseen and unfamiliar trouble on set and help protect your crew from potential danger. Also, be honest and straightforward with everyone on set about any possible risks that you think they could incur. Everybody needs to be 100 percent comfortable and okay with anything they are asked to do on set. (And if they aren't, it's a clear indication that what you are asking for should probably not be done and be completely rethought, replanned, or reconceived instead.)

Electricity Considerations

Be careful not to overload the electrical circuits on location. (See "How Not to Blow a Circuit" on page 158.) Check the circuit box before you begin plugging in lights to see which outlets are on which circuits. Kitchens are usually on their own circuit. You should also be aware that outlets on opposite sides of the same wall will often be on the *same* circuit.

If the circuit box is not clearly labeled, a surefire way to check which outlet is on which circuit is to plug a regular household lamp in an outlet and click the circuit breakers on and off. Label the circuit breaker switches as you identify the room(s) they control. If you overload a circuit later, this will make it easy to reset it. If you are shooting in an older location with a fuse box instead of a circuit breaker, make sure you have extra fuses on hand or you may find your entire shoot shut down for lack of a $2.00 part.

✔ *Match outlets to circuits and be prepared to reset a tripped circuit breaker or blown fuse if you overload.*

Safety Considerations

The most hazardous thing you will encounter on most sets are lights. Professional lighting instruments generally get very hot very fast. Apart from burning careless bare fingers on a regular basis, lights can and do start fires when mishandled. A fire can easily start if lights are placed too close to curtains, ceilings, or anything else flammable. Serious fire hazards can also arise if electrical circuits are overloaded. Not to mention the possibility of exploding bulbs, electrocution, or falling light instruments whenever simple safety measures are ignored.

Just like crossing the street, driving, or handling power tools, lighting *can* be very dangerous. However, by taking some basic precautions and treating lights and electricity with full respect, you can greatly reduce the risks of burning someone's home or business to the ground. Be careful and make safety a primary concern on set and you'll have few worries apart from getting your shot.

✔ *Lights can be very dangerous. Proper handling and safety should always be your primary concern.*

Listen up people. This is another one of those bull horn moments:

> *You can't be down and dirty with safety when the potential consequences are serious injury, fire, or an expensive morale-busting disaster.*

Following these safety guidelines will help you avoid most of the worst-case scenarios:

• Use heavy-duty extension cords

Use only heavy-duty extension cords. Check to make sure that the gauge or cable thickness will handle the full number of amps you run through it. (See "Extension Cord Loads" below.) Gauge can usually be found on the extension cord itself and wattage can be found on your light or light bulb base.

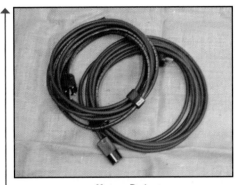

Heavy Duty

• Use gloves to handle hot lights

Film lights get very hot very fast. Go to the hardware store to pick up some leather electrical or work gloves for adjusting hot barn doors and light instruments.

Use Gloves

EXTENSION CORD LOADS

Gauge*	Length	Will Handle
12	50–100 ft.	10–15 amps
14	up to 50 ft.	10–15 amps
16	up to 100 ft.	10 amps

*It's tricky! The **lower** the gauge number the **more** power the cord will handle.

• Use sandbags to steady lights

Always use sandbags to secure light stands from careless crew members, wind, kids, or anything else that might accidentally walk into or knock over a light.

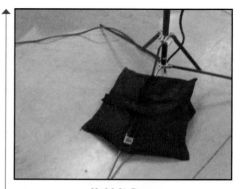

Hold It Down

• Screen open-faced lights

Make sure open-faced lights have protective screens or full **scrims** covering them to prevent hot shards of glass from scattering across the set if a bulb explodes.

Use Screens

• Stay clear of flammables

Never place a light instrument close to anything flammable or anything that may be damaged by heat, especially curtains, ceilings, and furniture. Stay at least 3 feet clear of anything that could catch fire or be damaged by heat—including ceilings.

Stay Clear!

• Be careful moving hot lights

Turn off lights whenever you aren't shooting or adjusting your lighting. Avoid moving tungsten lights when they are turned on. Your bulb **filament** is more likely to break or blow out when it's hot and jostled around. Similarly, be gentle with **spot** and **flood** controls. Any sudden jerk or bump to a hot light could cause a blow-out and cost you a good 15 to 20 minutes of time waiting for the light to cool down and the bulb to be changed. (Also keep in mind that quartz bulbs cost more than $25 each, even for small light units!) Always bring spare bulbs or back-up light gear to a shoot.

Be Gentle!

• Make sure lights are secure

Always double check to make sure that your lights are securely tightened to their stands. A loosely mounted light can easily fall off its stand or swing out of place.

Tight!

• Never operate lights in the rain

If a storm or sudden drizzle catches you off guard, immediately cut off power to your lights, unplug them, and get them out of the rain. DO NOT plug in or use again until *completely* dry. Dry off wet lights as soon as possible to avoid rusting. (A hairdryer is useful for quickly drying out wet gear and rain-soaked crew.)

Dry

• Never touch a quartz bulb

The oil from your skin can dramatically shorten the life of these very expensive bulbs or even cause them to explode in rare cases. Handle bulbs carefully using the protective foam wrapper normally found with the new bulb, gloves, tissue . . . anything, but your bare fingers. Inspect quartz bulbs for telltale bubbles caused by fingerprints or broken porcelain connectors (both pictured right).

Bubble = Trouble

By dividing your total light wattage by the voltage of the electrical outlets you can calculate how many amps of electricity you will need to power your lights and tell whether you're likely to blow a circuit or fuse. Here's the formula:

Watts ÷ Volts = Amps

Most modern houses in the United States have 15 or 20 amp circuits. Check the circuit breaker or fuse box to see what you're dealing with on your location. Voltage in the United States ranges from 110–120 volts. However, rounding the voltage down to 100 makes it much easier for people who suck at math (like me) and, more important, it leaves a comfortable margin of safety when calculating the above formula. Let's run through two examples:

500w + 250w + 250w + 200w = **1200 Watts**

1200 watts ÷ 100 volts = 12 Amps

Conclusion: In this case the total wattage of all lights adds up to less than 15 amps, so we're good to go with room to add up to another 300 watts of lighting on a 15 amp circuit or up to 800 more watts on a 20 amp circuit. (Don't forget to account for any *other* electrical appliances apart from lights that may be plugged into the same circuit, because they are draining precious juice too.)

1000w + 1000w + 220w = **2220 Watts**

2220 watts ÷ 100 volts = 22.2 Amps

Conclusion: This would be too many lights, or more correctly, too much *power* to plug into a room with a 20 amp circuit. The solution here would be to plug one of the 1000 watt lights into a heavy-duty extension cord plugged into a different circuit in another room, so that the electrical load on all circuits stayed comfortably under our 20 amp limit.

Fresnel Light

These lights have a focusable glass lens. The light beam can be focused into a spotted (narrow) or flooded (broader) beam. Mole-Richardson brand Inkie, Baby, and Baby Junior are all examples of Fresnel lights. Arri and Mole-Richardson brand Fresnel lights are the long-time industry favorites for their solid construction and reliability.

Open-Face Light

These are lights that don't have a glass lens in the front. Instead they have open-faced reflectors. You always want to have a screen or scrim in front of an open-faced light in case the bulb breaks. Examples of open-faced lights include Lowel's Omni and Tota lights.

LED Lights

LED lights are prized for several defining characteristics: they draw much less electricity than tungsten or even fluorescent lights—they can be easily powered by battery; the bulbs don't get hot, so they're much safer for location use and won't heat up a room after a few minutes; LED light bulbs last much longer than tungsten or fluorescent bulbs; and they are dimmable and they put out a lot of even light. Really, the only downside to using LED lights is that they are relatively pricey.

Fluorescent Light

Fluorescent lights, often referred to as **Kino Flo**s, after the most popular brand, are relatively lightweight and cast lots of soft even light. Best of all for guerrillas, they require much less electricity than tungsten lights. You can experiment with homemade fluorescent setups of your own, but beware of potential flicker issues with household fluorescents. (**Note:** Fluorescents won't work properly on an external dimmer.)

Practical Light

This just refers to any location light fixture that is seen on-camera. Desk lamps, halogen floor lights, track lights, etc., all make excellent practical lights. A practical light can serve as your key, fill, hair, or background light depending on its position and brightness. If you can dim the light, aim it, or swap out different wattage bulbs, it's even more "practical." Using existing lighting should always be the first option you consider for lighting docs since it's natural and requires little or no extra setup time. Experiment with white balance, reflectors, diffusion gel, and different types of bulbs to get a more desirable look.

China Ball 	These are simply your standard, inexpensive, paper Chinese lanterns. They sell for $5.00–30.00, depending on the size you want. You can pick them up at any lighting store. These lights are highly portable since they weigh next to nothing and collapse flat. They create beautiful soft light for interviews using nothing more than a standard household light bulb and a socket unit. These are an indispensable tool for doc guerrillas. Get some.
Barn Doors 	Barn doors are used to control light. And that's the name of the game . . . *light control.* The simple act of turning on a light is not lighting any more than hitting the record button can be called filmmaking. If you are not in *control* of your lights, you're not light-*ing.* You must use barn doors and other accessories such as **blackwrap** (see the next page) to make sure your light goes exactly where you want it and nowhere else.
Reflector Umbrella 	This nifty device mounts onto the front of an open-faced light instrument (to cast a much softer, broad, and evenly diffused light. Reflector umbrellas work great to create **fill light**. They can also be used to form a soft key light. If you want to impress clients for a paid gig, reflector umbrellas are also great for making things look and feel "Hollywood" for them.
Extension Cords 	Get as many heavy-duty extension cords as you can get your hands on. At least one for every light. Standard skinny household extension cords won't cut it. The lower the gauge number on the cord, the more power it can handle safely. Extension cords are necessary to run lights to different circuits of your location, which are usually going to be in different rooms. (See "Extension Cord Loads" chart on page 155.)
Dimmer	This is one of the most valuable lighting accessories that you can have in your guerrilla kit. A dimmer will allow you to quickly and easily adjust the intensity of any light you plug into it, which will save you immeasurable time moving lights, adjusting scrims, and fussing with **ND gels.** If using household dimmers, make sure that any lights you use don't exceed the maximum wattage listed on the dimmer. (**Note:** Always **re-white balance** your camera *after* you dim a key light since dimming lights may affect light color temperature.)
Gels 	Gels, which affix to barn doors using clothespins, are another indispensable accessory. At the very least you want to have color temperature blue (**CTB**) and color temperature orange (**CTO**) gels to allow your lighting to mimic daylight or indoor light color temperatures in mixed lighting situations (common) and neutral density (**ND**) gels. After those, you'll want to get an assortment of colors that will allow you to accent and "paint" your lighting compositions to portray different moods and meanings. (See "Down and Dirty Gel Guide" on page 168.)

Diffusion 	You absolutely must have some diffusion if you're using professional film lighting instruments. Diffusion material allows you to turn a **hard light** source into a **soft light** source. Diffusion material comes in frosted white gels and also heat-resistant cloth-like material called **toughspun,** which resembles dryer sheets. (Please note that you should never use *actual* dryer sheets for diffusion as they will quickly burst into flames . . . Don't ask how I know.)
Snoots 	Snoots mount onto the front of a light to give you a "spotlight" effect by narrowing the size of the beam. They are useful for pinpointing key lights, highlighting props, and tabletop work. If you don't have a snoot, you can pretty much use a piece of blackwrap to the same effect (see entry below).
Blackwrap 	A few good-sized sheets of this handy material will *always* serve you well. Blackwrap is essentially extra heavy-duty aluminum foil coated in a heat resistant flat black paint to absorb light. It is primarily used to control and shape light much like barn doors. However, blackwrap is much more flexible as you can attach it to barn doors and mold it into any shape you desire within seconds to quickly adjust your lighting on the fly.
C47s (clothespins) 	A standard lighting tool for decades, *wooden* clothespins—known in the industry as C47s, are the most practical and inexpensive means of attaching gels and diffusion material to the edge of barn doors.
C-Stand 	C-Stands or Century Stands are tough heavy-duty metal stands and a primary tool of grips everywhere. These are all-purpose stands for rigging and hanging a variety of film tools—be it lights, flags, boom poles, backdrops or cookies. It's not always practical to set up heavy C-Stands with flags for many doc shoots, but when you have the time and crew, these are handy industry-standard lighting tools to have.
Gobo Head and Arms 	Gobo arms are thin, but heavy-duty rods that work in conjunction with gobo heads, which are made up of two thick interlocking grooved metal "wheels" that allow you to tightly attach them to gobo arms, cables, reflectors, and anything else that will fit. These are the "Erector Sets" of the filmmaking world. With the right combination of stands, gobo arms, and gobo heads, a skilled crew member could mount or rig just about anything.
Flag Kit 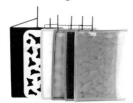	Flag kits contain several different materials in wire frames designed to be held in a gobo head. Flag kits usually contain some combination of: silks—white cloth diffusion; nets—net-like material for cutting down light intensity; flags—solid black material for blocking light and controlling shadows. Flags are usually color-coded as follows: Yellow=Silk, Green=Single Net, Red=Double Net, Black=Flag.

Introduction

Apart from a great location, few things will add production value to your documentary more than good lighting. Good lighting can be achieved with almost any type of professional lighting gear and even household lighting fixtures can be used to great effect. The art of lighting—and it truly is an *art*—is a subject unto itself that is well worth studying and experimenting with. I'm not going to get into a full-scale technical explanations of all the aspects of lighting you should be familiar with before shooting, but I will cover some specific lighting tips, tools, and setups useful for guerrilla docs.

Your setups will vary depending on the lights you have, the location, number of subjects, time constraints, and style of the piece. You can light locations and interviews effectively with one light source or using a full-blown formal **4-point lighting** setup once you understand a few basics. This is definitely one of those aspects of filmmaking that you can learn in a few hours, but it takes a lifetime to truly master.

Lighting can be a powerful tool in telling a documentary story. It sets the mood, style, and look of your film just as much, if not more, than your camera work and sound track. One of the key secrets to shooting professional looking video on any budget, any camera, and any time is to understand and strive to master the craft of lighting.

Learning and Mastering the Craft

The best way to learn lighting is to experiment. Try different types of instruments, accessories, gels, and reflectors. Play with them. See what they look like on video. Pay close attention to the lighting in your favorite docs and TV programs.

Intern or volunteer as crew for video shoots with experienced DPs or gaffers (lighting guys/gals). Observe what they do and which instruments and accessories they use. Look at the video monitor to see what effect each lighting tool has on the image. Ask questions. Take notes. Later, get your hands on the finished project, if you can, and study and analyze the lighting some more.

> ✔ *Good production value is good lighting. The best way to learn lighting is to experiment and observe.*

Setting Up Your Key Light

You can use a professional film light or **practical light** as a key or main source of light on your subject. You generally want to place your key light at roughly a 45 degree angle next to the camera on the same side that the interviewer will be sitting. Adjust the barn doors so that the light only falls on the parts of the frame you want. You may also want to take measures to reduce the light **intensity**. (See "Controlling Light Intensity" on page 167.)

Next, and most important, if you are using a hard light source such as an open-faced light or fresnel, you will probably want to place some **diffusion** material on the front of the light or **bounce** it off a white surface. I would never use either type of light on a subject without softening it, unless I *wanted* to portray a subject with a harsh look.

Finally, you should add **blackwrap** or **flags**, if desired, to narrow the beam or reduce any unwanted light from spilling onto other parts of the scene. Most of the

Diffusion gel mounted on a Lowel Omni light

time you will only want the key light on your subject's face and upper body and you would use another light to light the background. However, when pressed for lights or time, I often purposely aim or reflect the key light so that the same instrument can double as a **background light** or **hair light** to kill two birds with one stone.

Another option is to use a **light bank,** which is a tent-like housing specially designed to fit over hard lights. This does an excellent job of diffusing the light. Light banks are ideal for interviews, but they are also expensive and some models can be a pain to set up. I've found that I can get good results and more control with just some diffusion and black wrap, so I still keep it Down and Dirty. Go with what works for *you*. What's ultimately important for interviews is that the key light is soft, even, and only where you want it to be.

A light bank on a Lowel Rifa Light
(photo courtesy of Lowel Lighting)

Hair Light

The main purpose of a **hair light**, or **backlight** as it's also known, is to help separate subjects from the background. Hair lights add some dimensionality, **production value**, and compliment your subject. This is the light that gives the hair of your favorite Hollywood starlets like Zoe Saldana or Mila Kunis (sigh!) that magic glow in their close-ups. A small light source placed above and just behind your subject on the

opposite side of the camera from the key light will work this magic for you. Be careful that your hair light does not spill onto your subject's face or elsewhere. It should only form a nice rim around one side of the head, neck, and/or shoulders. This will be easy to tell if you are adjusting your lights one at a time . . . as you *should* be.

Background Light

A small or standard hard source will serve you well as a **background light**. One method is to create diagonal slashes of light across the background. These are easily formed by adjusting barn doors or blackwrap to form a small slit. Other popular options are triangular slices of light shooting up or down across the background. This effect can also be created using barn doors or blackwrap to narrow the beam then slightly twisting the light toward or away from the background. You could also use a cut-out pattern called a **cookie**. Cookies may come as part of a **flag kit**. You can also easily create your own cookies to cast interesting shadows by cutting a piece of cardboard or blackwrap to a desired pattern. Experiment to see which effects work best for your project.

The final touch to your background lighting will be to gel the lights an appropriate color that provides some contrast or otherwise compliments your subject. Again, use your own taste. (If you don't have good taste, ask a more fashionable crew member.)

The Cookie Effect

Cookies come in all kinds of patterns, from abstract (below), to window panes, to blinds, to leaves . . . you can always instantly cast interesting shadows, break up plain flat backgrounds, and add a new layer of visual storytelling.

**A light aimed through a cookie to create a pattern
on the background**

The cookie effect in a close-up

Avoid the common mistake of making your whole scene flat with **fill light**. Adjust your fill light to taste. Simply moving the light source closer or farther away from your subject or diffusing or dimming it can control fill light from a lighting instrument.

About half the time I find that I don't really need a fill light. All you want to do is fill in any harsh shadows and bring out some of the details hidden in the shadows, not blast the subject with light that will make your image look flat, two-dimensional, and lifeless.

Subject with "racoon eyes"

Pay particular attention to the eye sockets of your subject, which often require a fill light to eliminate dark eye shadows known as "raccoon eyes," which is particularly prevalent when your key light is at a high angle or when shooting outdoors in bright, midday sunlight when the sun is at its highest. In the illustration below right notice that the subtle fill light just fills in some of the shadow on the right side of the model's face. (Another quick solution to raccoon eyes is to shoot with the sun behind your subject forming a nice hairlight or to move out of the direct sunlight into a shaded area.)

Key Light Only

Key Light + Fill Light

Fill Light Alternatives

Rather than setting up a separate light for fill, you can usually do just fine and keep it low tech by using a reflector to bounce the key or hair light into dark facial shadows. Similarly, you may find that by simply opening up the camera's aperture a little more you can often eliminate dark facial areas without blowing out other parts of the image.

CONTROLLING LIGHT INTENSITY

In video, there's almost always more than one way to do something. When lights appear too bright or intense there are a variety of solutions that you can mix and match to get just the right look:

Spot and Flood Your Light

narrow beam

wide beam

Most film lights have a knob or dial to control the intensity of the light beam.

When a light is at its broadest beam setting it's flooded.

When a light beam is at its most intense setting it's spotted.

Add ND Gels

Use clear gray ND gels to cut down light intensity.

Use Different Bulbs

You can also switch bulbs of different wattages to control intensity.

Use a Dimmer

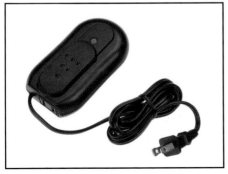

Whether built-in or add-on, dimmers are hands down the fastest, easiest way to control intensity.

Use Scrims

Scrims are little screens that are used to cut down light. They come in full or half sizes and single or double thickness.

Diffusion Gel

1. This is a must for interviews when using a hard source of light. Diffusion gels soften the texture of a subject's skin and will always look better than hard light shined directly on a subject.
2. Use to soften or diminish harsh shadows.

Color: frosty white

ND Gel

Color: light to dark gray

1. Use to cut down a light that's too bright. These gels come in various shades of light and dark gray and do not affect color temperature.
2. Use on one-half of a light to balance lighting between a light- and dark-skinned subject under the same key light. Adjust your lighting and exposure for the darker subject, then use an ND filter on one side of the light to get a good exposure on the light-skinned subject.
3. ND gel can also be taped to the inside of a lamp or china ball that is too bright on-camera.

CTO

Color: light to dark orange

1. Place CTO (color temperature orange) gel on a daylight-balanced light, such as an HMI, or LED light or KinoFlo, to match it to the color temperature of indoor light.
2. Use a large CTO gel sheet to cover windows in the background or behind your subject to make the normally bluish daylight appear be the same color temperature as tungsten (indoor) light. Carefully tape the gel into the window frame. Composing a tighter shot or using shallow depth of field will make a gelled window less noticeable to the camera.
3. CTO can also be used to "warm up" an interview subject's skin tone. This is an easy cure for pale faces and an all-around simple way to make just about anyone look more healthy and attractive on video.
4. You can also use CTO on light instruments when shooting outdoors with your camera balanced for daylight to give subjects a strong warm contrast to their cooler background.

CTB

Color: light to medium blue

1. Place CTB (color temperature blue) gel on a tungsten-balanced light indoors to supplement natural sunlight being used in a scene. Place your light outside a window shining in or anywhere off-camera, pointing the same direction as the sunlight.
2. Use to create "artificial sunlight" by placing on any powerful tungsten (indoor) source of light. You can create "sunlight" in a studio or on location in the dead of night with this handy gel. Shine through a set of blinds or cardboard cut out (a.k.a. cookie) in the shape of a window to create a more interesting effect. (See "Cookie Effect" on page 165.)
3. Place on a tungsten-balanced (indoor) light to match it to the color temperature of daylight when shooting outdoors to supplement daylight without having a blue/orange contrast in color temperatures between your subject and the background.
4. Use to "cool" a scene or subject that looks too warm. You could also white balance the camera to a warm card for a similar effect. (See the Crazy Phat Bonus Website for this book at www.focalpress.com/cw/artis)

Amber Gel

Color: yellow/orange

1. Use these gels to warm up a scene or a subject's face.
2. Use to create a sunrise or early morning sunlight effect. (**Note:** Lighter shades of CTO gels can also be used as a substitute.)

---

1. Use these gels to add a little color to hair/back lights.
2. Use to change the color of the background to match or contrast with your subject's clothing, hair, or skin tone.
3. Use to accent "props" in a scene.
4. Use for coloring any scene where appropriate.

Party Gels

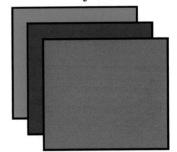

Color: various—reds, greens, purples, etc.

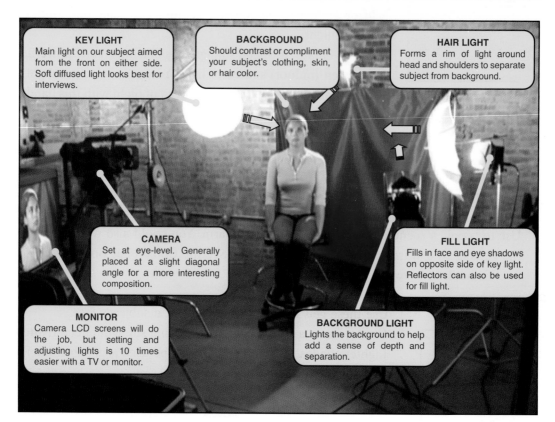

KEY LIGHT
Main light on our subject aimed from the front on either side. Soft diffused light looks best for interviews.

BACKGROUND
Should contrast or compliment your subject's clothing, skin, or hair color.

HAIR LIGHT
Forms a rim of light around head and shoulders to separate subject from background.

CAMERA
Set at eye-level. Generally placed at a slight diagonal angle for a more interesting composition.

FILL LIGHT
Fills in face and eye shadows on opposite side of key light. Reflectors can also be used for fill light.

MONITOR
Camera LCD screens will do the job, but setting and adjusting lights is 10 times easier with a TV or monitor.

BACKGROUND LIGHT
Lights the background to help add a sense of depth and separation.

The cost of your lighting kit is almost irrelevant. The most important factor is your understanding and mastery of your lights. I have consistently achieved great results lighting interviews using a simple, Lowel Omni 3 Light Kit, which consists of three 500 watt lights, and supplementing with whatever practical lights (lamps, desk lights, etc.) on location that I found useful. More recently, I've come to favor the popular Lite Panels 1×1 LED units. Although pricey–about $1000 and up–they are lightweight, highly-portable, bright, and have a built-in dimmer, all of which makes them quick and easy to set up for docs.

A light is as a light does and if you learn to bounce it, diffuse it, reflect it, dim it, or otherwise find ways to control the quality of the light ... anything can be a key light. A Chinese lantern like the one pictured above creates beautiful soft warm light.

For more formal setups using four-point lighting, a China ball or fluorescent light is a good addition to your light kit. In addition, a smaller light such as a Lite Panels mini or Pro-Light light may also be desirable. These small but powerful lights are useful as hair lights, prop lights, or even background lights. With most cameras you can even get away with one as your key light for tight shots. (See also "Lighting Tools of the Trade" on page 159.)

3 TIPS FOR SHOOTING IN LOW LIGHT

One of the unavoidable realities of documentary work is low-light situations. Some subject matters unfold almost entirely in low-light and dark environments. Adding more light or using an onboard camera light is the *technical* ideal, but this often compromises the *natural* action on-screen. What's a Down and Dirty filmmaker to do?

1 USE THE GAIN OR ISO FUNCTION

Video and DSLR cameras each have a function to artificially brighten the image. On pro video cameras it's "gain" and on DSLRs it's ISO. However, the big trade-off that comes with gain or ISO is video "noise," resulting in a lower quality, grainier video image. Use only as much as you need.

"The Education of Shelby Knox"—Incite Pictures

2 SHOOT WIDE

Longer telephoto lenses generally suck up more light. Shooting with a wide fast lens or with your zoom lens at the widest setting is another way to get more light into the camera. Rather than zooming in and out to adjust your frame, move the camera closer or farther away from your subject to reframe shots and still stay wide.

3 DECREASE YOUR SHUTTER SPEED

Taking your shutter speed down a setting or two from the normal shutter speed will increase the amount of light going into your camera, which will brighten your image. The trade-off is that faster motions may appear blurry or surreal if the shutter speed is lowered too much. (See "Shutter Speed Basics" on page 127.)

Reflectors

A carefully aimed reflector can double your lighting power and substitute for your fill, key, or hair light.

Blackwrap

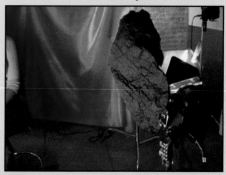

Blackwrap can be molded to barn doors to act as a flag. Barn doors, blackwrap, and flags all work to keep light only where you want it.

Placing Gels

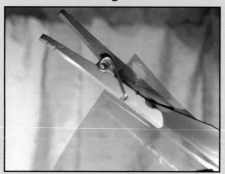

C-47s (a.k.a. clothespins) should be used to attach gels to the very edge of barn doors to avoid melted gels and burning clothespins.

Experimental Lights

Try making your own gear like this home-made fluorescent unit or experiment with different types of fixtures to expand your kit.

Lighting from Below

Lighting subjects from below can make them appear mysterious, spooky, or surreal.

Gold Reflectors

Apart from amber gels, gold reflectors can be used to warm up a subject's skin tone.

1 Decide Where You Want to Shoot

Ideally, the scene should communicate something about the person you are interviewing, but practical and technical issues may sometimes trump this desire.

2 Set Up Your Camera and Monitor and Choose a Frame

Adjust color bars on your monitor accordingly. (See "How to Adjust NTSC Color Bars" on page 139) It is pointless to adjust lights for video without looking at a monitor, because what your naked eye sees has almost nothing to do with how the scene will actually look on *video*. Use a stand-in model (i.e., crew, P.A. or bystander), preferably one with the same skin tone and height as your subject.

3 Take Control of the Light In the Room

Turn off all lights on set (unless you're using them as work lights). Block out any unwanted sunlight using curtains, dark cloth, garbage bags, or newspaper.

4 Assemble the Lights

Plug the AC cable into each light, tighten onto a stand, add barn doors, and plug light in. Call out, "Spotting!" to warn crew and test. Set light in desired position and weigh it down with a sandbag. Secure cables on floor with Gaffer's tape.

5 Adjust the Lights and Set the Final Frame

Lights should always be set one at a time, so that you can see what *each* light is doing. I'd start with the key light, then background light or prop light, then hair light, and finally the fill light. You want to

a. Aim, spot, and flood each light to desired intensity
b. Adjust the barn doors
c. Add scrims and/or diffusion as desired (NO colored gels yet)
d. Use blackwrap and flags as necessary to control light spill
e. White balance the camera
f. NOW you can add colored gels as your heart desires

I suggest that you set lights in order of importance just in case you run out of time. That way, your subject will still have a good key light if you didn't get to tweak everything else the way you'd like to. Now have your actual subject sit in and tweak the lights one last time to accommodate their height, skin tone, etc. Apply makeup if desired.

Practical Lighting Setup

THE RECIPE:

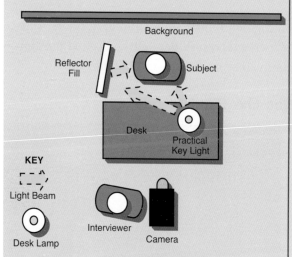

Background

Reflector Fill

Subject

Desk

Practical Key Light

KEY

Light Beam

Desk Lamp

Interviewer

Camera

SKILL LEVEL: Beginner

PREP: 5 Mins.

INGREDIENTS:

Practical Lamp

Reflector

OPTIONAL INGREDIENTS:

Dimmer

Lightbulbs

ND Gels

ALTERNATE RECIPES:

· Manipulate white balance or use a gold reflector for warmer look

· Use track lighting as a hairlight

NOTES: Down and Dirty DV is all about keeping it simple, resourceful, and practical. Any light that's already on location and appears on-camera is called a practical light for obvious reasons. Pay attention to the lighting on location and look for lamps or other light fixtures that you can use to your advantage. It doesn't have to be a key light either. Practical lights can be used as background lights, fill lights, or even hair lights in the case of track lighting. Cut and neatly tape a piece of ND gel to the inside of a lamp shade that looks too bright on-camera. If you also carry a few different sized bulbs and/or a dimmer you can easily create a variety of attractive looks with household bulbs.

4-Point Lighting Setup

THE RECIPE:

Background

Cookie

Background Light

Subject

Hair Light

KEY

Light Beam

Light Instrument

Key Light

Interviewer

Camera

Fill Light

SKILL LEVEL: Intermediate

PREP: 30–45 mins.

INGREDIENTS:

| Key Light | Fill Light | B.g. Light | Hair Light | Color Gels | Cookie |

OPTIONAL INGREDIENTS:

Dimmer

ALTERNATE RECIPES:

· Omit background light for more isolated subject

· Try slashes or washes of light instead of cookie

· Reflector can be used for fill

NOTES: This is the standard interview setup used by formal documentaries, magazine news shows, and other projects seeking a polished or broadcast look. By using a cookie or other patterns on the background and/or gels on other lights it can be quite stylized and dramatic. These setups add a certain professional production value, but also call more attention to the filmmaking process, look less natural, and take the most time to set up.

Simple Lighting Setup

THE RECIPE:

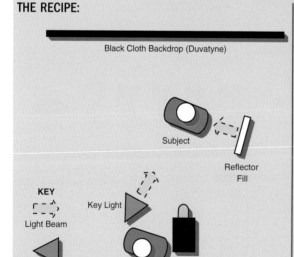

Black Cloth Backdrop (Duvatyne)

Subject

Reflector Fill

KEY

Light Beam

Key Light

Light Instrument

Interviewer   Camera

SKILL LEVEL: Beginner

PREP: 10–15 mins.

INGREDIENTS:

Key Light   Reflector (Fill)   Black Backdrop

OPTIONAL INGREDIENTS:

Amber Gels   Dimmer

ALTERNATE RECIPES:

· Add hair light for more separation from background (b.g.)

· Use darkened natural surroundings instead of backdrop

NOTES: Simple, elegant, and natural. In the setup pictured here, we hung a large piece of Duvatyne (non-reflective black fabric) on the wall and lit the subject with a single diffused open-faced key light, then propped up a reflector to fill in the shadows on the right side of her face. Alternatively, you can get the same look sans black cloth by placing your subject in the center of a large room. The key to both methods is angling and flagging off your lights so that no light spills on the background and gives away the illusion. Four-point lighting is great, but one- or two-point lighting can be just as effective, and look more natural. You don't have to get fancy to get great lighting results.

Window Lighting Setup

THE RECIPE:

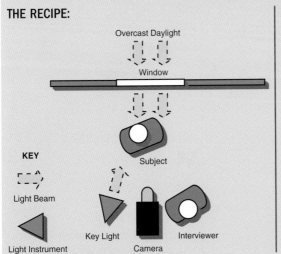

Overcast Daylight

Window

Subject

KEY

Light Beam

Light Instrument

Key Light

Camera

Interviewer

SKILL LEVEL: Advanced

PREP: 45 mins.

INGREDIENTS:

Window (Overcast)   Key Light   CTB Gels   Polarizer Cam Filter

OPTIONAL INGREDIENTS:

Dimmer

ALTERNATE RECIPES:

· Open window if exterior noise is acceptable

NOTES: This setup is a little unorthodox, but it's a perfect example of using creativity to overcome a lame shooting location. This room was just plain white walls and windows, but had a decent view down onto the street. Pulling off this setup is tricky on three accounts: (1) a polarizer camera filter is needed and the key light has to be carefully aimed at the right angle to light the subject to minimize reflections, (2) the camera and interviewer have to be at a high angle to get the street below in the background and maintain a decent eyeline, and (3) the sunlit background is much brighter, so we needed a very strong key light to get a good exposure on our subject after first exposing for the exterior view. Using a dimmer may make it easier to balance the key light with the outdoor light.

Anonymous Lighting Setup

THE RECIPE:

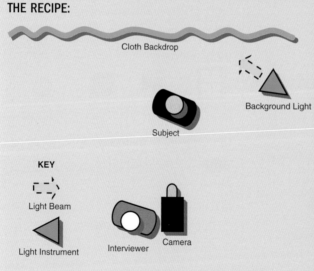

Cloth Backdrop

Background Light

Subject

KEY

Light Beam

Light Instrument

Interviewer

Camera

SKILL LEVEL: Beginner

PREP: 10 mins.

INGREDIENTS:

 B.g. Light

 Cloth Backdrop

OPTIONAL INGREDIENTS:

 Hair Light

ALTERNATE RECIPES:

· Light and use the room as your background instead of a backdrop
· Put subject behind a backlit screen
· Shoot subject's shadow only

NOTES: This setup is for subjects such as whistle-blowers, victims, or crime figures who agree to an interview, but wish to remain anonymous for reasons of safety, legality, or privacy. The key to this setup is to only light the background. This will produce a sharp dramatic silhouette. You'll probably also want to gel this light a color that works for your scene. Keep in mind that different colors can convey very different messages about your subject to your viewers. You can add a hair light if you'd like a little more definition of your subject, but be careful that it doesn't spill onto her face and reveal her identity. If safety is really a concern, you can also disguise her voice in post-production, add a hat or wig, or just shoot her torso.

2-Subject Lighting Setup

THE RECIPE:

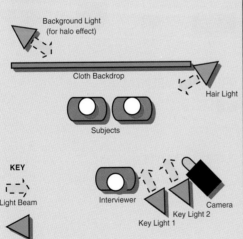

Background Light
(for halo effect)

Cloth Backdrop

Hair Light

Subjects

KEY

Light Beam

Light Instrument

Interviewer

Key Light 1

Key Light 2

Camera

SKILL LEVEL: Advanced

PREP: 45-60 mins.

INGREDIENTS:

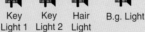

Key Light 1   Key Light 2   Hair Light   B.g. Light   Amber Gels   Cloth Backdrop

OPTIONAL INGREDIENTS:

Dimmer   Gels

ALTERNATE RECIPES:

· Light backdrop from front instead of rear
· Use a single key light for both subjects
· Give each subject their own hair light
· Move camera and key lights left of interviewer

NOTES: Lighting two-subject interviews with a small light kit calls for one or more of your lights to do double duty to light both subjects at the same time. It's not uncommon to have subject's shoulders touching. If they sat in their normal personal space comfort zones, there would be a huge empty spot in the middle of the frame and I'd need to compose a wider (i.e., less intimate) shot and use a much bigger cloth backdrop to pull off the setup. The backdrop doesn't have to be iridescent like the one pictured above, but you will at least need a translucent material if you want to get a halo effect like the one here when lit from behind.

Night Exterior Lighting Setup

Photo: *Paper Chasers* – Son #1 Media

THE RECIPE:

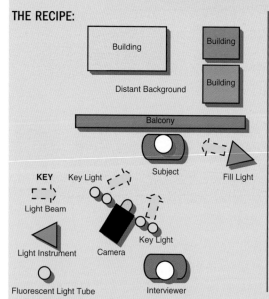

Building

Building

Distant Background

Building

Balcony

Subject

 Fill Light

KEY   Key Light

Light Beam

Light Instrument   Camera   Key Light

Fluorescent Light Tube   Interviewer

SKILL LEVEL: Beginner

PREP: 30 mins.

INGREDIENTS:

Key Light   Fill Light   Color Gels   Dramatic View

OPTIONAL INGREDIENTS:

Hair Light

ALTERNATE RECIPES:

· Use a China ball as a key light

NOTES: The above setup was lit with a homemade fluorescent unit that I like to call the "Kino-Bro" created by my man, D.P. "Black Magic" Tim. The Kino-Bro consists of four small fluorescent light tubes attached to an open frame with a space in the middle for the camera lens. It's designed to wrap soft even light around the face. You could achieve a similar effect with standard fluorescent units on either side of your camera. Night exterior setups work best with a strong well-lit background. The camera's low angle provides a more dramatic composition that takes full advantage of the vivid Manhattan nightscape behind the subject.

TV Monitor Lighting Setup

Photo: *Paper Chasers* – Son #1 Media

THE RECIPE:

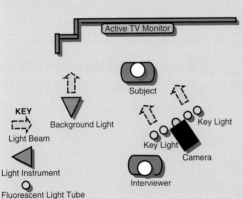

Active TV Monitor

Subject

KEY
Light Beam

Background Light

Key Light

Key Light

Camera

Light Instrument

Interviewer

Fluorescent Light Tube

SKILL LEVEL: Intermediate

PREP: 35 mins.

INGREDIENTS:

Key
Light

B.g.
Light

Color
Gels

TV
Monitor

ALTERNATE RECIPES:

· Use a standard tungsten key light
· Window with curtains in place of monitor
· Use shallow depth of field to "soften" background

NOTES: This is another setup using the homemade "Kino-Bro" fluorescent light unit cited on the previous page. The pictures on the wall are lit using barn doors on an open-faced light to form a slash of light across the corner. Swap out different colored gels to create different moods and play with subject-background contrasts. The lighting here is easy enough, but using an active tv monitor in the background can be tricky on a few accounts: (1) You need to be *sure* that you have the legal right to show the video playing on the monitor; (2) the video must be long enough or looped; (3) it should not overshadow your subject and, very important; (4) there's a good chance that you will get a nasty flicker common when shooting video and computer monitors. To reduce this flicker: (a) see if you can adjust the monitor's refresh rate; (b) check the camera menu for a "flicker reduce", "scan sync", or "50Hz/60Hz" function; and/or (c) experiment with slightly higher or lower shutter speeds.

Blacklight Setup

Photo: *Paper Chasers* – Son #1 Media

THE RECIPE:

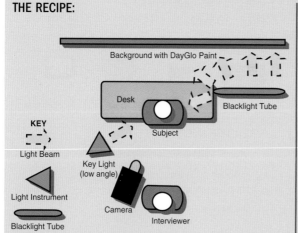

Background with DayGlo Paint

Desk

Blacklight Tube

Subject

KEY

Light Beam

Key Light
(low angle)

Light Instrument

Camera

Blacklight Tube

Interviewer

SKILL LEVEL: Beginner

PREP: 20 mins.

INGREDIENTS:

Key Light   Blacklight

OPTIONAL INGREDIENTS:

Dimmer   Fill Light   Reflector

ALTERNATE RECIPES:

· Use shallow depth of field to "soften"
background

NOTES: You always want to try to take advantage of location lighting first and supplement or add light as necessary to set the right visual mood. In this dark music studio, a practical black-light on location is acting as a background light and providing a cool purple fill on the right side of the subject's face. DayGlo graffiti on the walls pops a funky burst of color behind our subject and separates him from the neon background to add depth to the shot and set the perfect tone for the interview. A single key light is angled up from below creating a stark contrast to the purple fill light on our subject's face. Also, note that D.P. Eric McClain lowered the camera some to give our music C.E.O. subject a more powerful and imposing screen presence. By carefully observing the creative options on location, you can save time and better portray your subjects in their natural environment.

CHAPTER 5

SOUND
RECORDING

It's absolutely essential that you have some audio gear apart from the camera's built-in mic. To get professional-quality audio, you're going to need a professional-quality mic at the very least. **You simply can't record good sound from crappy mics.** Buy used sound gear, if you can't afford it new. Unlike cameras, good name-brand professional mics (and lights for that matter) will easily serve you for a decade or more if they are not abused. Here's the minimum gear I recommend for a doc.

Shotgun Mic

You want the best shotgun mic you can afford. These extremely sensitive and directional mics are used to isolate the sound source they are pointed at and minimize background noises. The *Sennheiser 416* shotgun mic pictured here is a popular workhorse among indie filmmakers.

Boom Pole with Shock Mount

The lighter and longer the pole, the better. A decent shock mount is a must for location audio. I don't recommend it, but it's okay to cheap out on the boom pole if you have to. A heavier, homemade paint pole boom will require more muscle, but can get the mic just as close as the pro models. Search the Internet for do-it-yourself boom pole designs if you go this route.

Headphones

You need the padded kind that completely cover the ear. The Sony 7506 headphones pictured here are an industry standard. Professional-quality headphones will cost at least $50 to $200. Make sure the plug (stereo or mini) is the right one for your mixer or camera. If not, you may need to use an adapter plug. If you need to shoot more low-key, you could go with *professional* sound-isolating earbud headphones which completely plug your earholes.

XLR Cables

Take at least 15 feet of XLR cable for every mic. You can't have too many XLR cables. Beware, with rough handling, XLRs may develop shorts, which cause static and sound drop-outs. If you will be recording live events such as concerts you will want to use extra-long 25–50 feet XLR cables. Test for shorts by linking all your XLR cables together, hooking up to a mic and jiggling the cables while listening for static.

Windshield

A fuzzy fur windshield or wind protector that slips over your shotgun mic is a must to combat wind noise common during exterior shooting.

Once you've scrounged up enough cash to get the basics, you'll want to add these items to expand your sound package and take your recording to the next level.

Wireless Lav Mic

For many doc scenarios a wireless lav is the only thing that will do the job. They are indispensable to cover wide shots and people on the go. They are also pricey, but you're better off sticking with a shotgun mic or using a hard-wired lav, rather than getting a cheap (i.e. unreliable) wireless unit. Save up and get a quality wireless mic when you can.

Zeppelin with Pistol Grip

These little mic housings are pricey, but they are hands down the most effective solution for blocking wind noise when shooting exteriors. The pistol grip acts as a sound shock-absorber for the mic and also allows you to use boom-mounted mics in small spaces without a boom pole.

Windjammer

To make your zeppelin even more effective at blocking wind noise, slip on a windjammer (also affectionately known as a "**dead cat**") for *maximum* wind protection. This is the combo the pros use. Not cheap, but extremely effective in windy conditions.

Mixer

I like the *Sound Devices 302* pictured here for doc work, but you can go with any quality mixer as long as it's portable, battery-powered, has the number of inputs you need (3 to 4 inputs is plenty), has a peak meter to read levels, provides **phantom power** to mics, and has the ability to send a 1 kHz reference tone.

Adapters

These are a must if you'll be mixing equipment from different sources or want to plug into the main sound feed of a live event such as a press conference. Stereo to mini plug adapters, XLR male-to-female adapters, and XLR to RCA adapters and cables are commonly needed. (While you're at the store, you'll also want some gaffers tape to secure your XLR cables safely to the floor.)

Introduction

Sound is one of the least appreciated, but most important parts of filmmaking. It's as much a part of telling your story as the cinematography, art direction, or acting. And if you screw it up, the audience won't forgive you. They will forgive a blurry shot, a boom mic in the frame, and they'll even let a weak performance slide, but no one will forgive bad sound. And it's very time-consuming and difficult, if not impossible, to fix most sound mistakes made on location. So listen and learn, people . . .

There are four basic types of microphones to consider for documentary production: boom mics, lavalier mics, handheld mics, and wireless mics. Each has unique advantages and drawbacks depending on the specific production situation you are in.

Boom Mics

These are mics mounted on a boom pole, which is held by a boom operator. Although you can use any type of mic that will fit on a boom pole, **shotgun mics** (a.k.a. hypercardioid mics), which have a very directional and narrow **pick-up pattern**, are most often used on boom poles. Shotgun mics focus on sound only in the direction they are pointed and greatly diminish most sounds from the rear and sides. Because of this, they are great for isolating your subject's voice from a noisy or crowded environment.

Boom mics are handy for "run-and-gun" shooting, when you may have multiple or spontaneous interview subjects, and also when your subject is very active and you don't have a wireless lav. I avoid boom mics for interviews, because they are very distracting to subjects who sometimes have a natural tendency to steal a glance at a phallic object hovering just above their head every few seconds or so.

Carbon fiber boom poles like this one are the most lightweight (and expensive)

✔ BAD AUDIO is an UNFORGIVABLE video sin.

(1) Check your frame line with the camera person before shooting, then get the mic as close as possible without getting it in the frame.

(2) Keep the mic pointed "on axis"—directly at your subject's mouth.

(3) Always wear over-the-ear headphones.

(4) Regularly check for visual cues and feedback from the mixer and camera person.

(5) Allow enough XLR cable slack to move as freely as necessary, but not enough to trip. Try to get an assistant to wrangle cable if there will be a lot of unpredictable movement.

(6) Anticipate your subject's movement and be prepared to quickly follow. Keep your eyes on the cameraperson and mixer to avoid getting in the shot or yanking the XLR cable.

(7) Spiral XLR cable around boom pole and secure all loose cable to help avoid cable noise, handling noise, and trips.

(8) Assume comfortable feet and arm positions. Relax.

While it may not be rocket science, booming is a skill that can make the difference between professional quality sound and amateur radio hour. A good boom operator must have stamina, a good ear (and eye) for detail, and should keep the following in mind.

This is an example of how NOT to boom. Keep your mic pointed at your subject's mouth.

Pay attention to lighting to avoid boom shadows on your background or subject, especially their face as pictured here.

Manned boom mics can be distracting to subjects. Use a boom mic stand or a lav mic instead for stationary subjects.

Spiral the XLR cable around your boom pole. Secure with gaffer tape or elastic hair ties to avoid cables clanking against the boom.

When booming more than one person, gently twist the boom pole to mic each person as they speak.

If shooting solo, mount a shotgun directly on-camera to shoot B-Roll or use a mic stand for interviews.

BOOMING TECHNIQUE

There are a variety of ways you can hold a boom and each has distinct advantages and drawbacks depending on shooting circumstances. Once you try out a few of these stances you will discover what works best for you in different production situations. I generally find that over the course of a production, I will use several of these techniques.

Overhead

Pros: This is the best overall position to operate boom from, mainly because it allows you to easily twist the mic to keep it on axis, to quickly follow moving subjects, and it's up high, so doesn't impede people's movements.

Cons: The biggest downside is that the boom gets very heavy very fast, so this is hard to hold for long takes. Booms are also not practical in crowds, tight spaces, or when you're trying to stay on the down low—*"Nope, nothing unusual here. Just somebody waving around a 10 foot pole with a mic on it."*

Shoulder

Pros: This position has many of same advantages as the overhead position, except that you can hold it comfortably a lot longer. For long takes, with a little finesse you can smoothly switch between the shoulder and overhead positions as you need to give your arms a break.

Con: The downside to the shoulder position is that it's considerably harder to follow moving subjects since you have to twist your whole body to move the mic and you're also very limited in your field of vision on one side.

Below

Pros: This position is a good choice to avoid any issues with boom shadows or mics dipping into your frame. It's also a good position to use when you need to hold the boom for a long time.

Cons: This position completely hinders subjects' movement—*Limbo time everybody!* Apart from that, pointing the mic upwards will make any unwanted noises from above, such as planes and air vents, more prominent on your soundtrack.

Pelvic

Pros: With the boom positioned near the top of your left or right pants pocket and one arm extended you aren't so much holding the boom pole here as *balancing* it. This allows you to easily hold the boom for a very long time and you can one-hand it, freeing up your other hand to signal the director, operate the mixer, write a note or just scratch that itch.

Cons: Apart from looking a little obscene, this position sacrifices some mic-to-mouth distance, is not good for following movement and could cut off the frame diagonally if you boom from a side position away from the camera.

Pistol grip

Pros: Pistol grip shockmounts give you the option to remove the mic from the boom pole entirely, which allows you to be much more mobile, maneuver in tight spaces, and record audio more inconspicuously. It's also a little less intimidating for subjects.

Cons: Of course you sacrifice reach and some distance with a psitol grip position and you definitely don't want to use a pistol grip in any situation where it may be likely to be mistaken for a gun pointed at someone.

Lavalier Mics

Also known as "lav mics" for short, "lapel mics" (because of where they are commonly placed), or "plant mics" (because they are easily hidden or planted in a scene), the lav mic is another mainstay of documentary production—especially for interviews. These tiny mics mount on a shirt, lapel, or tie and do an excellent job of picking up the speaker's voice because of their proximity to the throat and chest

cavity where the sound is being generated. Lav mics are a good choice for car scenes where they can be taped to a dashboard, rear view mirror, or sun visor to pick up conversations in the front seat. Lavs are also handy for wide shots where their tiny wire and mic can be hidden behind just about any object in the frame that's close to your subject.

Handheld Mics

The term is self-explanatory. These are the mics passed around the audience on talk shows and used by talent on location to do "man-on-the-street" interviews, news, and live events. They are simple and easy to use. Apart from the above they are also good for speakers on stage and open talking forums such as town hall meetings.

Wireless Mics

These little beauties are an indispensable part of any serious documentary sound kit. The most common units come with lav mics, but you can also get units with a "butt plug" (Yes, that's the real name) to make boom mics, handheld mics, mixers, or just about *any* sound device wireless. The beauty of going wireless is that your subjects are free to move about, run, perform, or do just about any other activity completely unhindered by cables, so it is considerably easier to get candid interviews and **B-roll**. Your subjects essentially forget that they are wearing a mic because it's so small and unrestrictive. This means a less guarded subject and more candid and honest footage for you.

Time and again, documentary makers and reality TV producers have captured personal scenes, closed-door fights, and whispered conversations with these unobtrusive mics. Using a good wireless unit, the most intimate moments can be recorded from a distance word-for-word with crystal-clear sound even when your subject is behind closed doors, whispering, or in complete darkness. For most, the big deterrent to using wireless is price. At $500 to $4000 on up, good wireless units are not cheap. Cheap VHF wireless units are not worth bothering with as they get way too much interference from radios, walkie talkies, and other wireless audio signals. If you go wireless, stick with UHF models and don't be cheap. It *won't* pay off.

Sennheiser's G3 wireless mics are a long-time indie film favorite.

Professional lav mics come with a "tie clip" for mounting them onto your subject. The important thing is that the mounted mic is not too low and doesn't distract the audience. A sloppy mic mount or wire dangling down the front of your subject is the distracting hallmark of inexperienced amateurs. Even if you don't, act like you know . . . The technique outlined below takes a little fussing and practice to get right the first few times, but it's easy once you learn it.

Put the mic into the clip mount, screen side facing out. Form the wire into a loop and place the loop inside the clip.

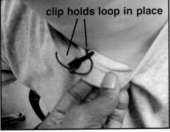

clip holds loop in place

Put the clip into place on a shirt lapel or the neck of pullover shirts. Use the clip to hold your loop in place *inside* the clothing.

Hide the wire by having your subject drop it down *inside* their clothing, then tuck the excess wire into their waistline or pocket.

Stash the mic capsule in subject's pocket or on the floor. If they need to get up, disconnect the XLR and leave the mic in place.

This is how you would mount a lav vertically on a jacket, tie, or collar.

For T-shirts and other clothing without a place to mount vertically, just turn the whole thing 45 degrees and mount it sideways.

Handling Subjects

You always want to *ask* a subject if it's okay before you start pulling, clipping, and adjusting things on them. Let subjects know what you need to do and why, especially if you're a guy dealing with a female subject. Give subjects a minute of privacy to run the wires down their clothing, then readjust the mic as necessary.

2 SUBJECTS, BUT ONLY 1 LAV MIC

What do you do when you're shooting solo and need to record two subjects at the same time? A boom mic is well-suited for capturing the back and forth between two subjects, but it requires an operator. A lav for each subject is always ideal, but time or equipment limitations may dictate that you have to make due with one mic. One mic is all you'll need if you get Down and Dirty with it . . .

Solution #1—Mic Opposite the Biggest Mouth: When recording two people with one lav, mount the mic on the softer spoken of the two subjects and on the side closest to the louder person. Make sure your subjects are sitting close to one another. You may have to ask the subject without a mic to speak a little louder, or pay more attention to your mix in post to make sure things even out, but this technique will generally work fine in a pinch.

Solution #2—Hide a Lav in the Scene: You can hide the mic in the scene between the two subjects if you can find an appropriate prop or another object to mount it to—a cup, pencil holder, or desk decoration. Make sure the mic screen is facing your subjects. It's normal and acceptable to see lavs mounted on a subject, but they look like crap just taped onto something in frame. If you have to do so, hide it.

Solution #3—Dangle a Lav from Above: If you have enough XLR cables (and you *should*), you could also dangle the mic just above frame using a mic boom stand or a C-stand and gobo arm. If you're keeping it real down and dirty, you can just string it from any light fixture or other object you find on the ceiling. Make sure the mic is centered and about a foot in front of your subjects with the tiny mic screen facing them. Beware, this configuration is more susceptible to ambient noise because lav mics are omnidirectional. This technique is best suited to quieter locations.

Solution #1   Solution #2   Solution #3

	BOOM MIC	LAV MIC	HANDHELD MIC
Best Use	■ Run-and-gun shooting ■ Subject can't wear lav ■ Unpredictable or dynamic scenarios	■ Controlled interviews ■ Very wide shots ■ Car interiors ■ Need to hide mic ■ Wireless use	■ Man-on-the-street interviews ■ Open forums (i.e., talk show, town halls, etc.) ■ Live reporting
Pick-up Pattern	■ Hyper-directional (shotgun)	■ Omnidirectional	■ Cardioid (semi-directional)
Advantages	■ Subject free to move ■ Isolates dialogue ■ Can be mounted on camera	■ Low profile ■ Small size ■ Easily hidden in a car or wide shot	■ Easy to use ■ Can cover multiple people in succession
Drawbacks	■ Large and distracting ■ Booming requires another person ■ Sensitive to airplane noise	■ Time-consuming to mount ■ Prone to noise from clothing or touching ■ More delicate than cables	■ Sound quality usually not as good as boom or lav mics ■ Must be held at correct distance for good sound
Beware	■ Operator and camera going separate directions ■ Improper handling creates noise on sound recording	■ Subject walking away still attached to camera ■ Radio interference (on wireless lavs)	■ Subjects seizing control of mic

Crisp, clean sound can only be achieved by recording at *optimum levels*. You can use a great mic or boom as close as you can get, but if you're not mindful of where that level meter should be on your screen, you may still screw yourself in the end. So where should your levels be? I've got six words for you, baby . . . The Super Happy Fun Sound Zone!

The Red Zone of DEATH This is where audio levels go to die. If you try to fix low levels in post by simply boosting the volume, you will *also* be boosting the level of any background noise and hiss. Over-modulated audio is distorted and unintelligible. Badly recorded audio is almost always unfixable in post. It's fine to let naturally sharp loud sounds (i.e., gunshots, a slammed door, etc.) "kiss" this zone for a quick moment, but anything more is problematic.

Acceptable Levels It's okay to have your levels hang out in this zone for a while during recording, but it's preferable to keep them more toward the center. If this is where most of your audio is recorded, you can still work with it in post, but count on spending more time tweaking levels and mixing audio.

Super Happy Fun Sound Zone!!! Hey, the name says it all. This is the good stuff. This is where crisp, clean audio is recorded. You will have much more flexibility to raise or lower these healthy audio levels in post. Moreover, you'll have super happy fun sound!

The DIGITAL Audio Sweet Spot

On *digital* equipment (such as your camera or digital recorder) you want your audio levels to peak roughly between **–20 dB** and **–12 dB** on average.

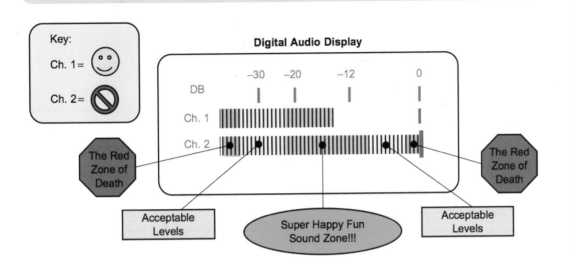

The ANALOG Audio Sweet Spot

On *analog* equipment (such as certain models of mixers) you want your audio levels to peak at **0VU** on average.

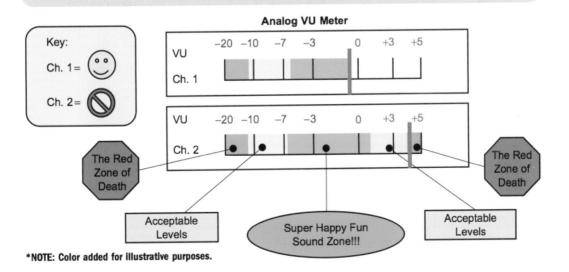

*NOTE: Color added for illustrative purposes.

Riding Levels

The term "riding levels" just means adjusting your sound levels during recording. Don't make the novice mistake of *constantly* adjusting levels for every minor fluctuation in sound level. Most people's conversation and speech fluctuates in volume to a predictable degree. Try to set levels while people carry on with *normal* conversation rather than doing the old "Mic check 1-2-3." I always ask

people to tell me what hey had for breakfast as a sound check. This will make it easier to hone in on the subject's *natural* speech pattern and volume levels.

If you've done your job right, you should only have to adjust your levels sparingly during most recording. Pay attention to what's being said and the tone of the conversation so you can anticipate when things are going to get softer or louder.

Where Should Your Needle Peak?

On digital cameras and digital sound equipment you want the levels to peak at around −12 dB. That is to say, the meter should just "kiss" −12 dB at the highest points of speech. (On analog devices that have peaking needles instead of digital meters your levels should peak at 0.) It's okay, if during the quieter reflective moments your levels hang out near −30 dB. And it's also okay if during animated storytelling or normal laughter they jump a little over −12 dB. What you're primarily concerned about are loud bursts of laughter, shouting, quiet whispers, or very soft-spoken comments . . . basically anything that lingers in the red zones of death at either end of the spectrum. (See "Recording Sound Levels" on page 196.)

Analog vs. Digital Peaking Meters

I think the easiest way to understand digital versus analog audio measurements is to think of it as the difference between the metric system (meters, milliliters, etc.) and the English or "Imperial" system (yards, inches, etc.) of measuring. They are simply two very different scales to measure the *exact same thing*. However, just like the metric and English systems, the important point is to always be aware of exactly which one you're dealing with and to know how to translate one into the other. So let's start with how you can generally tell the difference.

DIGITAL VERSUS ANALOG AUDIO		
COMPARISON	**DIGITAL AUDIO**	**ANALOG AUDIO**
Ideal Peaking Level:	–12 dB or –20 dB*	0/VU
Audio Measured In:	dB (decibels)	VU (volume units)
Display Type:	LED Lights, LCD	Moving Needle
Scale Ends In:	0/dB	+3 VU or +5 VU
Response:	Instantaneous	Slight delay

*See "Why Are There Two Different Digital Standards?" below.

Exceptions to the General Rules

Now mind you, not everything on the above chart is a 100 percent hard-and-fast rule, as devices vary from manufacturer to manufacturer. For example, some modern analog equipment may actually use LED lights to measure VU levels, such as the Sound Devices 302 Mixer, and some scales will end past +3 dB.

However, if you look at the where the peaking scale ends and whether it's measured in VU (analog volume units) or dB (digital decibels), you can pretty easily tell what type of audio scale you are dealing with and know where to set your levels. If you are ever completely clueless or working with a scale that has no markings (common on consumer equipment), you generally won't go too wrong keeping your levels a few marks to the right of center on horizontal meters or a few marks above center on vertical meters.

Exceptions to the rule—some analog mixers like this *Sound Devices 302* have LED peaking meters instead of a peaking needle.

Why Are There Two Different Digital Standards?

In short, the reason digital equipment is set at –12 dB or –20 dB (as opposed to strictly one or the other) is personal preference. If you want to play it pretty safe and have a little more headroom in case of sudden loud noises, you should let your audio peak at –20 dB. If you like to live life a little more on the wild side, you can do what I do and let that baby peak out at –12 dB to give yourself a better chance of capturing healthy levels for quieter sections of speech.

If you ask any two audio people, they'll each have their own preference and reasoning why they go with one or the other. Even though the two numbers sound vastly different, if you look at the distance between –12 dB and –20 dB on a digital audio scale, it's actually fairly negligible.

TWO MICS ARE ALWAYS BETTER THAN ONE

One big thing you can do to increase your chances of quickly recovering from an audio mistake is being redundant in your setups. Even if a scene only calls for one mic, I still recommend using two mics as often as possible. These dual-mic setups take more time and effort, but once you've been burned a time or two with bad audio, they won't seem like nearly so much trouble as reshooting the whole scene or slinking over to the director with your tail between your legs.

Here are a few common tricks of the trade that can save the day. If there is a cable short, low batteries, an actor accidentally hitting the mic, wind noise, or any other unfortunate (but not uncommon) occurrence that may ruin a take, a second mic may still get the shot crisp and clean . . . or at least usable. Your options will be limited by your equipment and shooting circumstances, but here are a few common backup mic strategies.

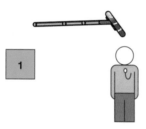

Mic #1 – Shotgun Boom
Mic #2 – Lav Mic

Mic #1 – Shotgun Boom
Mic #2 – Shotgun Boom

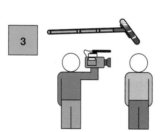

Mic #1 – Camera Shotgun Mic
Mic #2 – Shotgun Boom Mic

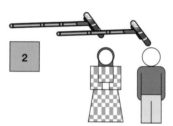

Mic #1 – Shotgun Boom
Mic #2 – Hidden "Plant" Mic

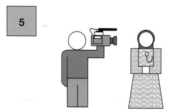

Mic #1 – Camera Shotgun Mic
Mic #2 – Lav Mic

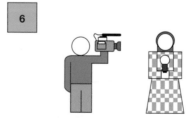

Mic #1 – Camera Shotgun Mic
Mic #2 – Handheld Mic

WHY USE A MIXER?

You may ask yourself: "Why would anyone ever *want* to use a mixer when the camera already has two XLR mic inputs and audio level control?" Ask no more . . .

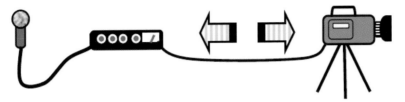

Separate Sound from Camera

A mixer serves as an extension of the camera's audio controls by allowing a sound person to monitor and adjust audio without having to touch (i.e., shake) the camera or get in the camera person's way during shooting. It thus preserves the delicate relationship between the sound department and the camera department.

Use Multiple Mics/Devices

Mixers allow you to use and power multiple microphones or other sound sources, usually three or four, at the same time. Using a video camera alone you are limited to just two sound sources and audio is much trickier to monitor and adjust using camera controls, which often cause you to shake the camera *during* shooting!

Control Over Sound Quality

A field mixer will give you control of the volume of each mic or sound source that you feed into it, and it may also permit you to pan the sound to the left or right channels, filter out background noises, use a **limiter** to prevent distortion, and hook up a second set of headphones for a boom operator. Most DV cameras don't offer any of these options, because cameras were made to record great images. Mixers, on the other hand, were made to help you record great *sound*.

USING A FIELD MIXER

These instructions are for the *Sound Devices 302* field mixer. However, you can follow these same steps for any mixer that has similar features.

mixer sound inputs

STEP 1: Hook Up Mics

1. Use XLR cable to plug each mic or sound source into a mixer input.
2. If your mic needs power, turn on the mixer phantom power switch(es) marked as "PH", "+48V" or "MIC +48V".
3. Set your input signal level to "mic" for microphones or set it to "line" for most other devices.
4. Plug in your headphones. Turn mixer power on. Use only fresh premium brand batteries and keep at least two extra sets of batteries on standby.

camera sound inputs

STEP 2: Hook Up Camera

1. Run XLR cables from the mixer's right and left outputs into the matching camera inputs. (*On cameras left = Channel 1 and right = Channel 2.)
2. The *302* mixer is already set to output "line" levels, but on others you may have to switch the output to "line".
3. Next, set your camera signal level the same as the mixer output at "line".

(*If you are ever unsure of which type of signal level to use, listen to your headphones as you switch between mic and line. Only one will sound normal, the other will sound very soft and faint or very loud and distorted. Go with the normal one.)

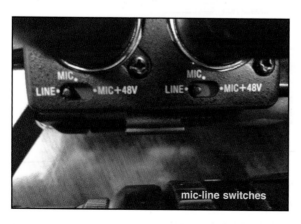

mic-line switches

camera sound meter

STEP 3: Send Out "Tone"

1. Turn on the "1K" tone switch to send a "0" level. (Other mixers may need output manually adjusted to "0".)
2. Adjust the level on your camera until the meter reads "–20 dB".*
3. Once set, turn off the tone and DON'T TOUCH the camera controls again. You will now ONLY use the mixer to control all your audio levels.

camera sound audio levels

STEP 4: Adjust Audio Levels

1. Set the pan switch to: (a) "L" to send the mic only to the left output, (b) "R" to send the mic only to the right output, or (c) "C" to center it out to both outputs. Using two mics send one "L" and the other "R". Using one mic, it's okay to use "C".
2. Have each speaker talk into their mic at his or her normal voice level. Adjust the input level for the mic as they speak, so that the mixer levels mostly linger in the area just before the "0".
3. Repeat for each mic input. If the level is still too soft or loud after adjusting mic input, adjust the gain knob for each input as necessary for good levels.

camera levels display

(*If your camera's meter doesn't have numbers for decibel levels, but does have an automatic gain function, you can turn on this function in the camera's menu, observe the level that auto gain sets for the mixer tone, then manually adjust your camera's gain to the same level.)

Limiter

The limiter is a function on the mixer and other sound devices that keeps your sound from getting so loud that it distorts. All limiters are not created equal. Some limiters will sharply cut off loud sounds rather than smoothly dampen them down. (Shown in the off position here.)

Lo-Cut Filter

This little switch, also found on some mics, helps filter out low-frequency background noises such as wind, idling engines, air conditioners, etc. (Shown in the off position here.)

Pan

Use to assign the sound from each mic input to the left output (L), the right output (R), or center (C) to send to both outputs simultaneously. (*Remember, on cameras L = channel 1 and R = channel 2)

Return

This is where you would plug in a mini to mini stereo cable (See "Cable Guide" on page 211.) from your camera's headphone jack to listen to the sound recorded by the *camera*, rather than just the sound coming out of the mixer, through your headphones.

Tone Generator

Use to send a 1 kHz (kilohertz) **reference tone** to the camera. Adjust the master volume until the needle is at 0. Digital cameras should be set to your preference of either –12 dB or –20 dB to match mixer levels. (See "Recording Sound Levels" on page 196.)

Slate Mic

Push and hold the same silver switch used for tone (above) to the left "MIC" position to activate the built-in mic. This is so you can leave audio notes at the beginning or end of a take. (Note that the camera must be recording.)

Down and Dirty "Wireless"

POOR MAN'S WIRELESS MIC

Wireless mics are invaluable for capturing good audio of certain types of documentary footage. However, the reality is that good wireless mics are still a luxury item for many doc filmmakers, so I want to share this little filmmakers trick for getting decent audio of a wide shot sans wireless mic. The only thing you need is a smartphone.

Download or open up an audio recorder app. Adjust the settings to your preference.

Start recording and place the recorder in the shirt pocket of the person you want to record.

Slate the shot and shoot your scene as normal, but make sure you still also record audio to camera. Don't forget to name each audio file after recording.

Import the digital audio files and use the slate clap and camera audio you recorded to help you sync the audio file to the video in your timeline.

This will work with any smartphone with a decent mic or other small stand alone digital recorder. Believe it or not, the audio recording quality of the iPhone is surprisingly clear and crisp. Here are some additional tips:

- Most phones will have a voice recorder app pre-installed, but I recommend more robust recording apps like Tascam's PCM Recorder pictured above.
- If there are two people, best to have a recorder on each or one will be much softer.
- Don't forget to name the digital audio files as you go, to make life easier in post.
- You can also get higher quality third-party mics to attach to your iPhone.

5 SOUND RULES TO LIVE BY

Some rules were meant to be broken. The following were NOT. Break these rules at your own risk.

RULE #1   Get the Mic as Close as Possible

The most basic rule for recording dialogue is to get the mic as close to the action as possible without being in the shot. The closer the mic, the better the quality of the recording. This is why boom mics so often end up creeping into scenes; the sound person was trying to get as close as possible and accidentally allowed the mic to enter the frame. The sound person should always confirm the **frame line** with the DP *before* shooting starts to avoid this problem.

RULE #2   Always Use Headphones . . . Always

There are a wide variety of things that can ruin your sound that can *only* be heard by listening to your sound with professional over-the-ear headphones. Simply watching sound levels on a meter or relying on your naked ear will not reveal the following: a cable clunking against the boom pole, air conditioner noise, hum from a computer, a distant plane, a loose mic in the zeppelin, excessive street noise, etc.

If using a mixer, you should monitor the sound being recorded by *the camera*, as opposed to only monitoring the sound coming from the mixer. The sound could come out of the mixer perfectly, but still be ruined by bad levels or other settings on your camera. Many mixers have a "return" or "monitor" jact to monitor sound from the camera. The bottom line is to always listen to the sound from it's *final recording destination*, regardless of whether you run through a mixer or other sound equipment.

RULE #3 — Monitor the Sound Levels from the Camera

Not even the most skilled sound technician can do anything to fix over-modulated sound in post. If you record sound that is too loud, you've just jumped on a one-way train to Stinktown. If you are using a mixer, remember to match levels between the camera and mixer. Once your levels are set, use the mixer controls. Be sure to monitor sound from the camera by feeding it back to your mixer through the return jack, because *that's* what's actually being recorded to camera and *that's* what counts. If you can't feed it back, keep an eye on the sound levels on the camera LCD.

The only audio that really counts is what's recorded to *the camera*.

RULE #4 — Scout Your Locations for Sound

It is vital to carefully observe every location, inside and out, for any source of noise or sound problems that could interfere with your shoot. Murphy's Law—whatever can go wrong will go wrong—is always in full effect when it comes to location shooting. If you don't take sound into full consideration when location scouting, or even worse, if you haven't observed your location beforehand, you are personally inviting Murphy to wreak further havoc on your shoot.

This subway bridge is a great *visual* location, but constant loud train noise makes it crappy for *audio*.

Always think about sound in addition to those beautiful images in your head. Do that cool director viewfinder thing with your hands . . . then cup your ears and *listen* to your location.

Recording **wild sound** or **room tone** is simply recording the natural sound of any location—all the little buzzes, hums, birds, traffic, and background noises that often go unnoticed in production. The purpose of recording wild sound is to smooth out audio inconsistencies in editing. This comes into play in two primary situations:

> **Situation A:** You need to do additional dialogue recording (**ADR**) after a scene was already shot. The ambient sound under the dialogue that you record during ADR will not match the shots you recorded on location unless you lay in the ambient sound from location or "room tone."
>
> **Situation B:** During location recording, background noise elements that you have no control over or failed to notice, such as air conditioners or computers, were there for certain takes but not for others. You'll need to restore that particular noise for certain shots for them to sound the same as the other shots when edited together in the same scene.

The procedure is simple. During a break or as soon as picture is wrapped, have everyone on location be silent and freeze where they are. No packing or adjusting equipment—no nothing for at least one full minute while the sound recordist captures the natural ambient sound of the location that will save your butt in the edit room.

It's pretty hard to recreate the sound of these distant waves in post—better record some wild sound!

Don't Just Look, *Listen* to Your Location

You can generally dress up even the lamest of locations by using a combination of interesting background lighting, tight framing, and/or shallow depth of field. However, one area you CANNOT compensate for is sound. If you're recording dialogue and your location is a noisy factory, an apartment over a loud bar, or next to the airport, you might as well find another location or pack it in for the day, because your audio is *more* important than your video.

> ✔ **Your audio is _MORE_ important than your video.**

Did I just blow your mind? Did the needle just skip off the record? For some people this notion is filmmaking heresy and I would be run out of town on the first train (probably headed to Stinktown). But let me break it down real simple: There are probably a dozen different things you can do in editing to cover up, cut out, or cut around bad video. However, bad *audio* (i.e., audio that is too loud, too soft, too noisy) is pretty much unfixable, not to mention unbearable on the ears.

Bad sound sabotages everything else, even compelling content. People can't enjoy your compelling content, if the sound is too awful to ignore. If you have whack sound, you have a whack project. Your location *has* to be good for sound. Period. Careful attention to sound always separates the pros from the hacks and the festival winners from the festival selections. The only thing more effective at telling your story than the camerawork, lighting, editing, and location is the voice of your subject who actually is *telling the story*. If the audience can't hear what they have to say, crisp and clean, what's the point?

The chart on the next page will help you anticipate and resolve some of the most common location sound problems.

The lake pictured here is beautiful to *look* at, but it's next to a noisy highway near an airport flight path, which makes it horrible for *sound*.

> ✔ *Don't just look at your location. Listen for anything that may cause sound problems when shooting.*

SOURCE	PROBLEM	SOLUTIONS (IN ORDER OF PREFERENCE)
Refrigerator	■ Cycle on and off creating low rumble noise	■ Unplug, but don't forget to plug back in ■ Use low cut mic/mixer filter to reduce rumble
Air Conditioners	■ Cycle on and off or make a continuous hum	■ Turn off when shooting ■ Try low cut filter on mic or mixer
Fluorescent Light	■ Can sometimes emit a buzz if mics are close or pointed at light	■ Keep mic away from lights ■ Avoid booming from below ■ Turn off the fluorescents
Subway Train	■ Periodic train noise or rumble	■ Change locations ■ Stop whenever train passes ■ If train runs under building, placing sound blankets on floor may help soften train noise
Traffic Noise	■ Excessive car/plane traffic outside of location	■ Close all windows ■ Put sound blankets over windows ■ Change locations
Noisy Pet	■ Yipe! Yipe! Yipe! ■ Meeeow! Meeeow! ■ Hoooooowl!	■ Put pet outside ■ Take the pet for a long walk ■ Have crew hold and comfort pet ■ Let subject hold pet on camera
Noisy Neighbors	■ Talking, watching TV, playing music or video games loudly	■ Politely ask them to lower volume, turn off or use headphones ■ Sweet talk/negotiate ■ Send them out for a walk ■ Flat out bribe them
Wind	■ Loud rumble on audio ■ Overpowers speech	■ Use zeppelin with windjammer ■ Add windshield over mic ■ Use lo cut/wind filter on mixer or cam ■ Mount lav mic under clothing ■ Remove low frequencies in post

The world of prosumer video has matured considerably over the last decade, leaving us with a wide variety of groovy gadgets and digital do-dads. If you're going to do this video thing for real, you're going to need to call on a variety of cables to help you connect your various cameras, mics, mixers, hard drives, and computers. Knowing and having the proper cable can make the difference between being the project hero or the project heel and save you time and frustration. So Down and Dirty DV is giving you the hook-up—the cable hook-up that is. Here's a guide to the most common audio and video cables/connectors:

CABLE	PORT	AUDIO	VIDEO	CONNECTS TO	COMMENTS/USAGE
RCA		A	V	■ Cameras ■ Monitors/TVs ■ Projectors ■ Consumer A/V gear	■ Yellow = Video ■ White = Left audio ■ Red = Right audio ■ Analog—NOT digital signal
BNC			V	■ Cameras ■ Monitors/TVs ■ Projectors ■ Professional video gear	■ Mostly used for high-end broadcast equipment and cameras
Firewire 4-pin 6-pin		A	V	■ Cameras (4-pin) ■ Small electronics (4-pin) ■ Hard drives (6-pin)	■ Also known as IEEE 1394a or Firewire 400 ■ Fast transfer of video files ■ Use 4-pin to 6-pin cable to connect camera to computer ■ 6-pin connects Firewire drives together
S-Video			V	■ Cameras ■ Monitors/TVs ■ Computers ■ High-end video gear	■ Does NOT carry audio info ■ High-quality analog video signal

CABLE	PORT	AUDIO	VIDEO	CONNECTS TO	COMMENTS/ USAGE
Firewire 800		A	V	■ Hard drives ■ Computers	■ Twice as fast as standard Firewire (IEEE 1394)
Coaxial		A	V	■ Monitors/TVs ■ Cable boxes ■ Older analog cameras	■ Screw-on or push-on types
USB/USB 2.0/3.0 mini standard		A	V	■ Cameras ■ Hard drives ■ Printers ■ Flash drives ■ Computers ■ Small electronics	■ Mini and standard connectors ■ USB 2.0/3.0 is even FASTER than Firewire ■ Standard USB format is too slow to carry HD signals, but can be used for very slow file transfers
Component			V	■ HD/HDV cameras ■ HD Monitors/TVs ■ DVD Players ■ HD Cable Boxes	■ Next best thing to HDMI cables for best quality display ■ Best option for standard DVD picture quality
HDMI		A	V	■ HD cameras ■ HD Monitors/TVs ■ HD Cable Boxes	■ Used to view HD footage on HD display at full resolution ■ Best HD signal possible ■ Expensive cable

CABLE	PORT	AUDIO	VIDEO	CONNECTS TO	COMMENTS/ USAGE
XLR		A		■ Pro cameras ■ Mixers ■ Most pro audio gear	■ Most common pro audio cable ■ Use adapter such as Beechtek DXA box to go from XLR—mini-stereo
1/8" Stereo		A		■ Headphones ■ Cameras ■ Electronics ■ Wide range of pro A/V gear	■ a.k.a. "mini-stereo" ■ Get a 1/4" adapter for more versatility—a.k.a. "3.5 mm"
1/4" Stereo		A		■ Headphones ■ Some pro audio gear ■ Musical instruments	■ Standard on older audio gear ■ Get a 1/8" adapter for more versatility
Thunderbolt		A	V	■ Computers ■ Monitors ■ Hard drives	■ Extremely fast ■ 10 GB/second transfer speed ■ Can also power devices
HD-SDI		A	V	■ Pro HD cameras ■ Pro HD monitors ■ Pro HD video recorders	■ Used to view uncompressed HD ■ Best HD signal ■ Found on pro gear ■ Expensive cable
DVI			V	■ Computer monitor ■ Some TVs	■ Apple devices may require additional adapters
VGA			V	■ Computer Hard Drives ■ TVs ■ Projectors	■ Apple devices may require additional adapters ■ Used to connect computers to projectors

Breakaway Cables

These combine two XLR cables, a mini-mini stereo cable (for a mixer return jack), and a headphone jack extension all into a single cable that separates with a twist to allow the sound operator to quickly "breakaway" from the camera when necessary. They are very handy for run-and-gun doc shooting.

Coiling Cables

Knowing how to coil cables properly is something that separates the wannabes from the pros. (You won't even be able to keep a P.A. gig if you don't know how to correctly coil cables!) The most important thing to keep in mind is that the cable must be able to unravel quickly without getting tangled up. The second thing to remember is that every cable has a natural coil known as the cable's "history." In other words, it will only coil and uncoil neatly and correctly in that direction and will ultimately become a tangled mess if you coil it any other way. Here's how to do it:

1	2	3	4
Find the natural "history" of the cable by seeing which way it forms and holds a 1 to 2' foot loop easiest.	Give the cable a slight twist at the top of each loop to form a spiral and keep its "history."	Repeat, stacking each loop in your hand so it will easily unravel without snagging.	Secure the coiled cable with Velcro, a twist tie, or small piece of sash rope.

Hiding Mics

wide shot with hidden mics

shotgun mic
lav mic

lav screen facing out at subject

Often it won't be possible to use a boom, particularly for wide shots. In these scenarios consider hiding a lav, table, or even a shotgun mic within the scene.	The possibilities for hiding mics are as open as your imagination. Any object in frame can be used to obscure a mic.	Lav mics are tiny and can be taped or mounted to almost anything. Make sure the screen on the lav mic is facing your subject or else you'll just be recording a cup of coffee!

Shooting in Rooms with Echo

Bathrooms have perhaps the worst acoustics of any interior you will ever shoot in. Because there is often no furniture, curtains, or rugs to absorb sound, bathrooms are hollow echo chambers of hard surfaces that bounce sound off the tiles, floor, and ceiling.

The quick and easy solution to recording sound in bathrooms or any other echo-y space is to simply hang or lay some **sound blankets**. These are the same thick, rough, quilted blankets that movers use to wrap furniture. (If you're keeping it down and dirty, a thick household quilt or blanket will also serve the exact same purpose.) Use as many sound blankets as necessary to cover large hard surfaces and "soften" echo-plagued rooms by the desired amount. (If you ever need to steal a power nap during down time, a few sound blankets can also be fashioned into a cozy guerrilla bed.)

How to Mount a Sound Blanket

Method 1: Clamp or drape the sound blanket over the top of a stall or shower curtain rod (bathrooms).

Method 2: Clamp blanket onto a backdrop stand or a frame of two C-stands with long gobo arms locked together (pictured above).

Method 3: Use gaffer's tape to hang it on the wall.

Method 4: Simply lay it on the floor like a rug.

How to Eggroll a Sound Blanket

Here's a cool trick for efficiently packing and storing sound blankets.

1
Lay blanket out flat.

2
Fold into thirds.

3
Roll up tightly on floor.

4
Tuck the rolled end into the open end.

5
Bam! You've got yourself an eggroll!
Strike a pose.

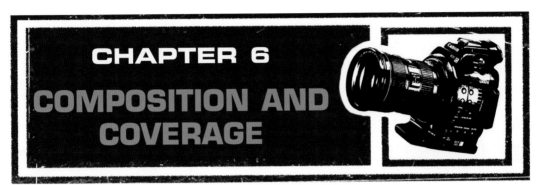

CHAPTER 6
COMPOSITION AND COVERAGE

Introduction

Your composition (i.e., framing) and choice of images are the main elements of visual storytelling. How you frame your shot will help communicate to your audience the tone of the scene, the perspective of the piece, and how they should feel about your subject, just to name a few. Below are some basics to keep in mind when shooting docs.

The Rule of Thirds

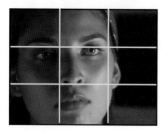  

When framing your shots you want to follow the "rule of thirds" wherein the screen is divided into thirds, horizontally and vertically, forming a tic-tac-toe pattern. Your subject should be framed so that they fall on one of those lines, ideally at a point where two lines intersect. In close-ups, it is also important that your subject's eyes be framed along the upper horizontal line as well.

Look Room

Make sure you leave enough "look room," or extra space, in the direction your subject is facing. If you don't allow for this, your subject will appear crowded and the composition may subconsiously bug your audience. (Which is okay if that's what you *meant* to do.)

COMPOSITION BASICS

Head Room

Too Much Head Room

Good Head Room

Similar to look room, mind your "head room," or the space above your subject's head. Too much head room will make your subject appear diminished, insignificant, and lost in the frame. Again, using the rule of thirds will help you avoid poor head room.

Severed Body Parts

Cut Off at the Knees

Better Framing

Be careful not to cut off your subject at the knees or in other ways that unbalance your frame or awkwardly "sever" body parts.

COMPOSITION TRICKS

Hiding Undesirable Backgrounds

In documentary, you will often have to make do with the settings you have to work with. However, there are a few tricks you can use to make those settings work better for you. Distracting or undesirable objects such as the boathouse (circled) can be "flagged" out using a foreground object such as a leaf or sign. This also has the added benefit of creating a more interesting composition. If you need to block out a crowd of people, an ugly setting, or other large area, you can always raise your subject or lower the camera and shoot tilting up so the sky is your background. (Be aware that this technique could also have the effect of making your subject more imposing and possibly backlit, but either is less distracting than some kid making faces in the background!)

Cheating Backgrounds

Sometimes you will need to "cheat" or move a piece of furniture to get a more pleasing shot. In the illustrations above I was stuck with the doc maker's worst nightmare—a plain room with white walls. My best option was to find a way to use the scene outside, but I thought showing just the building fronts was a boring composition. So I raised up the camera tripod high enough to tilt down to the more dynamic street background with people and cars and used the window as a **frame-within-a-frame**. Then, I cheated my subject's chair by raising it on some apple boxes. Finally, I raised my own chair to maintain the same **eyeline** as my subject during our interview. (See "Window Lighting Set-up") on page 177 for more details on this set-up.

LENS FOCAL LENGTH

A sometimes overlooked, but major factor of composition is your choice of lens focal length. DSLRs and pro video cameras have removable lenses and can accept prime (fixed focal length) lenses, while other video cameras have a zoom lens permanently affixed to the camera. To adjust focal length on any zoom lens you simply zoom in or out to wide, normal, or telephoto lengths. In the footage below, the model stood in the same spot while I adjusted a fixed zoom lens, then moved the camera forward or backward to maintain the same subject framing.

Normal

Zoom Technique: Zoom lens to midpoint
Prime Lens Equivalent: 50 mm

❏ Both foreground and background remain in focus
❏ Most resembles the eye's natural perspective

Telephoto Lens

Zoom Technique: Zoom fully in
Prime Lens Equivalent: 70 mm

❏ Background soft-focused
❏ Much less of the background is visible
❏ Distant objects appear closer and more compressed

Wide-Angle Lens

Zoom Technique: Zoom fully out
Prime Lens Equivalent: 14 mm

❏ Objects close to lens are distorted
❏ Distance greatly exaggerated
❏ Much more background is visible
❏ Background objects shrink in size

Which Focal Length to Use for Which Shot?

There's no straight answer to this question, because it partly depends on your particular shooting situation as well as what you wanna show and how you want to show it. Want to show that a downtown street is really crowded? Break out the telephoto lens and compress that mass of humanity for the audience. Need to cover a convo of two subjects in the front seat of a moving car? Better have a wide angle lens in your kit. Gotta cover a short one-time-only event? No time to be switching up lenses during a firefight! Use a zoom lens to get full coverage with close-ups, mediums, and wide shots in three minutes flat.

NORMAL   **TELEPHOTO**   **WIDE**

Your choice of focal length is as much a creative choice as your framing or location. You can make the same street seem congested and teaming with cars or desolate and empty. The above shots were all taken during a one-minute period shooting the same group of cars coming down the street from the same camera position. However, notice the dramatic difference in the images and the way that distant and foreground objects are portrayed at each focal length.

NORMAL LENS   **WIDE LENS**

If you know you'll be shooting in tight quarters like cars, small rooms, or just a packed crowd, a wide lens is a must.

DON'T JUST TELL 'EM, SHOW 'EM

The Audience Wants to See Your Story

The constant challenge of the documentarian is to find a way to *show* the audience, not just tell them. Remember those people? The audience? The whole reason you're making this doc? Well, they want to actually *see* what your characters are saying.

Even mundane things like a subject discussing mailing a letter at the post office can become poetic moments with the right images. Was it a wintery day? What kind of post office was it? Was it a small town post office off a dirt road? Was it the main post office in Manhattan? Crowded? Empty? What did the clerk look like? What did it sound like? They'll never really know unless you *show* them.

Photos: *Death of Two Sons*

   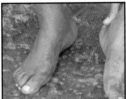

| 1. This subject tells an anecdote involving a religious rite. | 2. We *watch* a man praying before the rite. | 3. We *see* the kettle used for the rite. | 4. We *hear* the sound of the water spattering on the dirt. |

POV Shots Put the Audience There

Not only does your audience want to see it, but they want you to help them *experience* it. Put them in the shoes of your character. What did it *look* like from the plane when they dropped the bomb on that village? What did the woods *sound* like before the bear attacked? How did it *feel* to be there? When you're stuck for images ask yourself these types of questions. The answers will help you use your camera and imagination to put your audience in your subject's world. Shooting from a subject's point of view (a.k.a. POV) is a potent way to put your audience inside a story.

Photos: *Death of Two Sons*

| This is what it looked like from a subject's room when it rained. | This is how a subject scanned with his finger as he recited verses. | This was a subject's daily climb up a ladder inside the mosque. | This was the view from the taxi on the day of that tragic last trip. |

✔ Shoot the sights, sounds, and viewpoints of your subject's world. If your subject <u>talks</u> about it, try to find a way to <u>show</u> it.

Cover Your Scene (and Your Butt)

The term "coverage" refers to the variety of shots you use to visually tell your story. Think of it not just as covering your scene, but covering *your butt* in editing. Apart from just breaking up the monotony of a single, long camera shot, getting more shots or additional coverage will provide plenty of opportunities to cut away from your main shot in the editing room. This makes it easy to condense time and work around problem shots. With good coverage an editor can easily condense interviews, events, and demonstrations down to a smooth few minutes to tell a story that's visually dynamic and one that conveys more info using the visual language of filmmaking. Freestyle and experiment as much as you want when shooting and editing, but know that the filmmakers that get the best results from breaking the rules of screen grammar already *know* the rules inside and out. Here then, are the rules ...

ESTABLISHING SHOTS

These shots open a scene to let the audience know where you're at.

These are often wider exterior shots. An office tower, a subject entering the room, street signs on a city corner, the room the interview is taking place all are examples of typical establishing shots. However, establishing shots can also be as tight as a street sign, a colorful taxi, or any other shot that gives your audience some sense of the *flavor* of the location. You can use a single shot or show a brief sequence of shots that establishes the atmosphere and activity of a location. Generally, you'd start with your widest shot, then bring the audience into the scene with progressively more intimate shots. A sequence of establishing shots of an African marketplace might run like this.

The Establishing Sequence:

Photos: *Death of Two Sons*

PRE-VISUALIZING YOUR SCENES

MIKE ATTIE & MEGHAN O'HARA, CO-DIRECTORS
incountryfilm.com
(In Country, a documentary film about Vietnam War re-enactors)

Meghan: When we were shooting "In Country" I'd fly to Seattle and we'd drive to Salem, Oregon, which takes three or four hours. We would talk through the shoot that we were about to go to. "OK, we're going to this character's house. What's the important part of this shoot?" and we'd write it out. "What's the theme? What is this character?"

We really talk in narrative terms, like, "What is this character? Who are they in the story? What do they bring to the scene?" You prime yourself for all the things you're going to look for when you're there.

You imagine, you pre-visualize a best-case scenario where, I'm making this up, this isn't from our film, but let's say that you need to show that the relationship between your character and his wife is strained.

So you're going to dinner and you're hoping that you're going to be able to see their interaction and catch looks that kind of show this part of their personality.

You think that all through ahead of time and maybe none of those things will happen, but I think the more you think about what your themes are, your story elements, your character and also the practical things, like shots and audio, the better it will go.

If we're going to a place, we start thinking we need a picture of a sign, we need a picture of this or that. We talk through all the coverage and shots. Talking through all that beforehand makes you able to *see it* when you're there with your camera.

WIDE SHOTS (WS)

Wide shots or master shots are your conservative "safety" shots that will save your scene if that funky creative framing you tried doesn't work out. It's the one shot that you can always count on to cover all the action. No matter who's speaking or what happens–it's in the master shot. Looking at a master shot we should get some sense of the setting and a full sense of the scale of the main action whether it's children playing in a stream or simply a subject talking on the phone. If two or more subjects are interacting, try to get an angle that includes all the participants.

Until you fully understand the visual language of docs (and probably even after that) you should make it a habit to get a good master shot *first*. Then go in for tighter and more creative angles as the scene dictates. Ask yourself this question on location: "If I had to communicate this whole scene to an audience with only one shot–what would that shot be?" Whatever you frame up in your monitor in response to that question will probably make for a good master shot.

MEDIUM SHOTS (MS)

Paper Chasers   *Death of Two Sons*

Medium shots are basically framed from the waist up. Medium shots bring the audience in closer to further inform them of what people are wearing or doing. Most notably, medium shots show us a subject's gestures and body language. You should never underestimate the incredible power of body language in storytelling. Body language and gestures communicate more information in a matter of seconds than speech alone ever could. (That's why us New Yorkers always gesture to other drivers with one hand when we get cut off on the road . . . it's more communicative.)

CLOSE UPS (CU)

Medium Close Up (MCU)
Framed from the shoulders up.

Close Up (CU)
Framed from the neck up.

Extreme Close Up (ECU)
Framed tight on facial features.

Now that you've told the audience where you are with the establishing shot, and you gave them a medium shot to show them your subject's dress, action, and gestures, it's time to get intimate with some close-ups. Close-up shots range from the chest or shoulders up and are often used to capture dialogue, show expression, and otherwise bring your audience close to the character or object on screen. Apart from intimacy, close-ups draw our attention to specific details onscreen. (See below.)

In Country

Death of Two Sons

1-SHOTS

1-shots are shots of a single person. These are generally going to be the master shot of your subject. For interviews, 1-shots are usually medium close ups (MCUs) with enough room at the bottom of the screen to overlay a graphic of their name and title. Within this shot you can also zoom in to a CU or ECU when appropriate.

2-SHOTS

Any medium or close shot that frames two people at the same time is generally referred to as a 2-shot. A 2-shot is an ideal master for covering the interaction between two people.

OVER THE SHOULDER SHOTS

Photo: Double 7 images

The name says it all here. This is another shot designed to help the audience determine the positioning and eyeline of the people on the screen. Over the shoulder (OTS) shots show the perspective of one side of a situation and highlight the reactions of subjects to each other. During interviews you can steal these shots whenever there is just chit chat, a break in the shooting, or a question is being asked, then smoothly push in for a tighter shot on your subject. Apart from interviews, OTS shots are a good choice for any conversation or interaction between people and for showing a character's point of view (POV).

REACTION/REVERSE SHOTS

Photos: *In Country*

These shots show how a subject responds to a person, thing, or situation. For single-camera interviews you can actually "cheat" these after the interview by having the interviewer restate specific questions, or just recreate a series of their responses (nodding, smiling, etc.) for the camera. Similarly, a reverse shot shows the opposite angle or viewpoint of the shot before it. When shooting be mindful of your subject's left–right look direction, so it always appears they are looking at one-another on-screen.

DUTCH ANGLES

If you're going for something stylistic or edgy or trying to portray a subject in an unusual way, a Dutch angle, where the frame is slightly diagonal, can be used to create tension in the frame or impose a flashy artsy look. MTV, reality shows, and some high-energy sports and entertainment shows frequently use this technique. Nothing's more imposing than a 360-lb. linebacker ready to charge onto the field, other than a 360-lb. linebacker ready to charge onto the field shot in a Dutch angle!

DOLLY SHOTS

The Losmandy Spider dolly breaks down into a suitcase and is designed to roll on rubber Flextrak, which can be laid down in minutes.

Any shot that rolls the camera on wheels is a dolly shot. **Dolly** shots smoothly follow a moving subject or roll to reveal a character, object, or some other new visual in a scene. They can go left or right, in or out, or weave a fluid path through scenes. Well-executed dolly moves are a guaranteed way to break up static camerawork and make your film look and feel like it actually has a budget.

You can use any variety of portable and lightweight dolly systems, make your own, or create dolly moves by putting your camera on almost anything with wheels and a smooth enough ride. One Down and Dirty mantra is "a tool is as a tool does." Wheelchairs, cars, subway trains, skateboards, rollerblades, bikes, shopping carts, and more can all be made to serve as dollies with some practice and the right surface. When it comes to dolly surfaces, the smoother the better. Soft rubber tires are also best for more textured surfaces.

Photos: Leyla T. Rosario

The Classic NYC MTA Dolly

The Skateboard Dolly

The "Rollercam" Dolly

The Drive-by Dolly Shot

Regardless of your equipment, dolly shots will almost always take more time to get right. Plan it out carefully. Estimate how long you *think* it will take—then *double it*. But when you do eventually get that smooth few seconds of hot moving footage, it's pure filmmaking gold called **production value**.

DOLLY AND SLIDER MOVES

Kessler's Phillip Bloom Pocket Dolly

The modern day (and easier) alternative to the dolly shot is the slider shot. As the name implies, sliders are camera support systems that smoothly slide the camera from point A to point B—left to right, front to back, or whatever you're into. Most sliders use some type of rails and/or pulleys to smoothly move the camera a short distance of 3–6 feet.

Although 3–6 feet is far shorter than the length a dolly typically moves (a typical Hollywood dolly move starts at 6 feet and could easily go 60 yards or more—if the budget's big enough!)—the trick is all in the lens you use and the shot you choose. If you experiment with different focal lengths, slider moves can add just as much production value and cinematic drama as dolly moves for a fraction of the cost, set-up and space. Some sliders can even execute vertical moves that mimic a jib. Another big low-budget plus of sliders is that a single person can easily operate a slider.

Relatively small and light sliders have risen in popularity along with small form factor DSLR cameras, but there are plenty of models that can also handle many medium-sized pro video cameras. This is definitely a luxury accessory that will give you a lot of production value bang for your buck. Apart from shooting more cinematic B-Roll and establishing shots, sliders are also good for visually spicing up the camerawork for interviews.

Another very cool feature of many sliders is that you can also rent or buy a special motor that can execute moves at precise speeds and intervals and allow you to add eye-popping motion to time-lapse footage if your camera has time-lapse capabilities. These time-lapse motors can be programmed to move the camera on your slider in tiny increments, so you could time out a 4-hour slider move over 3 feet of track for some dramatic perspective changes as the sun makes its way across the sky.

Photos: thomsondipalma.com

The Slider/Dolly In Move

Left to right moves are cool, but front to back slider or dolly shots that smoothly glide in or out of a scene, are also an effective way to pump up production value. Although they might seem the same, there's a big difference between the feeling of a zoom in and a slider or dolly move in. The zoom in is Tito, but the dolly in is Michael! (Crotch grab!)

Dolly/slider moves work best when something is also framed in the *foreground* of your shot to add a sense of depth and movement.

If there's not something naturally in the foreground, you can place something there. Peep the 'Branchosaurous" a favorite film trick to add some custom foreground drama.

Weighing down your slider with shotbags or sandbags will help reduce shake.

You may find it easier to slide the camera along the rails by hand rather than using the crank. Experiment with your particular model and see which is smoothest at different speeds.

Adjust the tension control of the slider for the particular weight of your camera and speed of the move you want.

Some higher end sliders like the Matthews DC Slider can even execute vertical moves that mimic a jib.

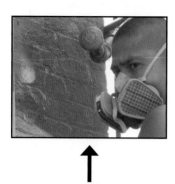

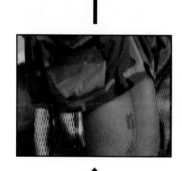

The Full Tilt Boogey

Tilt shots are camera moves that scan the scene up or down. Tilts can be used to: (1) follow action vertically as in an elevator going up, (2) emphasize or take in height as in scanning the length of a redwood tree, (3) reveal new information in a shot as in the example on the left, or (4) open a scene with a more dramatic establishing shot as in look at the shot on the right.

Left: The camera tilts up from a stool on the sidewalk to reveal a pair of sneakers, then a mysterious masked youth. Is he a rebel soldier? A toxic clean up worker? No, wait, he's got a spray can in his hand. It's an artist.

Right: "Death of Two Sons" cinematographer, Cary Fukunaga, imparts an ominous mood with a gentle tilt down from an eerie yellow sky to a wide-angle shot of a rural hospital to open this scene in which a doctor discusses a tragic accident.

Zoom moves in or out should be motivated. Amateur video is typically full of pointless dizzying zooms in and out on a subject without any clear rhyme or reason. Apart from adjusting your frame, zooming camera moves should be used sparingly and only when they will add some dramatic effect and help to tell (here's that word again) the *story* unfolding before the lens. For example, your documentary subject is telling you the sad tale of how their puppy, Scrappy, fell through the thin ice on a pond and how helpless they felt watching little Scrappy bravely struggle. Just as that tear begins to well up in their eye you're going to ever so gently zoom in, slow and steady, from your medium shot to a close-up as the tear rolls down her cheek. If you've zoomed just right and look very closely at that tear, you may even see the reflection of your own Sundance Award for Best Cinematography.

To pull this off you have to be able to anticipate and time where your subject is going with a story *before* they get there then meet them at just the perfect moment for the height of drama. (Basketball fans should think of it as a video alley-oop.) Even if you don't win anything it's still extremely gratifying to pull off a smooth and perfectly timed dramatic zoom.

Executing the Move

It's easy to botch a zoom by stopping too soon or zooming in too close to a bad composition. Make sure you practice this move and are familiar with the sensitivity of your camera's zoom control. Keep your pan and tilt tripod controls comfortably loose and use the tripod handle to smoothly adjust the frame as you zoom in. Otherwise, if the tripod is locked into place and you do a dramatic zoom-in you may end up on a close-up of your subject's forehead!

Other than the above, your zoom control should be used primarily for readjusting your frame with the intention of editing out the zoom movement itself. However, when shooting live events, it's a good idea to always zoom as though you may have to use the whole shot just in case some unexpected, but crucial action unfolds in the middle of your move.

> ✔ *When shooting interviews and B-roll use zoom moves sparingly to heighten drama and intimacy.*

CUTAWAYS

CU cutaway shots allow you to condense interviews by giving you a transition shot.

To smoothly edit your subject's comments and condense time without using **jump cuts**, you will need to insert completely different shots during the editing process that will allow you to cut away from one part of the interview and move to another. Hence, we get the term "cutaway."

I can't say enough about the importance of cutaways. If you want to avoid suicidal thoughts in the edit room, get lots and lots of cutaways. Time after time they will help you out of difficult problems during editing. They take such little effort to shoot, but can add so much to a finished scene.

Cutaways are generally individual shots of anything relevant to your interview or location. Most often they are close-ups, but medium and wide shots can also work. A family picture on the wall, your subject's nervous hand gestures, the trophy case behind them, the scene nearby . . . anything that captures the character of your location, says something about your subject, communicates more info about the scene, or helps you tell your story more effectively will make for a good cutaway. Shoot as many and as much as you can, even if they seem mediocre or don't really seem to help you tell your story, because you will always need *something* to cut away to in editing.

I've often shot what I thought were too many cutaways only to find that I needed every single one in the final cut to make a project work. Listen, there is no such thing as *too many cutaways*! If you don't shoot enough cutaways you'll find yourself doing one or all of the following: (1) using the same one or two decent shots repeatedly, (2) putting in jump cuts out of necessity, rather than as a creative choice, or (3) dressing a corner of your bedroom to shoot a "fake" cutaway. Say it and live it: Cutaways. Cutaways. Cutaways . . . Always. (See also "Bedroom B-Roll" on page 237.)

Subject's hand gestures make great all-purpose cutaways.

CUTAWAY	COULD COMMUNICATE
Reaction shots of others in the room	How the subject is received
Family photos	Happier days in a failed marriage
A factory billowing smoke	This is a blue collar town
A nervous hand gesture	Subject is uncomfortable with topic
Shaky hands cracking open a beer	Subject has alcoholic tremors
	Subject is shaken up about something
	Subject is a drinker
A clock	Subject is late for appointment
	It's unusually late
	A certain amount of time has passed
A big toe poking out of ragged shoes	Subject's financial/social status
	Subject's trendy fashion
	Subject's humble nature
A political bumper sticker	Subject's politics or sense of humor

How to Shoot Cutaways

If there's one golden rule of cutaways, it's to hold any shot for at least 10 seconds *after* you're focused and adjusted. When I shoot cutaways I always get several different shots, because I'm never quite sure how they might be needed in editing. The more creative choices the better in my book.

STILLS

CU, MED, WIDE, hold each for 10 seconds. Vary by racking focus at front and end of each shot.

ZOOMS

Zoom in and out at various speeds. Hold on end shots. (These holds can double as your still shots.)

PANS

Pan left, then right, letting subject enter and exit the frame *cleanly*. Pan left then right holding on subject in frame for each. Pan at various speeds.

> ✔ Shoot stills, zooms, and pans of cutaway shots as time allows. Hold all shots for at least 10 seconds.

YOUR B-ROLL IS YOUR "A" ROLL

The term "B-roll" comes from the world of film where editors used to use an "A" and a "B" roll of identical footage, before the digital age changed everything. B-roll shots are similar to cutaways in that they help break up the static interview shots, but B-roll plays a more major role in telling a visual documentary story.

A long-time documentary filmmaker I know actually refuses to use the term B-roll, because she feels it diminishes the importance of these visuals—and she's right. B-roll should not be a secondary or low priority. It really should be thought of as "A-roll," because it is the *action* of your story, which serves to reveal character. Without it, you've just got a bunch of talking heads . . . booor-ing.

Even with an engaging storyteller speaking, the audience still needs to see visuals of the scene, settings, characters, and action of the story. An interview or voice-over itself is the narration or literal *telling* of the story. The B-roll is the *showing* of the story. Together they can complement each other by painting a more complete picture.

That amazing guitarist could *tell* us what it was like to play Woodstock (the real one), but we've only got half the story until we cut in the B-roll shots that *show* the multitudes of free-spirited, mud-covered hippies swirling to the music as far as the camera lens can see. A soldier could tell us what it's like to be in combat, but when we cut in a shot of explosions and a chaotic firefight, his story takes on real human meaning. Now we've got a much stronger sense of story than either an interview or B-roll footage alone could have given us.

If you only have a short time with your subject, you're going to have to figure out how to best get some supporting images. Often, I'll try to grab some B-roll, immediately before and after an interview, of the subject doing whatever they would naturally do in the environment. As with cutaway shots, any B-roll you shoot may be needed by your editor to make a problem segment work, to cover up a problem with another shot, or it may be just the right shot to make visual poetry.

Ideally, the B-roll relates directly to the topic at hand, but often you'll have to settle for mundane activity that just shows your subject in action in their environment(s). The best-case scenario is to schedule some separate or additional time to follow your subject and shoot action shots. If you arrange this with them ahead of time, you'll be able to determine the most appropriate and visual activities and events to capture for your project.

> ✔ **Shoot lots of B-roll and cutaways.**
> ✔ **Look for visuals that help tell your story.**

Think of ways to have subjects *demonstrate* the subject matter. If he's a chef, show him cooking. If she's a vet, show her treating an animal. Show us the A-roll . . . the *action* of your story.

THE DARK ART OF BEDROOM B-ROLL

Just like every industry doc filmmaking has it's dirty little secrets and little-known practices. One of the black ops tricks we occasionally have to employ, especially when the clock is ticking, is something I like to call **bedroom B-Roll**.

There will inevitably come a time when you have some great content, but really could use an appropriate visual to (a) visualize the content, (b) cover up a mistake such as a camera bump or someone crossing into frame, (c) give you footage to cover up a **jump cut** that resulted from cutting two different soundbites from your subject together, or maybe you just need a few more shots to make a transitional montage work.

Whatever the cause, the bottom line is that you're blurry-eyed in front of your computer for the sixth hour straight and you have to finish your project in the next 48 hours, but you really need a shot that doesn't exist. Well, with your chief Down and Dirty weapon—a little imagination and creativity—it's not too difficult to create some quick cut-aways or B-roll without ever leaving your bedroom.

The secret is to think of "generic" shots that don't do much to reveal specific time, place, or people, but that serve as an appropriate visual reference for the content at hand. Extreme close ups, POV shots, and still life shots are some of the common tools of this dark doc practice. (Okay, it's not really *that* dark or secret, I'm just being dramatic and using gratuitous alliteration.) With a little imagination and the right location you can often conjure up some appropriate B-roll without staging an entire production.

COMMENTARY	IMAGERY
Someone discussing research	Hand writing on a note pad
Subject discusses why they don't trust ingredients in non-organic products	Pan across the ingredients of various products in your pantry
A journey abroad	Passport and some plane tickets

DOC STORYTELLING
WITH ANIMATION

JOHN CANEMAKER, ANIMATOR/FILM HISTORIAN
(*The Moon and the Son:* An Imagined Conversation)

"Documations" or "Animentaries" (to coin a bad term or two) are wonderful hybrids that can challenge filmmakers and keep audiences on their toes. Mixing moving images of reality and fantasy is yet another way to find the truth.

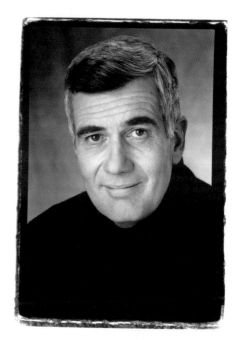

I think audiences are more accepting, less guarded, more open to information and subject matter via animation. The fun and good feelings received from animated fare when we were kids holds over to adult years. Serious subject matter can be broached through this trust held over from childhood, and the material can be understood more easily (and deeply) through animation with its penetrating concentration of energy and design.

Animation can go places live-action cannot. For example, it can personify abstract thought and emotions in a direct, immediate way. It can use symbols to get under the skin of the viewer, or into his or her mind and heart. It can discuss and explore subject matter that might be too personal or sensitive or complex for a live camera. It can deepen perceptions of the truth.

I warn potential clients that they must have a good reason to use animation in a doc; the animation should push beyond where live-action can or should go, not reiterate or imitate reality, but move forward into new areas of believable visualization. It was easier for me to do *The Moon and the Son* (2005 Academy Award— Best Animated Short) in animation since that is the medium I know best. I think the film would work in live-action as a documentary, or as a straight, live-action dramatic narrative. But I wanted to push the perimeters of the animation medium to encompass documentary-like storytelling. I wanted to go beyond the physical limitations of live-action.

DEPTH OF FIELD DEMYSTIFIED

"Shallow depth of field" refers to the visual effect where your subject is in sharp focus, but the background and/or foreground is soft-focused or vice versa. It's a very pleasing and dramatic cinematic effect that goes a long way to making video look more like film, which more naturally has a shallow depth of field. The term "depth of field" simply refers to how much (deep depth of field) or how little (shallow depth of field) of the picture in front of and behind the subject is in focus. In addition to just looking cool, using shallow depth of field keeps your audience's attention focused on the subject and blurs out distracting backgrounds.

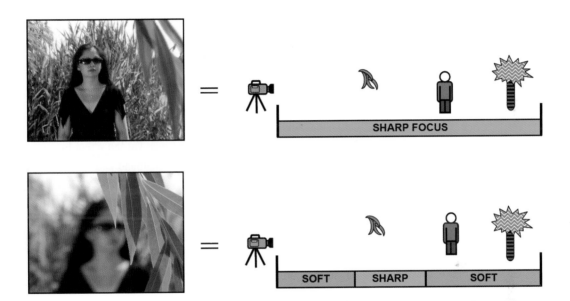

Racking Focus

Shifting focus between a foreground subject to a background subject using shallow depth of field is known as **racking focus**. It's a potent storytelling device for filmmakers to reveal new, information, introduce a character, or direct the audience's attention.

SHALLOW DEPTH OF FIELD

So now that you know what shallow depth of field is, how do you get your camera to do it? Contrary to popular belief, even low-budget guerrillas can simulate or get impressive shallow depth of field from any regular old prosumer camera. Here are several different ways to pull it off. And most won't cost you an extra dime.

Open Up Aperture

If you **open up** your lens aperture (iris) to a low f-stop such as f/2.4, you can get dramatic depth of field over shooting at higher f-stops. Using an ND filter or increasing your shutter speed slightly will also allow you to shoot at a lower f-stop to get a more shallow depth of field.

Zoom In to Telephoto

Zooming all the way in to the lens telephoto setting is the easiest way to simulate shallow depth of field with prosumer cameras. This method requires moving the camera farther away from your subject to get a normal composition. You may also need a wireless mic or extra cable to run from the camera to your subject's mic. For the effect to work best, place your subject as far from the background as possible to help create depth.

Move Camera Closer

The closer the camera is to your subject, the more shallow the depth of field. The more distance between the things in your frame—foreground objects, subject, and background—the more dramatic the effect will be, so for more cinematic rack focus moves, spread your subjects apart.

Use a Big Sensor

CCDs or imaging chips are the actual electronic gizmos that capture an image in video. Image chip size can be thought of like negative size in still photography. The bigger the chip, the better the image. Cameras with big ol' chips like the Canon 5D DSLR series or the Sony F5 35 mm video camera take in a lot of light which makes for a more shallow depth of field.

Use an App

Even if you're just rocking with the cellphone filmmaking crowd, you can still get a sweet piece of the shallow d.o.f. pie by using an advanced video camera app like Filmic Pro that allows you to manually focus and set exposure. Lock in your exposure on a darker part of the frame to open the iris. Then lock in your focus to your subject close in the foreground with plenty of depth behind them . . . Better right?

10 TIPS FOR SHOOTING LIVE EVENTS

One of the more fun challenges you may encounter is shooting live events. Whether it's a stage show, concert, wedding, or speaker at a podium, there are some basic tips you should apply every time.

1. Scout the Venue First

Before the event, try to scope out the venue. Most events will usually have some type of rehearsal beforehand. The earlier you can get a look at the venue and/or performance, the better. Before you shoot, take notes on the performance, available electrical outlets, best camera placements, venue layout, lighting changes, sound system, venue rules, etc. Write down all of your questions and any ideas for coverage as they come to mind. Find out who the technical point people are in case you have questions or need adjustments to the lighting or audio. Think and walk yourself through every step of the production from setup to show to wrap. Will you need a wide-angle lens to shoot the whole stage? Is the lighting too dark or bright? Is there an outlet you can plug into or will you need enough batteries to last the entire show? If possible, try to shoot some test footage. This may be your only chance to discover and fix major issues *beforehand.*

2. Arrive Early and Get Establishing Shots

Give yourself ample time to set up, speak with organizers, and scout the venue if you haven't already done so. As soon as you have your camera ready, go outside and pop off some exterior and establishing shots while you still have daylight and things are quiet. Simple establishing shots are easily forgotten in the hurried energy of a live event. I will often shoot exteriors before I even walk into the venue. If the actual event is taking place in the evening, you'll probably want to get more establishing shots of the venue after sundown with the audience arriving.

Remember to shoot establishing shots of the venue.

3. Know the Agenda

Make sure you get a program, set list, or whatever script they're using that will tell you what's happening, when it's happening, and who's involved. Frantic organizers will often forget to tell you about last minute changes, so pay close attention to changes or additions during rehearsals and warm-ups. Write notes on your agenda and keep it in your pocket or taped to your camera at all times. One

key to covering any live event is *anticipating* what's going to happen and being prepared to cover it. If you don't know where and how the performers are entering, when the vows are going to be said, or when the pyrotechnics are going to go off during the big finale, you're probably going to blow some of the most important shots of the event.

4. Shoot Like a Video Ninja

Wearing all black helps you blend into the dark and avoid distracting the performers or audience as you move around to get your shots. When placing stationary cameras, try to shoot from vantage points that allow you to get a good shot, but also allow the audience to have a clear view. If you have to set up your tripod among the audience to get the best viewpoint, ask if it's possible to block off the immediate seating area around your camera to prevent people from bumping your tripod. Beware of venue

areas that become shaky when filled with people moving, dancing, stomping, or tapping their feet. A tripod planted on a shaky surface is pointless. The other alternative is to go handheld. Keep moving when doing handheld work so you don't block any one person's view for too long. For long events, vary your handheld camera positions and use stationary objects to steady the camera to give your arms a break. Plot and time move across the stage to minimize distraction.

Note the visibility of the photographer in gray vs. the DP wearing black next to him.

5. Check Sound Early and Often

Most shooters will tell you that picture is usually not too much of a hassle to set up, but *audio* at live events and performances can drive you insane. Strange hums, low levels, or simply no sound are common issues when setting up for these types of shoots. The culprit in these instances is usually an incorrect setting, crossed wires, weak batteries, close proximity to other electronics, or incompatible equipment. It may take significant time to diagnose and fix an unexpected sound problem, so set up and check your audio *early and often*. If you've arranged to plug into the main sound feed, make sure you have enough XLR cables to run from the main mixer to your

camera position. If you're using wireless mics, you want to allow yourself extra time to deal with any sound interference or problems mounting the mics on performers' costumes. Always use brand new premium batteries (Duracell or Energizer) for wireless units and don't commit the cardinal sin of forgetting to turn on or "un-mute" a performer's mic before they walk out! Someone in the wings should be dedicated to making sure all wireless mics are turned on (and off) when necessary.

When possible, try to plug into an output from the main mixing board for the best quality sound.

6. Shoot with Multiple Cameras

It's difficult to cover a concert or other dynamic live event adequately with a single camera. Shooting with two or three cameras will help ensure plenty of creative choices in the edit room. Decide and communicate what each cameraperson will cover (i.e., main performer, audience, master shot, close-ups, instruments only, etc.).

It's best if (1) all the cameras are the same brand/model, (2) all the camera menus are on the same settings, (3) all cameras are white-balanced on the *same card* in the *same light*, and (4) all cameras are shooting at the same f-stop, if possible. If you can't do these things, count on living with inconsistent images between cameras or spending a lot of time tweaking the video during editing. Another huge issue to work out is how to sync the audio from all these cameras. **Plural Eyes** is a popular program that takes a

Use identical menu settings and white-balance all cameras on the same card in the same light for picture continuity.

lot of the hassle out of syncing in multiple cameras. But even without specialty software, you can still do it Down and Dirty with an old-fashioned **slate** (a.k.a. clapper board) to mark the beginning of the performance then keep all cameras rolling until the end of the performance, so that you'll only have to sync each tape once during editing.

7. Beware of Battery and Media Card Changes

Properly timing the changing of batteries and media cards involves planning, skill, and a little luck. Even if you can change batteries as fast as Clint Eastwood can draw a gun, you're still going to miss anywhere from 20 to 40 full seconds of the action, because the computer that runs your video camera takes a little time to boot up an down and load data. If it's during the big show number, the kissing of the bride, or

any other crucial moment, you're screwed. Follow the agenda and anticipate when important moments are coming up. Keep a vigilant eye on your "media remaining" indicator on the LCD screen. Always have a media card or fresh battery ready to go in your pocket as your current one nears the end. It's better to do changeovers at the first break in the action, during the last three to five minutes of your final media storage, than to get stuck changing out cards, drives, or batteries in the middle of a crucial shot.

Keep an eye on record time remaining and strategically plan the changing of media when shooting live events.

8. Cover the Whole Event

Don't just shoot the main event or performance itself. You are a documentarian. You are a *storyteller*. The real story of the event involves more than just what happens between curtain up and curtain close. Use your camera to tell the story of the *whole* event from A to Z. Even if the performance is all you're really interested in, you should still get a few decent shots of the setup, audience, backstage activity, and anything else of interest that will help your editor tell the whole story in pictures. Before the event, make a shot list of all the action you'll want to cover. If you do this, take a breath mint when you screen your **dailies**, because I promise you that your editor will kiss you for having such foresight! (See also "Live Event Gig Sheet" on the Crazy Phat Bonus Website for this book.)

Shots such as the audience arriving help communicate more about the event.

9. Inventory Your Gear at Wrap

It's not uncommon for there to be several different sets of technical equipment or gear on a shoot like this: your own personal gear, rented gear, the venue's gear, and other video crews' gear. It's also not uncommon for this equipment to get mixed up or misplaced during a long day of shooting in a large space. Use labels, tape, paint, or engraving to clearly identify your equipment. Try to keep all of your gear together near your location or in a secure staging area. Make sure all items that you'll need for the main event are on your person or at arm's reach. Keep a checklist of all the equipment that you brought with you and check your gear against this list as soon as you finish breaking down. Also, make sure you return any cables, adapters, or other gear you may have borrowed from the venue or other shooters.

Mark your gear and do inventory at wrap to avoid mix-ups with other equipment on site.

10. Don't React . . . Anticipate

Learn the art of anticipation. Over time as you shoot more and more documentary footage you will learn to read body language, facial expressions and the rhythms of speech and conversation to the point that you will instinctively be able to anticipate and be prepared to follow the action as people move, sit and stand, do something dramatic, or just start or stop talking. You will eventually develop a sixth camera sense that will guide you to pull out, tilt, zoom in or hold at the exact right moment. Anticipation of live action is one of the things that really separates doc camerawork from narrative camerawork. We don't know exactly what the people in front of our camera will do at any given moment . . . but whatever they do, we need to be on point with a solid composition in our frame no matter what. To quote a memorable line from an intimidating inmate with an eye patch of one of my favorite docs, *Scared Straight*: "If I decide to jump on that [bleep] ceiling you better not take your eyes off of me!" . . . I'd listen to him if I were you—**anticipate and follow your subject's actions**.

Whether it's a stage dive, signature dance move, or the big pyro-technic finale . . . Your job is to anticipate it and be ready to cover it with the perfect shot every time.

CHAPTER 7
INTERVIEW PREP

Introduction

If everything was properly thought out and prepared ahead of time (and I'm sure it was, now that you've read this far), shooting interviews should be the easiest part.

If you've got a good crew that you trust, you probably won't need to worry as much about your sound and picture. However, if your crew is inexperienced or (worse) you just showed your reluctant roommate how to use a mixer or operate the camera the night before, you better keep a close eye on the monitor and sound levels.

> ✔ You should only be focused on two things: your subject's answers and the technical quality of your sound and picture.

Basic Considerations of Shooting Interviews

1. Writing list of questions
2. Choice of location
3. Equipment prep and travel
4. Prepping subject
5. Framing and background
6. Getting coverage
7. Monitoring technical problems
8. Asking questions and responding

Get Yourself Together

Remember, your subject is taking all their cues from *you*, so relax. Take a drink of water. Glance over your opening questions. Smile, if it's appropriate. Make sure all your crew is ready. (I like to imagine that I am *channeling* Oprah Winfrey, but you should do whatever works for you.) Briefly meditate on the goal of your interview, but most important . . .

> ✔ Relax and have a real conversation with your subject.

Equipment Prep

You should always thoroughly check and test shoot with your rig before any type of shoot, especially documentary. The absolute last place you want to find out that you have a problem with a piece of gear is on location during your shoot. In the best case scenario, you will just be thrown a little off your rhythm. However, in the *worst case scenario*, you may not be able to shoot at all and you could lose your only opportunity to get that interview. This is easily avoided by checking and double-checking everything beforehand.
(See "Documentary Shoot Checklist" on the bonus site for this book.)

✔ Check and double check all equipment beforehand.

Travel

Make sure you know where you are going. Even if you have a GPS unit, I still recommend printing out a local map and taking a look on Google Streetview, so you'll know what the building looks like. If you're driving make sure you've got gas or time to get it. And most important, arrive on time

Always take directions *and* a map to a shoot.

(Source: Google Maps)

or a little early. Your best bet for a big interview is to arrive an hour early and sit down at a local coffee shop, review your questions and crew details, and gather your thoughts. You will be much more relaxed than if you scramble out of the car 15 minutes late apologizing to your subject and rushing your setup. I have done both more than once and I can tell you that the former makes for a much better and enjoyable interview.

✔ Know where you're going and allow time for traffic. Arrive early and gather your thoughts.

The first thing you should do when you arrive is greet your subject, preferably without the equipment and never with the cameras rolling (unless this has been previously discussed with your subject).

Introduce your crew members, then do a quick walk-through with your crew. Discuss where you want to set up and any furniture or props that will need to be adjusted. Always *ask first* and explain if you need to do any major adjustments like move a sofa or take a picture off the wall.

Setup Time

Be realistic about your setup time. This will largely depend on the size and experience of your crew. I generally like to allow an hour to get lights, camera, and sound all set up, but I have often had to do it in half that time when pressed. Lights will always take the longest, so once you've got your camera picture up, start with the lighting. Adjusting your lighting should be done with a stand-in whenever possible (usually a crew member), preferably one with the same skin tone and height as your subject.

> ✔ Greet your subject, then walk through the location with your crew and decide where you want to set up.

Warm 'Em Up

If you aren't too involved with the setup, this time should be spent just "warming up" and briefing your subject. If they seem particularly anxious, save the briefing for the last minute and just have a normal friendly conversation to help put them at ease. Be careful not to get too deep into the topic of your interview during this time. You don't want your subject to give his best answers and responses before the camera even rolls, because their answers are rarely as good the second time around.

Once the tape is rolling the first thing you want to do is get your subject to state their name and title and spell their name out for you. (You'd be surprised how often I've been editing something two weeks later, but couldn't remember who an interview subject was, let alone how to spell their name!) If you're not around, your editor will still have all the info they need for titles. I also always get subjects on tape saying that I have permission to use the video for my project even though I also get a written release as well. (Always cover your video assets!).

> ✔ Before you start, warm up your subject with some casual conversation. get them to relax.

CHOOSING INTERVIEW BACKGROUNDS

Storytelling Through Framing

Many times, the very first time we get to see the location is an hour (or less!) before our scheduled interview, in which case an office or living room is generally the best you can expect under the circumstances. No sweat. The same goal applies–try to find some element(s) of that space that help visually tell your story and get them in the frame.

Going back to our earlier example, if your subject is a boxer, get her trophies in the background. Frame that autographed poster of Muhammad Ali so it's partially visible behind her. Turn out the lights in the basement and light the punching bag in the frame just over her shoulder. Use your awesome guerrilla skills of observation and imagination to help tell your story. You get the point.

Using Props and Cheating Furniture

Use whatever visual elements you have on location to help tell your story. Don't force the issue or rearrange the whole room, but if it's already there, move it or frame it and use it. Don't worry, the Documentary Police won't come to arrest you. No one will know where that poster was before and it's a long accepted practice to do a *little* creative art direction on location.

A chair "cheated" to show view of street

Remember, if the props or visual elements aren't lit they won't be seen and, effectively, aren't in the frame. You may find that you have to **cheat** your background light or a practical light to illuminate your props if you are short on lighting gear. Ideally, you would also have a smaller light fixture to highlight props.

Using Depth and Busy Backgrounds

Another way to spice up your interview is to stage it so that the shot has a lot of depth behind your subject. However, be very careful when using distracting or busy backgrounds such as television sets, crowd scenes, bright flashing lights, etc. Generally, these should be avoided, but this isn't a hard and fast rule since having greater depth and action in the background of your shot can be a great aid in storytelling and a more dynamic composition as long as it doesn't overshadow your subject. If you really think a particularly busy background will aid your story, follow the procedures from "Hot Tip: Shallow Depth of Field" on page 240 to throw the background out of focus and minimize the distraction.

> ✔ Use and light the "props" in your shot. Avoid shooting busy or distracting backgrounds.

EASY DO-IT-YOURSELF BACKDROPS

A large piece of fabric will make a great and inexpensive all-purpose background. It'll come in handy especially when you don't have a decent location to work with or want to create a uniform look to your interviews even though they take place at a variety of different locations. The network shows use this technique all the time. I think so-called "professional" backdrops are an overpriced waste of money. Any fabric store will yield a multitude of more attractive artistic choices, one of which is sure to work for you. Look for something that's at least 12 × 12 feet that has an interesting texture or pattern. The bigger the piece of fabric, the wider the shots you can compose with it. The possibility of the looks you can achieve are endless.

Lighter colored fabrics such as standard canvas are more flexible because you can gel the lights on them so they appear any color you like. Darker fabrics such as rich red or blue velvets will give you a more formal look, but will require more light. Reflective fabrics also create an attractive and dynamic look. You probably even have some old Ikea curtains lying around that might do the trick. Thicker, more opaque fabrics look better. Bed sheets and other thin fabrics are usually pretty cheesy looking, but you may be able to get away with it if they are wrinkle-free, rigged and lit well, and sufficiently out of focus.

Unless your fabric has an intentional wrinkled look, you're going to need to have an iron handy. Allow time to iron out wrinkles on smooth fabrics such as satins. (Check the iron for

the proper setting for your type of fabric.) Use a backdrop stand or hang backdrops between two C-stands using long gobo arms connected. A cheap portable clothing rack may even work on a tight budget. Make sure you've arranged it to create some interesting ripples in the fabric. These ripples will add to the overall texture by creating some depth and interesting bands of shadow.

Light your fabric from an angle for the best results. You can use barn doors to create a diagonal slash or oval pattern. Some fabrics will also look good lit from behind. Experiment with different light positions and cloth ruffles. Each will create a unique pattern of light and shadow. You can also place a cookie on a light to create an interesting pattern if the fabric is still too boring.

Finally, you might try out different gels to see what best contrasts or compliments your subject's clothing and skin tone and decide if you want to use shallow depth of field to throw the backdrop a little out of focus. The last step is to place your subject at least five feet from the backdrop. Set up your camera and experiment at home.

Subject Positioning

You should generally position your subject facing slightly left or right. A dead-on angle makes for a more flat and boring *visual* aesthetic. However, a subject looking and speaking dead-on into the camera can also make a more stark and powerful *emotional* connection with the audience. Ideally, you want to place them 5–10 feet from the background to avoid their shadow or to achieve a shallow depth of field as discussed earlier. The closer your subject is to the background the more you will have to raise your key light to angle shadows down out of the shot. Also, avoid swivel chairs.

Interviewer Positioning and Eyeline

It's important when framing that you pay attention to your subject's "eyeline," which is simply a term to describe where your subject *appears* to be looking in the frame. You should instruct your subject to look at the interviewer not the camera (unless they are directly addressing the audience). Eyeline issues can be avoided by placing the interviewer very close to either side of the camera lens. I have found that between the key light and the camera works best. (It's a tight fit for the interviewer and it will be more difficult for the subject to see you next to the light, but man that's a sweet eyeline!)

Good Eyeline

Bad Eyeline

And it's of equal importance that the interviewer's eyes are at the same level as the camera. A few inches of difference between the interviewer's eyeline and camera angle can easily make it appear that the subject is looking awkwardly off camera. You generally want them to look just off to the side of the lens they are facing. For example, if your subject is framed more on the right side of the frame, they should be looking just to the left side of the camera and vice versa. This will appear most natural.

Otherwise your audience will completely forget about the subject of your interview and just keep asking themselves: "What the heck is that guy looking at?!" They will want to see it too.

✔ *Check your frame to make sure your subject's eyeline appears natural and not too off camera.*

HOW DO I LOOK?

Improving a subject's appearance in documentary work is a stylistic, or arguably, even an ethical choice. You have to decide what's right for your project and what, if any, impact it will have on your audience and story. In my experience, otherwise perfectly composed people, even those used to being in front of a live audience, are often somewhat nervous and self-conscious in front of a video camera, even with a tiny crew. One of the things these subjects are most concerned about is their appearance. With this being the case, a subject will inevitably ask you how they look. The correct answer is always, "Great!" And with a little bit of Down and Dirty DV know-how, you will be able to say it and mean it.

Clothing

If it's appropriate for your project, you may want to suggest specific clothing to your subject, such as a uniform or traditional costume. However, it is very important that you tell subjects what type of clothing NOT to wear when you speak to them ahead of time to make your arrangements. There are a few types of clothing and accessories that are very uncamera-friendly to video. Clothing with logos is obviously a potential legal issue and may need to be blurred out in post, particularly if your piece will

eventually be broadcast or released theatrically. However, a much bigger problem is certain patterns and colors, usually found on shirts, that can be very problematic for video.

Often these problems are **unfixable** in post-production, so whenever possible they should be avoided like a student loan bill collector. However, there will inevitably come a time when you'll have to tape someone wearing problematic clothing. The chart on the next page will help you figure out how to handle it on set.

Subjects with glasses or hats can be tricky to shoot.

HAZARD	VIDEO PROBLEM	SOLUTIONS
Bright White	May "blow out" under the lights making it hard to get a good exposure without making your subject's face underexposed, especially, with darker skin tones	■ Wardrobe change ■ Tone down with a jacket, vest, or sweater ■ Frame most of it out ■ ND gel light on shirt
Bright Red	Bright saturated reds can "bleed" or glow on video (darker reds such as burgundy are usually okay)	■ Wardrobe change ■ Frame it out ■ Cover up with a jacket or sweater
Thin Stripes	Will cause your video to produce a "moiré effect," which is a crazy, vibrating, rainbow-like pattern; ditto for herringbone patterns as well	■ Wardrobe change ■ Frame it out ■ Cover up completely with sweater ■ Adjust detail in camera menu
Hats	Will put your subject's eyes and face in shadow	■ Remove ■ Move key light to lower position ■ Fill shadow with reflector or light ■ Tilt brim up ■ Turn around backward
Sunglasses	Will obscure subject's eyes and reflect lights and crew	■ Remove sunglasses ■ Adjust to minimize reflection ■ Try polarizer filter on camera
Glasses	Will obscure subject's eyes and reflect lights and crew	■ Adjust to minimize reflection ■ Have subject wear contact lenses ■ Try polarazier filter on camera

✔ *Brief your subject about video-appropriate clothing in advance. Know how to resolve clothing problems.*

Hey, everybody can't look as good as me and you. Thankfully for them, there are several simple techniques that you can employ to make any subject look more attractive to the camera using a combination of lighting, makeup, camera angles, and filters.

ISSUE	LIGHTING	MAKEUP	CAMERA
Wrinkles	■ Soft diffusion ■ Fluorescent lights	■ Powder ■ Full makeup	■ Avoid extreme close-ups ■ Soft FX filter ■ Decrease video detail
Acne/Scars	■ Use soft diffusion ■ Fluorescent lights	■ Powder ■ Full makeup	■ Avoid extreme close-ups ■ Soft FX filter ■ Decrease video detail
Pale Skin	■ Warming gel	■ Powder ■ Full makeup	■ Warming filter ■ White balance
Blotchy Skin/ Freckles	■ Warming gel	■ Powder ■ Full makeup	■ Avoid extreme close-ups ■ Soft FX filter ■ Decrease video detail
Large Nose	■ Place key light at same angle/ height as camera lens ■ Adjust to avoid nose shadow	■ Powder	■ Shoot from dead-on angle ■ Avoid shooting wide or low
Double Chin	■ Angle key light so chin is in shadow	■ Powder (one shade darker) below jaw line	■ Shoot from slightly higher angle

EASY POWDER MAKEUP

Always carry some professional-quality, **translucent powder** makeup in a few different skin tones when shooting interviews. If your subject's face or head is shiny, a few quick brushes of this magic dust will take care of it quickly. If they (or you) are concerned about how they look, dust on some professional translucent powder makeup.

I swear it takes off five to ten years of age, helps to mask blemishes, and gives subjects a natural more even complexion that doesn't look too made up. Moreover, it's just powder, so you don't need any special training or hours of practice to apply it. And it comes off easily with soap and water. First, cover up your subject's clothes with a makeup apron or towel. Ask them to close their eyes and very lightly dust their face with the powder.

Keep your powder nearby during the shoot. Your first application will probably start to wear off after 20 to 30 minutes under the lights or as your subject begins to sweat. If there is a P.A. or someone else on the set who knows how, have them quickly reapply the powder to the shiny spots, usually the nose and forehead.

A little makeup can work wonders on subjects who are nervous about how they will look on video. When I show them the final picture on the monitor, subjects often can't believe how *good* they look. However, make sure you've got the right skin tone or else you could easily make them look like a madeup corpse! (I've done that, too.)

I like the Ben Nye theatrical makeup brand, but lots of companies make professional-quality translucent powder. Just don't get anything cheap. You will also need a few good powder puffs or pony hair brushes to apply it. Brushes are much better, but some subjects will be picky about using a brush that's been used on someone else's face. For this reason, it's also a good idea to keep disposable powder puffs at the ready. Yet another solution is to buy little books of disposable paper sheets of powdered makeup.

Before Makeup

After Makeup

TALENT RELEASES

Get a Signed Talent Release Form

It's crucial that you get a signed talent release form from your subject. These forms give you legal permission to use the person's physical likeness and voice for your project. It's always a smart practice to get releases signed *before* the interview. Doing so will ensure that you don't forget and the subject won't get cold feet and deny permission after the interview. There is a sample talent release in the back of this book. Consult an entertainment attorney to draft a release form to fit your needs.

Talent Release Form Essentials

- ❏ **Name of subject**
- ❏ **Subject contact info**
- ❏ **Title of project**
- ❏ **Producer and production company**
- ❏ **Compensation (usually none for subjects)**
- ❏ **Usage (documentary, Web site, ads, etc.)**
- ❏ **Signature of subject**
- ❏ **Signature of filmmaker**
- ❏ **Date**

Getting Releases from Major Figures

Sometimes you will be fortunate enough to score a big interview on the spot with a major celebrity or important figure. In this case, you may have to wait and contact your subject for a release after the fact, as such figures aren't keen on signing anything (apart from an autograph) on the spot. They have agents, managers, assistants, and lawyers (a.k.a. "people") that screen and handle this type of paperwork. If you don't already know, casually ask them who you should forward the release form to so that you can use the interview. If they are amenable to signing it they will do so, or tell you whom to contact. They may want to see a copy first.

Verbal Releases

Either way, I try to always get a **verbal release** from my subjects as soon as the camera starts rolling. To get a verbal release, have your subject state and spell their name, then say something to the effect of "Does [name of production company and filmmaker] have your permission to use this interview for [title of your documentary]?" Whether or not this will hold up in court is another story, but it's far better than *no* release at all and a good extra measure even with a signed release.

> ✔ *Try to get a signed release form beforehand when possible. Always get a "verbal release" on camera.*

FAIR SUBJECT PORTRAYAL AND RELEASES

ALBERT MAYSLES, DIRECTOR/DP
mayslesfilms.com
(Grey Gardens, Gimme Shelter, Salesman, Lalee's Kin, etc.)

I think that it's important to feel confident that you're gonna get the release. When we made *Salesman*, each time we'd film in another person's house we waited until the end to ask for the release and we didn't have any problem. But you can run into that problem. That's why [it's best] earlier on, rather than later on to get the release. But basically, you don't want to get a release from a person who feels that they don't want to be in the film. You'd rather not show the film if they're unhappy with it . . .

You don't want to cut off yourself from the opportunity to film somebody in a very profound way because it's a little embarrassing or whatever. But at the same time, there are moments where it would be exploitive, where it would be a damage to that person to film them, and I don't film under those circumstances. Sometimes you're in a borderline situation where it might be damaging, might not, and you go ahead and film it, knowing that you have the responsibility in the editing not to include it if it's embarrassing. Oftentimes it's a good idea to show the film to the person in the film before the film is finally released, because there may be something in that film that you didn't know would hurt that person and you wouldn't want it as much as he wouldn't want it either.

The basic thing is that I believe in what I'm doing, in that I believe that I'm not going to do harm to the people that I'm filming, but rather that it will be a benefit to them. Several years ago I helped to make a film of a very poor black family in the south, (*Lalee's Kin*), and they had everything to be embarrassed by . . . but, because I shot with love in my heart and with an open mind, I ended up with a film that when I showed it to Grandma, she turned to me having just seen it and said, "That's the truth." Then she went on to say, "But couldn't you have made it longer?"

That kind of affirmation is what I get all the time because what I do is good for the people that I film. It sort of is an answer to Arthur Miller's plea, "Attention must be paid." I think we have to pay attention to our neighbors, and to people far from us as well. And in paying attention to end up understanding them and loving them because of the desire to understand them and the love that we give people in filming them.

Remind your subject of the focus of your interview and tell them approximately how long the interview is going to be. Be considerate of any time constraints they give you. Be forthright and honest about your approach and what is expected of the subject in terms of answers and candidness. If there are sensitive personal issues at hand, discuss how they will be treated.

If complete spontaneity is not necessary for your interview, you might even tell your subject a few of the questions you will be asking ahead of time to allow them time to think of how they will respond. The more they know in advance, the more comfortable they will feel with the interview process. Just before the interview starts, give your subject some basic instructions that will help them relax and, more important, keep you from pulling out your hair in the editing room.

Also, don't forget to ask your subject and everyone else in the room to turn off their cell phones. However, if your subject doesn't turn off their phone and they take a call, keep the camera rolling. You never know what you might capture in that little human moment—an angry tirade to a lawyer, a tender moment with their kid, a big deal going down, good news, bad news . . . drama. See "Instructing Subjects" on the next page for specific instructions to give to your subject just before an interview.

> ✔ Before you shoot, give your subject instructions that will help you to shoot and edit the interview smoothly.

You want to minimize "directing" real people, but you gotta give them a few basics to make sure you shoot something you can easily edit.

INSTRUCTING SUBJECTS

1 | **Just relax. Ignore the camera and lights and just talk to me. Don't look into the camera. Just look at me.**

You want to impress upon your subject that the interview process is just a *conversation* between you and them. Looking directly into the camera or stealing glances is disturbing to the audience, which is accustomed to people looking at the interviewer, just off camera. (In certain situations, such as introductions, confessionals, and emotional pleas, addressing the camera directly is acceptable, but when a subject does *both* in the same shot, it doesn't work.)

2 | **Please wait until I complete my question to answer, then answer in complete sentences. For example, if I ask you where you're from, instead of just saying "Chicago," you would say "I'm from Chicago."**

This will give you the ability to isolate the subject's answer in post-production and omit your own question/voice from the edited segment. This will keep the focus on your subject and give you more choices in the editing process. It's also always a good idea to mic yourself as well, so you can clearly hear your own questions and preserve the option to add them in later if you change your mind.

3 | **Don't worry if you make a mistake or misspeak. This is all going to be edited down for the final piece.**

Remind your subjects that nothing they say is being broadcast live (unless it actually is!) and that you will be cutting out any obvious mistakes, misspoken words, or anything else that would portray them unfairly or is irrelevant to your film. So they should just reeelaaax.

4 | **Would you like some water or anything else before we begin?**

Even if they say no, keep some water at the ready. Talking for twenty minutes straight or longer will test anyone's voice. They may want some other creature comforts such as a cigarette or a beer. The more relaxed a subject is the more they're going to talk freely, but be careful here—shooting someone who's under the influence poses ethical questions. Use your own ethical meter to decide what's appropriate for your project and for a fair portrayal of your subject. You can say no or ask that they keep the item in question off camera, if their request is not appropriate. Also, keep some tissues handy if you think things could get emotional. Always take care of your subjects.

KEEPIN' IT "REAL"

1 SHOOT WITH THE RECORD LIGHT AND BEEP OFF

One of the keys to getting good doc footage is to get people to be more natural and less self-conscious. Whenever you hit the record button, most video cameras beep and activate a little red **tally light** on the front of the camera. This makes people even more aware that they're being videotaped. Turn both of these functions off in the camera menu.

2 USE LAVS OR MIC STANDS

Manned boom mics are distracting and take more manpower. Interview subjects not used to being on camera may be considerably more self-conscious with a large boom mic swinging a foot or two from their head. A tiny lav mic on the lapel or a boom mic on a stand has the *opposite* effect. They more easily forget that they are being recorded and are more likely to relax and open up.

3 GO WIRELESS

The only thing better than using a lav mic to keep subjects relaxed and natural is to use a wireless lav mic. When you go wireless, subjects are free to move about a considerable distance from the camera and still be heard clearly. You can get crisp audio of conversations that take place yards away from the camera, or even behind closed doors. This is a doc staple for capturing unguarded, intimate moments.

A good UHF wireless mic kit like the one above will cost at least $500.

4 KEEP THE CAMERA AT A DISTANCE

Another technique you can use to record more natural doc footage is to keep the camera at a healthy distance from your subject. This is most practical when you are doing a sit-down interview or using wireless mics to shoot cinema verité style. This technique, coupled with a wireless mic, is the easiest way to capture intimate, personal moments on video. Out if sight, out of mind.

WHEN SUBJECTS WANT TO WALK

ROSE ROSENBLATT & MARION LIPSCHUTZ, PRODUCERS/ DIRECTORS

(The Education of Shelby Knox, The Abortion Pill)

Rose: So you're an outsider, and you start out as an outsider and you can't help that. You are the outsider and they have all their prejudices, and here's what happens . . . there are stages to cross. And this has happened in every one of our films. At first they're really interested, they want to do it, and then you move into their house in a matter of speaking, I mean, you're shooting a lot, and you want to get good stuff—and then they freak, they're freaked . . . "Uh oh . . . This is too much."

Marion: And then they want you out and they're pissed. Meanwhile you're thinking, "I shot all this, they can't walk."

Rose: Right. And it looks like they're walking. You know, everybody gets to a point it looks like they're walking, and you go, "My God, I just spent, ten thousand, fifteen, whatever, five thousand, whatever, all the money I had, and they're walking." And you flip . . . And that's the test. You see, at that point, you don't give up. At that point you go, "OK, now I gotta really convince them that I'm really there on their side."

Marion: They may get that way, because once we move in, we may be the uninvited guest, but once we're there, we're so there. This may not be the case with everyone, but there's always this point when they're like, "What do you mean you're here? Please, outta my life." And then we behave and then it's fine.

Rose: And everybody has a different way that they'll do that. But that's what you have to do. You can't be scared off by that. You gotta know, this is supposed to happen, it's happening now, I'm at step two or step three and now this is the next hurdle. And then you make friends with them. And after you do that, they start to direct the film. And you gotta let them direct the film. They call you and say, "Oh you shoulda been here yesterday. Come here next week. This is happening, this is happening. You should do this. You should . . . "And it's part of the process to incorporate them, and their suggestions, because that's where their enthusiasm, that's where their energy is.

CHAPTER 8

CONDUCTING INTERVIEWS

Introduction

Okay, here's where we get to the heart of the interview process—your questions and conversation with your subject. Everything you've done up to this point, lighting, setting mics, framing, etc., will all have been for naught if you don't handle your questioning properly.

It's now up to you and you alone to elicit your subject's funniest anecdotes, most painful memories, long held secrets, mind-blowing theories, and candid opinions in a way that your audience will find compelling, whether your subject is talking about their first knockout or their last insurance seminar.

But how does one actually do this? Browbeat them? Trick them? Ask them for "the real scoop"? No, to all of the above. You simply have a real and candid *conversation* with them. You've already done this a hundred times over whenever you've met new people at parties, gone on a first date, or had a new roommate move in. You just need to employ the exact same social skills and principles to *consciously* lead your subject to your interview goal—only now you're doing it with a camera and lights.

> ✔ Ask questions, listen and respond to your subject's answers, always keeping your interview goals in mind.

The type of questions you ask will largely determine the quality and depth of your interview. Avoid asking leading questions or questions that can be answered with a simple yes or no. Remember, you want your subject to paint the picture, not just color in *your* preconceived lines.

Leading questions are okay as follow-ups to your main questions, especially when your questions will remain in the edited piece. But for the most part they will undermine your intention of having the subject tell you what they have to say in their own words and in full glorious detail.

Questions that begin with words such as *how, why, where,* and *what* will elicit stronger, more in-depth answers from your subject. Questions that begin with words such as *did, are, will,* and *was* will likely get you short, general, one-and two-word answers.

LEADING VS. OPEN-ENDED QUESTIONS

	QUESTION	TYPICAL SUBJECT ANSWER
Leading	1A) Did that bother you?	Yes.
Open-ended	1B) How did that make you feel?	Ticked off. I couldn't believe that my boss would ever say that to me!
Leading	2A) Are you a Communist?	No.
Open-ended	2B) How would you describe your political beliefs?	I'm a Conservative Socialist Libertarian who practices Capitalism.
Leading	3A) Was it scary?	Yes. It *was* scary.
Open-ended	3B) What was it like?	I was terrified and trembling all over. I literally wet my pants!

✔ *Ask open-ended questions to avoid short, lame answers.*

LOGICAL ORDER OF QUESTIONS

Let's go back to the example of interviewing your favorite guitarist. If your goal was to do a serious interview about his role in the rebirth of Funk music, the questions covered might run something like this:

Sample Question Sequence

1. Where are you originally from?
2. What bands have you played with?
3. What do you think got you into music?
4. Who are the pioneers of Funk ?
5. What was the first song you learned on the guitar?
6. How would you describe the sound of Funk?
8. What distinguishes Funk from other genres?
9. What keys do you usually play in? Why?
10. How important are electronic instruments to Funk?
11. What do you think fans enjoy most about Funk?
12. What do you think is the future of Funk?
13. Is there anything I *haven't* already covered that you think is important for people to know about Funk?

The number of questions should be determined by the length of time allotted for your interview, anticipated amount of screen time in the final piece, and how in-depth you want to get. You should always be respectful of your subject's time constraints. If your subject only has a very limited amount of time, ask one or two preliminary questions and get right to your point.

Be mindful of the pacing and length of your interview. Know when to move on to a new question. Also, be mindful of when your subject is getting tired and losing energy. Remember, they are amateur onscreen speakers under bright hot lights. Under these conditions people can expire much quicker than usual. Better to end on a strong point, rather than beat the topic (and your subject) into the ground. Finishing with a "soapbox question" will usually generate a good end note. Often the subject will say something poignant or revealing toward the end of an interview that will give it a sense of finality. These moments are documentary gold. (See "The Soapbox Question" on page 274.)

> ✔ *Order your questions so they logically lead to your goal. Beware of your pacing and end on a strong point.*

INTERVIEWING RESISTANT SUBJECTS

SAFIYA SONGHAI, PRODUCER

safiyasonghai.com

(Diamonds: The Price of Ice, Assoc. Prod.—Brown vs. Board of Ed.)

You have to go through it—not ask leading questions, but get them involved in a *conversation*, and then your subject will divulge more information when they know that you're not trying to catch them or trick them, but you're really just interested in hearing their side of the story: "How do *you* see things? How do *you* walk this earth?" You have to really tap into the empathetic side of yourself and not be judgmental, which is hard for a lot of people who are really tied into the mission of their documentary. They're like, "We are going to show that the whales off the coast of this country are being treated poorly, and we're going to go to these people and talk to them, and they're the ones who are responsible." You can't approach people that way. They're going to be defensive . . .

I think that with a resistant subject, oftentimes they *know* that you're on the opposing side, and the fact that they even granted you an interview is amazing, because a lot of times they'll just write you a very well-worded legal letter stating that they will not participate. If they are participating, it's usually because they have a very good public relations answer for anything that you're going to say. But you learn to work with that.

I think a lot of documentary filmmakers think that they need to have this person spill their guts and say, "I'm the one who did it!", kind of like an episode of *Law and Order*. They're not going to do that, but what they are going to do is cover their butts so much that it's going to *look* like what it is, and that's really all you need. You just need someone to look like they're trying to disguise something or hide something, or that they have something so well-worded that you can't punch a hole in it, which means that they have something to hide, and that's all that you really want to prove. They're not going to say, "I have something to hide." They're just going to try to hide it.

And you should really just let them stand on their own; stand as the person they are, and the audience will judge them, not just on what they say, but also their body language. They'll judge them on the way that they say it, and that's what you really want. You want people to have a visceral response to the players in your documentary, to the characters, to the people that were instrumental in whatever story you're trying to tell, whether it's an historical story, or cinema verité. You just let them be themselves.

HOW TO WORK A PRESS CONFERENCE

The opposite of a **one-on-one** interview is the press conference, premiere, or public opening. In these situations, you're competing with other media in a crowded room and are lucky to get in one question that matters to your project. Below are some ways to maximize the experience.

1 GET INVITED

Once you've identified the press event that you want to attend, email a written request including basic info about your project to the organizers. Follow up with a phone call or e-mail if you don't hear back in time to prepare for the event. If you have some graphic design skills, you might also want to make some professional-looking laminated "press passes" with your company logo and/or project title. Understand that these press passes give you no legal or official capacity whatsoever. However, they will make you and your crew *look* more legit and you'll be more likely to score an interview and be taken seriously.

2 ARRIVE EARLY AND STAKE OUT A GOOD SPOT

You need time to scope out the event, read the press packet, set up the best camera angle, and set up sound. If you arrive less than a half hour before an event, you will find yourself scrambling to figure out what's going to happen when and trying to shoot over the heads of other camera crews from the back row of the designated camera area.

3 PLUG IN TO THE MAIN MIX AND SET UP YOUR OWN MIC

Your best bet for sound is plugging into the main sound feed if it's provided. Ask the event sound engineer. Just run an XLR cable from the main mixer or feed box to your camera's mic input. (Ask, or switch between mic and line level on your camera to find the appropriate setting.) The other option is to set up your own mic at the podium along with the rest. When short on time (or mic stands) you can just quickly tape a lav mic onto or near the bundle of other mics facing the speakers podium.

4 TRY TO SNAG THE ONE-ON-ONE

After the main press conference there will sometimes be an opportunity to catch the featured CEO, celebrity, or public figure for an impromptu stand-up interview. (This is an area where those "press badges" I mentioned earlier can make a difference.) They can't talk to everyone individually, so you need to "sell" your project to their handlers or catch their ear with something appealing: "Mr. Mayor, do you have a quick minute to address Latino voters?" Try to be charming, then jump right to your main questions. You'll probably have one to three minutes or questions tops. Make them count and get the shot.

Brainstorm and Write Out Your Questions

How will you actually get your subject to talk about or explain the topic? Don't just wing it the day of your interview. Think about and *write* out your questions in a logical order. If you have thoroughly researched your subject, this part is easy. I recommend first brain-storming and writing down every question that anyone might possibly want to know about your subject or the topic, then go back to identify the questions that most pertain to

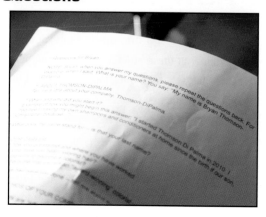

the goal(s) of your interview. Once you've identified these questions, trim them down more and put them in a logical order that will help your subject step up, pace, and narrate their story.

> ✔ Plan and write out your questions in a logical order.

Warm 'Em Up

I advise starting off with a few "softball" questions to get your subject warmed up. In an interview you're trying to get your subject to tell a story with a beginning, middle, and end. Make sure your questions logically lead them through each part and *build* to the main issue.

Warm-up questions should be easy questions about the person's general background as it relates to the topic–something that doesn't require too much thought or depth. After that, ramp up to the heart of the matter by covering some background material related to your topic. Finally, once your subject is fully engaged, delve deep into the heart of the matter. Then at the end, get your subject to reflect on what they just told you and sum it all up.

> ✔ Start off with some easy warm-up questions.

Remember, your questions are just a *guideline* to keep you focused on your goal. Don't make the novice mistake of just going straight down your list of questions one after another without regard to your subject's specific answers. You have to pay careful attention and "read between the lines" of what your subject is telling you, because it may be necessary to change, jump ahead, or skip some of your questions if the conversation dictates.

If your subject mentions something relevant that isn't part of your list of questions you need to follow up and explore that avenue.

Similarly, your subject will probably answer or touch upon some of your later questions before you ask them. That's fine. It means you've successfully steered your subject toward your goal. They just got there a little early.

To stay on track when your subject jumps ahead of you or brings up an unexpected but relevant point, I suggest one of three things.

When Your Subject Jumps Ahead

1. **Fugeddaboutit:** Skip the later question because it's already been answered or touched upon and isn't as relevant as other points you'd like to discuss.
2. **Go With It:** Seize the opportunity to segue into the later topic if you still need more details: "Now you just mentioned that boxers don't really make much money in the ring, so how does a boxer survive economically?"
3. **Get Back to It:** If you still want to explore the *current* question, tell your subject that you're going to get back to the later question: "You touched upon the subject of money which I'll get to in a minute, but before that I want to talk more about that first knockout . . ."

✔ *Carefully listen and go with the flow of the conversation, always leading it back to your interview goal.*

RESPONDING TO YOUR SUBJECT

Let subjects know you're listening. While interviewing your subjects you should give them verbal and nonverbal feedback to let them know you're paying attention, encourage them, and/or elicit a stronger emotional response. Obviously your verbal feedback should be geared toward your subject's previous comments, but there are a variety of common gestures, expressions, and brief comments that you can use to encourage your subjects and get them to explain more and do so with more passion and detail.

If you want to get a stronger narrative or more in-depth explanation from your subject, slightly embellish your feedback or "challenge" their answer (i.e., "Get outta here!"). If you amplify your feedback, your subject will naturally amplify his answer. Applying these everyday phrases and social behaviors as conscious interview techniques will help turn a perceived interrogation into a real and lively two-way conversation. (Hey, there's that word again!)

Give verbal feedback only when you're sure your subject is finished talking. You want to be careful not to "step on" your subject's answers, because he may have more to say and you won't be able to isolate the subject's answer from your comment in the editing process if necessary.

Don't rush to fill in every moment of silence. Your subject will naturally want to fill in the gaps by elaborating on their answer. Encourage people to speak and explain more with verbal and nonverbal cues.

> ✔ **Respond to your subject. Use verbal feedback and facial expressions to _engage_ them in the interview.**

GIVING FEEDBACK	
NONVERBAL FEEDBACK	**VERBAL FEEDBACK**
■ Good eye contact	■ "Amazing! You were only 9 years old?!"
■ Facial expressions (shock, delight, etc.)	■ "I can't believe they did that to you."
■ Head nodding	■ "No way!"
■ Hand gestures	■ "Get outta here! That really happened?!"
■ Head shaking (in disbelief or disgust)	■ "Hold on, are you saying that . . . ?"
■ Smile	■ "I don't believe you!"
■ Inquisitive look (like you don't understand)	■ "That _must've_ been really hard on your family."
■ Comforting hand pat	■ "I can't imagine ever being in that situation."

THE THIN LINE OF EXPLOITATION

SAM POLLARD, PRODUCER/EDITOR

(4 Little Girls, Eyes on the Prize II, When the Levees Broke, Slavery By Another Name)

You know it's a delicate thing, sometimes you can cross the line if you ask a person "So tell me how come your mother hated you so much?" And sometimes you can cross the line . . . even when you're the most sensitive.

For example when I was working on a project, initially I had a segment I was going to do about Attica. I interviewed one of the ex-prisoners, a guy named Frank "Big Black"

Smith. And he was like 280 pounds and bald and he had been taken by the authorities when they re-took the prison. They had stripped him naked put him out on a big table in the courtyard, burnt matches and cigarettes into his body and stuff, really tortured the guy. So part of my interview was to have him relive that moment. So when we asked him the first time on camera to relive that moment he did it like rote, something he had done a hundred times.

We said it was over. I said to my cameraman, "Cut." I turn to my assistant, my associate producer and camera and I said, "Do you think he really gave us his story? Did he really go back and relive that moment?" And they said, "No, he really didn't." So I turn to him and I say "Black, if you want this audience out there in Television Land to understand really what happened to you at Attica, really the struggle and the pain and the torture that you went through and how it affected you emotionally and psychologically, you've gotta really go back and really relive that. Just don't do it like rote, like you've done it a hundred times, really go back and live the experience again. Live it . . . if you can do it, then this will be fine. If you really want us to really understand what you went through . . . live it."

So we started the cameras again, I asked him a question about that day when they re-took the prison and we sat back and he gave it to us, and he gave it to us. My associate producer started crying, my camera person started crying, I started crying. Then it was over, we said cut. It was powerful. But when we wrapped up that shoot I felt like a real exploiter, even though he gave me my story, part of me was exploiting him. So it's a really thin line you can walk sometimes.

THE SOAPBOX QUESTION

Once you've exhausted all your questions, you always want to give your subject a final "soapbox question." Essentially, you're going to ask them: "Is there anything we didn't cover or anything that you'd like to say to people about [the topic]?" This is your subject's chance to get on their "soapbox" and deliver an opinion or commentary about any aspect of the topic they'd like. I have found that the soapbox question is often the most passionate part of the interview with the best quotes. It's also not unusual that even after all my well-thought out questions, the only soundbite that makes the final project is a subject's answer to my soapbox question.

Understand that even with a great set of well thought out questions, you're inevitably leading the conversation from *your* perspective. Your subject will probably still have at least one or two things she'd like to say that she thinks is important or may have been missed in earlier conversation. And ultimately, the *subject's* perspective is the one you really want to capture. The soapbox question also provides an opportunity for your subject to further explain any answer that was given earlier that she feels was unclear or incomplete.

The Double Bonus Soapbox Question

Sometimes it's also a good idea to throw the soapbox question out to your crew. After all, they are actually the very first audience for this interview. Both you and the subject are engaged in the conversation as participants, but your crew and the other people in the room represent fresh outside ears hearing things for the first time, as more pure observers. My crew have often helped me out, by catching important omissions or asking astute follow up questions that didn't occur to me or the subject in the moment. You should also make it a point to read the facial expressions, body language and other visceral reactions of your crew members as you conduct the interview. Chances are that your viewing audience will also react the same way.

> ✔ After you've exhausted your questions give your subject an opportunity to say whatever she wants about the topic.

INTERVIEWING CELEBRITIES

I freely admit that as long as I've been in this business I still get excited when I interview certain celebrities. However, for the celebrities themselves, the excitement just isn't there. Most of them have been interviewed a thousand times (some literally), especially if they're promoting a new project. And it's generally a tedious and boring exercise from their side of the microphone. However, I have found that by mostly avoiding the standard questions that they get ad nauseam, you can bring them to life and get past the standard canned answers.

My simplest technique to get celebrities to open up is to do my homework on their passions and just talk about the actual substance of what they do. So many celebrity interviews are about their social lives, salary, and lifestyle aspects, that most never get past the tabloid surface. There's a reason why everyone tunes in when master interviewers like Oprah Winfrey or Howard Stern interview a celebrity—they know they're gonna learn something *new and interesting* about that person.

A little bit of research—reading old interviews and articles, combing through their bio for interesting facts, studying their work—can go a long way to finding some obscure fact or some topic that that person feels strongly about, but has rarely had a chance to speak about. You'll know when this happens, because their eyes and voice will light up. More than once I've been on projects where some VIP who was very adamant that he only had 20 minutes for an interview, then went on to converse for an hour or more (and sometimes well after the camera was off), because the interview tapped into issues he felt passionately about but has rarely been asked about on camera. And *that's* what people want to talk about most; their passions, the things about which they feel strongest.

Even if your goal is more shallow, touch on those passions first and they're much more likely to open up and maybe share something new about a juicier aspect of their personal life or their new secret project once they know you've done your homework and respect and know them as a musician, actor, athlete, etc., and not just as a celebrity. Remember, a good interview is just an engaging conversation. Ask the questions that no one else has asked. Make people think. Demonstrate your deep knowledge and sincere interest in what they do and the things they love and you will get better results almost every time.

CORE—The Education Channel

Interrupting Your Interview to Solve Problems

Please do NOT be afraid to momentarily stop the interview and address any serious technical problems. If you have technical problems at the last minute or during your interview (and you *will* sooner or later), just play it cool. Reassure your subject and work with your crew to resolve problems quickly and *professionally*. Ideally, you want to wait and interrupt after your subject has completed their thought. However, if it's an emotional moment, a crucial point, or the climax of a story, it may be best to interrupt before they are done speaking, then ask the question again building back up to the moment and resetting the mood.

That great story they are telling, or that emotional moment you have carefully led them to, could be completely *unusable* if all we hear is the lav mic brushing against their scarf or all we see is a blinding reflection of lights in their glasses! I say it's much better to interrupt the flow and get it right than to capture something that's completely crappy or unusable. These issues will usually reveal themselves in the first few minutes of shooting, so the impact of an interruption will often be minimal.

Make sure you communicate to your sound and cameraperson that they should notify you, even if it means interrupting the interview, if any technical issue occurs that might make a shot unusable. This is particularly important if you don't have a monitor and/or headphones (It may be frustrating to be interrupted when you're on a roll, but it will be *infuriating* to discover an unfixable technical issue while editing long after the fact!). Here's another tip: If you and the crew agree beforehand on a simple set of hand signals for things like "pull out," "focus," "raise the boom," etc., you may not have to stop your flow at all.

> ✔ **Don't be afraid to stop and fix technical issues once you've started shooting. Your footage must be usable.**

Using a Monitor and Headphones

I highly recommend that directors use both a large monitor and professional headphones whenever possible. Any television with an HDMI, Component, or RCA jack will usually work as an impromptu monitor in a pinch. (While a TV set won't do much in the way of representing your true colors or showing you the exact edge of your frame, it will be fine for looking out for most common problems.) The larger the monitor, the

better, especially when shooting on DSLR's and other big chip cameras where it's more crucial to judge focus and detail. In lieu of a large monitor, a smaller portable monitor is still better than just using the 3.5" camera LCD screen. Remember to just glance over at the monitor periodically. You want to maintain good eye contact with your subject. And definitely keep the monitor out of your subject's view once the interview gets rolling.

Your sound operator should always have earphones, but whenever possible you should don a pair as well. Use only professional earphones that completely cover the ears and block out other sound. They may be awkward to keep on at first, but they will ensure that you pick up on the myriad of sounds that go unnoticed by the naked ear, but are picked up by mics and can easily ruin an interview.

✔ Always use a monitor and headphones to check the technical quality of your interview when possible.

Other Things to Look Out For

Once the interview has begun you need to be mindful of a few possible issues that could still crop up. It's common, especially during long interviews, that a camera or sound person may just get tired and zone out for a few moments, or even become so captivated by what's being said that they miss some technical issue that occurs during shooting. (I confess that I have been personally guilty of both.) The following chart lists some common things to look out for when the camera is rolling and gives some practical solutions for keeping your interview looking and sounding tight.

HAZARD	POSSIBLE PROBLEMS	SOLUTIONS
Shifting or Animated Subject	■ Subject shifts position causing focus to go soft or throwing off the framing ■ Subjects moves out of light	■ Instruct subject to limit movement ■ Signal cameraperson to watch focus ■ Loosen tripod pan and tilt and "roam" with subject ■ Readjust framing or lights to cover movement
Boom	■ The boom drifts into the shot or casts a shadow	■ Signal boom operator ■ Tighten frame
Loose Tripod	■ A loose tripod allows the camera to slowly tilt up or down	■ Signal cameraperson to readjust shot ■ Lock down tripod
Hitting Mic	■ Subject repeatedly gestures or scratches causing clothing noise on the lav mic	■ Instruct subject to be mindful of mic ■ Move lav mic to better position ■ Use boom instead of lav
Location Noise	■ Refrigerators, A.C. units ■ Traffic, planes, subway ■ Noisy neighbors, pets	■ See "Location Sound Hazards" on page 210
Reflections	■ Subject shifts causing an unwanted reflection on glasses ■ Picture frames on wall ■ Lighting is adjusted causing an unwanted reflection	■ Use polarizer filter on camera ■ Tilt glasses down by raising slightly above ears ■ Adjust angle of frame ■ Tape a small wad of paper behind frames hanging on a wall ■ Adjust angle of lights

5 WAYS TO DO A REMOTE INTERVIEW

A common scenario that many of you may encounter is that you want to interview someone who is in a completely different state or part of the world than you and your budget or time constraints won't allow you to travel there to shoot them. What's a Down and Dirty doc maker to do? Give up? Move on? Pick another subject? Not in my book! It's just another obstacle to be overcome with imagination, creativity and technology. Here are five ways you can capture an interview with a subject whether they are in the next city, country, or continent on the cheap . . .

1 SCREEN CAPTURE A VIDEO CHAT

I think the best option for remote interviews is to set up a video chat with your subject using any of the popular video chat programs and services such as Skype or FaceTime. This is pretty much the poor man's equivalent of a doing a satellite TV interview. In fact, it's pretty common nowadays to turn on your TV and see the cable news networks using this very simple and low-budget method themselves.

In most cases, these video conferencing programs are free to use and all you need is a free account and an internet connection. Keep in mind that the quality of the video is largely dependent on the quality of the connection—on both ends. In general these chat programs have decent, but not great video quality. Audiences have become accustomed to the lower quality of internet streaming interviews since they've become popular in the mainstream news media. However, one thing I've discovered is that if you're willing to shell out a little extra money to use a business video conferencing service like **GoToMeeting.com**, the video and audio quality is noticeably better and smoother.

So that's how you set up a remote interview itself, but how do you record it to video? There are just as many choices to capture the video as there are to do a video conference, so I'll cover a few of the most popular ones:

Snapz Pro (for MAC)

Snagit (PC/MAC)

A video/audio/stills capture program for Mac that allows you to capture and crop anything on your screen—including otherwise hard-to-capture flash videos. (Approx. $70.00)

Snagit is more or less the PC crowd's equivalent of Snapz Pro. Both programs have similar features. (approx. $50.00)

If a $50–$70 professional screen capture is still too tight for your budget, Mac users have another free screen capture option—**Quicktime Player**—which comes pre-installed on any Mac computer. Go to **File—New Screen Recording** and press the record button and you're off and running.

There are two big compromises with this low-budget method. The first is that Quicktime only records the video, *not the audio* playing from your computer, so you'll have to capture that separately and then sync them up in post production. And the second compromise is that Quicktime records the whole computer screen—menus cursor and all—not just a movie playing in a window, so you'll also have to crop the video in post. So Quicktime screen capture is definitely a case where you get what you pay for. (Not worth the extra hassle compared to the professional screen capture programs in my opinion, but I like to give you multiple creative options for any budget.)

2 DOWN AND DIRTY VIDEO

Software and screen capture add more expense and a few more steps to the process, so another way to capture a remote interview and keep it simple is to just shoot *the computer screen* itself as you conduct an video interview via Skype. Now just shooting the computer screen directly in a close up will work, but it will look a little janky. However, with just a little more forethought and art direction, you could compose a shot with some nice lighting and set dressing to help *visually* tell your story. Interviewing a nuclear scientist in Japan? How about a colorful little model of a molecule sitting next to the computer screen? A stack of science textbooks on the left? A diagram of a nuclear reactor lit and just out of focus on the wall in the background?

. . . Just because you're shooting an image on a computer screen doesn't mean it *has to* look whack. It doesn't take money or fancy equipment to make it look hot—it takes imagination and creativity. It's the most powerful free tool you have, but you have to take the extra time to *apply it* in every Down and Dirty production endeavor if you want to get production value on the cheap.

3 RECORD AUDIO ONLY

If recording video of the interview is not technically or practically feasible, then audio alone may suffice. There are also a variety of free and paid audio-only capture programs out there that work similar to the video/audio capture programs I mentioned above. Beyond the computer, there are also a variety of smartphone apps that you can use to record phone calls. **Google Voice** is a popular free service/app that allows Google account holders to record *incoming* calls only. However, some other phone apps let you record outgoing calls as well. In the case of audio-only interviews, you might consider editing the audio in your final project with a nice headshot or series of photos of the interviewee, B-Roll of specific subject matter at hand, an artsy topic-appropriate **montage** or any combination of these different techniques to keep things visually interesting.

4 RECORD AND TRANSCRIBE

Similarly, there are also online transcription services like **Speechpad.com** that will give you a 3-for-1 bang for your buck in that their Record-A-Call option allows you to: 1) make a phone call via your computer 2) Record the audio of that phone call and 3) Get a transcription of the full conversation. So that's pretty convenient one stop shopping for a remote audio-only interview. Speechpad.com is just the one I know, but there are also plenty of others out there if you do a little homework.

5 DOWN AND DIRTY AUDIO

Lastly, I know sometimes you just gotta keep it grimy and get what you can get, so at the very bottom of the remote interview list is the very simple option of just recording an online video or audio chat directly from a speaker phone or your computer's speakers. You can use a professional microphone hooked directly to your camera or even more grimy, you can just record the audio directly into an iPhone or iPad. I say grimy, because it seems so low-budget and cheesy, but in actuality the iPhones of the last several years record pretty high quality audio via the built in mic and audio recording program. I've recorded many remote audio interviews for my **Double Down Film Show** podcast this way and most of them sound pretty decent and many sound good.

So if you want to go this route of just recording directly from speakers playing the audio, you can try several different configurations. I highly recommend doing a test recording or two first to figure out the proper levels and distance to place the mic for best results. Otherwise, you may end up with 45 minutes of useless overmodulated audio.

Before You Call a "Wrap"

The wrap out is the last step of production where you pack up everything and tie up any loose ends. Before you officially instruct your crew to wrap, you want to make sure that you got all the coverage that you'll need to edit. Do you need any reaction shots? How about an establishing shot of the location? Did something come up in the interview that suggests a cutaway or B-roll shot? Check your shot

list and notes, then take a moment to think it through before you give the okay to wrap.

Thank Everyone . . . Profusely

Once you're confident you've got everything, profusely thank your subject for the interview. Subjects always want to know when a piece will be finished or broadcasted and when and how they will get to see the final project. You should have these answers at the ready for them. If they don't already have one, you should leave them your card or contact info. If you're produce a regular show or podcast, a classy move would be to create a simple business card with the dates and times the program will air in addition to your contact info. (This will save you from having to keep repeating the same info for every interviewee, especially for "man-on-the-street" segments.)

Equally important, don't forget to thank your crew, especially if they're working for free or dirt cheap. (Within a few days after you wrap on a big project, you should also send your crew a small gift, gift certificate, or at a minimum a simple thank you card.) You'd be surprised how much a sincere and heartfelt thanks can mean to crew members who are often ignored once a project wraps. If people went above and beyond the call of duty, let them know how much you appreciated their help. You'll want to keep them on file for your next shoot. (You do plan on shooting another project, don't you?) Lastly, thank your location owner, again, profusely, for helping you make your film. Here's another golden tidbit: Two of the most powerful phrases you can ever use on-set are "please" and "thank you."

> ✔ *Make sure you have all your shots before you call a wrap.*

Packing Up

Make sure your crew is careful and pays attention to details as they pack up. This is one of those times where novice filmmakers let their guard down, because they're exhausted and ecstatic that they pulled off the shoot. Everyone starts patting each other on the back and haphazardly rushes gear into the car, meanwhile some vital piece of equipment is left behind or the location is left in much worse condition than they found it.

The pros know that the shoot is *almost* done after the last shot, but it ain't done yet. You still have to account for and pack all of your equipment and restore the location to the same or better condition than you entered it. Always check your packed equipment against your original inventory list. Be extra careful removing tape and place all furniture and props back where you found them. (If you took pictures or notes before you started, this will be easy.)

> ✔ *Always leave your location in the same or better condition than you found it.*

CHAPTER 9
POST-PRODUCTION

"The higher the goal, the harder the climb,
But after that the bigger the muscle, the smarter the mind."
                                        —*Big Sean, "First Chain"*

THE POST-PRODUCTION PROCESS

Basic Elements of Post-Production

1. Viewing footage and taking notes
2. Logging footage and making transcripts
3. Paper outline and/or edit
4. Rough cut
5. Archival and stock footage
6. Animation and artwork
7. Narration
8. Revised Cuts
9. Music
10. Titles

It's All About Post

How do you know when you're done shooting a doc? This is always a tricky question. The practical answer could depend on your budget, your visa status, your production deadline or, more hopefully, on your story. But at some point, whether by choice or force, you must call an end to production and begin to lay out your story through the process of editing. This is where your project comes together or falls apart. The essence of documentary storytelling ultimately comes down to not so much how a story was shot, but rather how that footage is selected, edited, and treated during post-production.

Given the same 40 hours of raw-footage, any three directors would likely come up with three very different stories if faced with the task of creating a 90-minute film. A great micro-illustration of this concept is the phenomenon of online video "mash-ups" found like those on YouTube.com where the same raw footage is edited by different people to show multiple meanings and levels of artistry (and idiocy) depending on the editor and their intent. Post-production or editing is the greatest responsibility of the documentary process. It's the final phase where emphasis, meaning, mood, context, structure, and story are all assigned to your footage. It's the final phase where *your footage* is transformed into *your film*.

> ✔ *Editing is the greatest responsibility of the documentary. It's the phase when "your footage" becomes "your film."*

Viewing All Your Footage

Even if you've been viewing **dailies** as you go, you should still sit down once more after the dust clears from shooting to view all of your footage at one time. If you have a lot of footage, you'll want to schedule several sessions of 3 to 4 hours. Anything over that and your eyes start to glaze over. You may or may not want to have your editor or crew with you for this very first full viewing, but they should each be invited to view the raw footage at some point shortly after shooting. Zap some popcorn, dim the lights, and see what you've created. This is the moment of truth.

The treatment you wrote up is now irrelevant. Put it in your scrapbook. The film you wanted to make, planned to make, or thought you were making no longer matters—fugeddaboutit! What you watch now is the film you actually *made*. And it's all you've got to work with, baby. Now it's all about evaluating what you can do with it. The goal is to use your footage to create a compelling, dramatic, interesting, edge-of-your-seat, tear-jerking, awe-inspiring, and insightful documentary (or, at the very least, a coherent story).

> ✔ The film you wanted to make no longer matters. What you watch now is the film you actually made.

Taking Notes

First impressions count. Record your gut reactions to the footage as you view it. It's a good idea to speak your notes into a voice recorder, or have someone else take notes as you say them, so you don't miss some golden subtle moment onscreen. Note anything that makes you laugh, cry, smirk or otherwise draws an immediate emotional reaction. If something about a scene bugs you, write that down too. Your first impressions will often match those of your audience. Don't censor yourself or think too hard about it. Just note all your first impressions on the spot. You can mull them over later.

If watching with others, also note *their* first reactions and comments—the good, bad, and ugly. Also note favorite sound bites and any creative ideas you have for editing, music, or narration. Later, all these notes will help you make crucial decisions and refocus when you've lost perspective from days or weeks of staring at the same footage.

> ✔ First impressions count. Record your gut reactions to your footage when you view it all for the first time.

Why We Log

One of the most daunting tasks in documentary is **logging** and transcribing footage. Once you have somehow survived production and captured those magical moments on video, you will be left with a feeling of great satisfaction as you lovingly pet your pile of master video tapes (or P2 cards, or hard drives, etc.). That feeling will last for about two minutes until you realize that you have no idea exactly where those magical scenes are. It's time to go through each minute of footage and take notes as to what topics are covered, which shots are best, and most important, the exact tape (or folder) and time code of these scenes.

If you don't have a time code reference for each shot, you'll waste countless hours of post-production fast-forwarding and rewinding trying to find the specific shots and sound bites you need, because so much of what you shoot will likely be interviews and dialogue that have no visual cues as to what is actually being said.

Logging tapes isn't daunting because it's hard to do. It's daunting because it can be tedious and time-consuming, especially when you put it all off until the very end of shooting. The best way to avoid logging fatigue is to *log your footage as you go* and spread the task out into manageable sessions. It's also common for filmmakers to hand off their media to an editor, assistant, or intern who can begin logging while the project is still shooting. However, even if you farm it out to someone else, it's still wise to log the most crucial tapes yourself. Logging is the perfect opportunity to become more familiar with your footage before making countless editing decisions.

Organizing Your Shots

Label and organize your footage in a way that helps you begin to form a story. There are no strict rules here. Just find a way that works for you and your editor. Here are some suggestions.

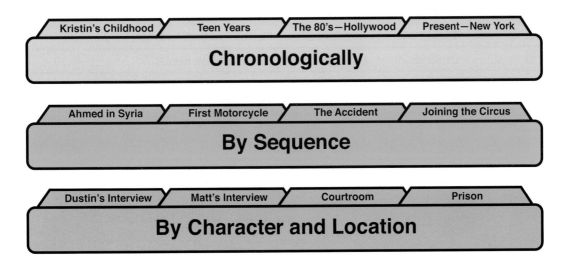

| Kristin's Childhood | Teen Years | The 80's—Hollywood | Present—New York |

Chronologically

| Ahmed in Syria | First Motorcycle | The Accident | Joining the Circus |

By Sequence

| Dustin's Interview | Matt's Interview | Courtroom | Prison |

By Character and Location

Logging Directly in Your NLE

Most editing programs have a logging feature that allows you to set the in and out points and type in a description. These programs automatically record the timecode and calculate the run time of each clip and let you to export your completed log as a sharable document.

Scene Detect

If you have a bunch of really long clips, the "scene detect" or "scene change detect" feature in some popular post software, such as **Adobe Premiere** and **DaVinci Resolve** will go through your footage as you import it and everywhere that it optically detects a new shot it will mark it and give you the option to divide the footage into subclips, even if you have an hour long clip. If your NLE doesn't have a scene detect feature built-in, there are also some stand-alone scene detect programs like **Scene Detector**, that can do the job as well.

Learning to "Log In Camera"

The easiest and smartest thing you can do to make logging easier is to always shoot with the tedious task of post-production in mind. Adopting the habit of regularly stopping the camera between takes or a series of shots will make life considerably easier when it comes time to locate your footage later. While it's often more convenient to shoot a lot of footage in really long clips without ever stopping the camera, it could make for more hassle and time in post than it saves you on set.

The Log Sheet

If you are working offline or just like to do it old-school, you can also easily whip up your own manual log sheet in MS Word, Excel or Pages. (You can download a blank log sheet on the bonus website for this book.) Your log sheet should include all the information listed below. You could also add two columns to take notes about the quality of audio and video for each shot or write down story ideas.

TAPE #	TC IN	TC OUT	COMMENT	RUN TIME
1	01:53:10:02	01:56:40:07	Pit crew meeting (noisy take)	3:30
1	01:58:35:20	01:58:54:10	Dale putting on helmet	0:19
2A	02:01:20:24	02:14:26:09	Dale's test laps (great shots)	13:06

| Starting time code | Ending time code | Description of shot and commentary | Total screen time in minutes and seconds |

Getting a Grip on Your Doc

As we've already discussed, one of the biggest challenges to shooting documentary and reality-based projects is capturing engaging content on video and shooting it in a way that's also *visually* interesting and complimentary. However, the other big challenge you'll soon discover is figuring out how to sort through all that material. Even with a short documentary project incorporating interviews, it's not at all unusual to end up with 3–20 hours of raw material. And if you're making a full-length documentary or TV program, you could easily have five to ten times that amount of material to sift through.

Anthony: And you, Rose? Why make a documentary?

00:48:53:24

Rose: I did both, and I prefer documentaries. I like them very much, and they're very, very different than working on doing features. I mean, I'd like the money for sure, and a bit of that celebrity ??? and glamour. But um, I was out in L.A. and you know, I mean I like it, but I really love making documentaries. I love struggling with footage, I love doing pro-social things, saying something important. I think more people need to do that, I think. You know, but I'm afraid that it's an art that may be dying slowly. It needs to be resuscitated.

Anthony: What are your most important skills as documentary filmmakers?...

Rose: I need to get the concept. I need to know, what is this about? Because when I know what it is about, I know how to do it. I know how to shape it. I know what should be in and what should be out. I know, I can select stuff, you know. I'm an editor, but I also, just need to know this is what it is about. Now it could be about a lot of things, but what's the big umbrella, and what's my point of view on it? I absolutely have to know that, and until I know that, I can't make choices that that don't have to get undone and redone. The more I know, the more I can immediately go to how I want to do it and how it should look and what's the right way to shoot it and who should be in it, all those kinds of things. And that, you know I want so much to know as soon as I can know it, and until I know it, I feel very lost in the desert. And once I have that "ah ha" moment, I'm a very happy camper.

00:51:46:10

Marion: Uh, I have to know whether, I have to be able to intuitively get the story. So, by intuitively, without a whole lot of thinking, presented with a set of facts, I can put them together in a way that I can imagine a story. Even if it hasn't happened, I can imagine what could happen from what I know. And then once I know something could happen that's interesting, then I've got it.

Anthony: Do you think that documentary can change the world?

Marion: No, I don't. I think um...

Rose: Well, um you know, *Supersize Me* changed the world a bit. *Fahrenheit 911* changed the world a bit. So and *An Inconvenient Truth* is changing the world a little bit. So actually, I think that it can change it a little bit, or it can reflect the zeitgeist, you know. So it comes at a time, it's it's an accident how it can happen cause there are a lot of good documentaries that get made that don't get out there quite the same way. There are so many things that go into it. The machine behind you, the time, you know, what's going on in the culture, whether you hit it right. This is all very ???. There's a lot of luck going into this thing, a lot of luck. Hard work, and luck.

Transcripts are the "road maps" to your raw material.

I mentioned the value of viewing your raw material and taking extensive notes to help you find the story. This is easy to do for a project with a single interview or two, but you'll probably still find it overwhelming to get any real handle on the full project and how to structure your story from just a list of notes. But, an easier and much more efficient way to tackle a large block of interview material, especially if you have a tight deadline, is to get written **transcripts** of all your interviews, then use those transcripts to quickly identify soundbites and make a "paper edit", which is exactly like it sounds—a written lay out of the soundbites and shots in order as they will appear onscreen. Transcripts are definitely one of those professional filmmaking conventions that if you've been working on doc and corporate projects and never had one made before, the first time you do you'll wonder how you ever edited doc footage without transcripts.

A simple edit log and notes are sufficient for many small and simple projects. However, feature-length docs, reality TV, and other large projects will call for full transcripts that contain every word said, who said it, and the timecode at which it was said. Making a transcript is the single easiest way to put together a final script and get a handle on your exact contents. You will be able to easily cut and paste sound bites into a paper edit and experiment with your story and structure.

In addition to helping you piece together a final script, a transcript of your interviews will make sure that you have not misrepresented what a subject said by editing it out of context. When you're pulling sound bites from interviews and juxtaposing them with other material, it's easy to inadvertently apply a different meaning than the one originally intended by the subject. Similarly, if you have everything down on paper, it'll be much easier to check the accuracy of the narration, statements made by subjects, and implied conclusions. So transcripts are also invaluable for fact-checking your final piece. If a company is interested in distributing your doc theatrically or on TV, they will almost always require a transcript of your finished project.

There are two ways to go about getting transcripts: the hard way and the easy way. The hard way is to put on a pair of headphones and just play, listen, rewind and type your way through each interview until you have every word spoken typed up. The obvious drawback with making your own transcript is that it's incredibly tedious if you aren't already a fast typist. So that's the downside. However, on the flip side–doing your own transcripts does have two big advantages: #1–you will be intimately familiar with the content of an interview by the time you complete the transcript yourself and #2–it costs you no money.

> ✔ **One of your biggest challenges is sorting through all your footage. Transcripts are incredibly useful to help find your story.**

Getting Transcripts Made

Of course, the easiest way to get a transcript is to pay a professional transcription service to give you a fully-typed printout and/or file of the contents and time code of each and every interview. The advantage of this route is that it saves time and energy. The only disadvantage is the cost.

Transcription rates vary widely by provider, quality, and level of detail offered, so shop and ask around, but you should expect to pay at least $1.00–$2.00 per minute for a transcript in most US markets. Prices will vary by how soon you need it turned

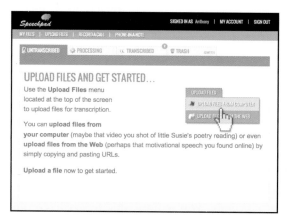

Speechpad.com is a popular web-based transcription service.

around and how detailed and accurate it needs to be—for example if you want the transcriber to include every "um", "ah" and background noise, it will take longer and cost you more. One important addition you want to ask for—is that the transcriber mark the time code or at least the run time 2–3 times on each page of the transcript. This may cost you a little extra, but will make the transcript *much* easier to use for editing purposes later. Of course, if you're trying to save every penny, you can always add timecode in yourself later, just make sure you get it in there one way or another.

In order to have a transcript made by a service, you are going to need to give them a video or audio copy of your interview. The easiest way is to use a file transfer service like **DropBox.com** or **WeTransfer.com** and upload a digital media file. Even more convenient, many transcript services, like **Speechpad.com**, now have interfaces that let you upload your files directly to their website. I recommend that you export and send just an audio file whenever practical, because it's a smaller file to manage and you want to keep tight control over your raw footage.

However, sometimes you'll need to send someone copies of your raw footage so they can also provide you with visual descriptions of the action or just better tell who's speaking. Whenever you do send a video file for transcription, I *highly recommend* that you only export a low resolution video with the time code burned in. This will make it much easier for the transcriber to note the exact time code at various points in the video. And a **timecode burn** will also make the footage undesirable should anyone come across your footage and decide they want to use it in a cheesy YouTube video.

Always burn-in timecode on raw footage submitted for transcription.

Anatomy of a Documentary Transcript

There are slight variations on how documentary transcripts are formatted, so let's take a look at the main things we'll want to make sure we've got on the page ...

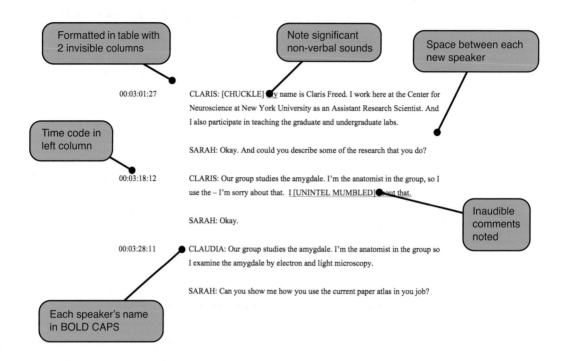

What Transcripts Do and Don't Tell You

Transcripts make it very easy to get a handle on the exact content you've shot. They serve as an accurate road map to easily locate, label, and arrange (and re-arrange) your footage in a precise and logical manner. They make it very easy to cut and paste and "edit" your material on paper before editing it on video. However, it's very important to remember that how something **reads** on paper can still be very different than how it actually **plays** on video, so you still have to actually watch and study your raw footage before you can make any final decisions. Peep the chart below for some examples of what transcripts do and don't tell you about your material.

WHAT TRANSCRIPTS CAN TELL YOU	WHAT TRANSCRIPTS CAN'T TELL YOU
■ Exact questions asked	■ Speaker's body language
■ Who was speaking	■ Energy level
■ Approximate length of comment	■ Awkward delivery
■ Exact timing/location of comment	■ Humorous vs. serious comments
■ General visual descriptions	■ Expressive or distracting gestures
	■ Bad focus or other visual issues
	■ Background noises

Step 1 — Read, Highlight and Subtitle

Read through the transcript and highlight all the best comments that stand out to you. Of course, which are "the best" comments is highly subjective and will vary from project to project–depending on the overall goal, the story you want to tell, and the new stories and themes you discover as you read through.

As you highlight comments, use *a different color for each speaker*, so later when you begin to cut, paste and re-arrange passages of text, you will get a quick and easy *visual* reference of who's speaking and for how long without having to read the name of each speaker.

Apart from highlighting as you read, I suggest also inserting bold subtitles at the top of each highlighted section. Titles such as "On Growing Up in Baltimore", "The First Day of Film School", "January 1969", etc. These subtitles will make it much easier to scan your transcript, locate footage and begin to group your comments by topic, theme, or chronology. These initial subtitles and groupings easily translate into editing bins in an NLE as you experiment with story and structure.

Note Comments That Are:

❏ **relevant to your story**
❏ **reveal new information**
❏ **concise and to the point**
❏ **well-said, poetic or just deep**
❏ **humorous**

Step 2 — Bold the Best of the Best

Okay, you've gone through the whole transcript and highlighted all the best comments, but chances are you've still highlighted way more material than you want to include even for a first rough cut of a scene.

Go through just the highlighted comments once again with an even more critical eye. This time bold only the very strongest and most concise comments within your highlighted material. Look for the one or two *sentences* that more succinctly sum up the entire *paragraph* that you've highlighted. (Yes, I'm essentially telling you to highlight the highlights!)

Example:

> Shemise: **My junior year was really good.** It was kind of split between fall and the spring. My fall semester, I think was the better semester. **I just gained a lot more focus about what I wanted to do. I took intermediate experimental sound mixing, and I was learning about Celtic music, and so that was all kind of pointing me in the direction of where I want to go, which is making musicals, and working with bands, and things like that.** So, the fall semester I really grew a lot as an artist, and just figuring out what I wanted to do.
>
> And then, the spring semester I had a lot more going on outside of school, so it was more like figuring out that balance between classes, and life and getting a job, and things like that. And I also started dancing, myself, which I don't **the Open Arts curriculum was really good. It's like we can take classes within film, but also classes in other art forms, so it allowed me to take special effects makeup and**

Step 3 — Cut and Paste into Paper Edit

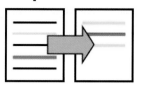

Now create a new document. This will be your paper edit. First copy and paste only the Subtitles you just inserted into the transcript. (At this phase we're starting to move things around a lot more and play with structure, so the subtitles make it super easy to see the order and relative length of time that we're devoting to each subject.)

Next, arrange the subtitles on the page in the logical order you think they should be presented and number each one. Viola! Without even thinking about it, you've got yourself a rudimentary outline of your scene or short project. This basic outline is the backbone that will form your project's structure.

Now you're ready to start copying and pasting the appropriate bolded comments under each subtitle. Choose wisely. Even at this stage, I think it's good to be fearless and only include the very best material that makes the very strongest points you want to make. There will be plenty of interesting side comments and humorous lines, but we only want to include the most interesting, to-the-point and concise comments.

Another advantage of this method of creating a paper edit is that you will have a quick color-coded visual reference as to how much screen time each person will be featured for. Screen time will vary from speaker to speaker, but a good general approximation is to count on 2–4 minutes of screen time per page of comments.

Step 4 — Pull the Selects

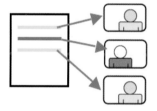

Now that we've selected all the strongest material, we're ready to locate those clips and put them into edit bins for easy assembly. If your transcript has notations for timecode, this process should be fairly quick. Create edit bins that correspond to each of the subtitles you created earlier and put the appropriate bolded and highlighted clips into each bin.

Step 5 — Rough Cut and Revise

Now you're ready to make an assembly edit. Using the paper edit as your guide, lay the clips out on the timeline in order. Watch the scene or short project several times through. You should read along from your paper edit to see if things actually sound and play onscreen the way you thought they would on paper. There are sure to be a few instances where they didn't. Words that read clearly on paper may actually be delivered poorly. There could also be technical issues such as background noise or a camera adjustment that make a comment less desirable. On the flip side, some things that may read as ungrammatical or non-sensical on paper, may be perfectly clear in the context of their delivery by a particular character in your story. For example, "Fo' shizzle, my nizzle!", makes no sense at all on paper, but when we hear Snoop Doggy Dog actually *say* it, his demeanor tone and facial expression make it understood that he simply means, "Yes, I like that, my good friend."

Decision-making in Editing

At its core the editing process is simply a very long list of decisions. Decision-making in the editing process can be motivated by all kinds of things from the technical, to the story-driven, to the practical. I think the process is best defined by asking yourself an interwoven series of questions about the information, story, and characters being presented onscreen. Questions such as these...

Questions to Ask When Refining an Edit

1. Has the same point already been made by someone else in your project? If so—from a *story perspective*—which subject is the best character to deliver this particular bit of info for your project?

2. Do you really need every sentence you have selected in the passage to make the point? Could you chop off the front or end of the sentence, or perhaps a phrase in the middle and would the point still make sense and come across?

3. Does the comment make sense in context? Or do we need another piece of information or specific visual to understand it?

4. What else might better help the audience to understand this particular comment—A graphic? Subtitle? Comment from another character? Animation?

5. Do you already have the visuals you need to clearly illustrate, show, or support the commentary at hand? If not, can you get archival or stock footage, shoot something else, use a still photo, magazine, or newspaper headline?

6. Have you arranged the selected comments in the most logical order to communicate the scene at hand? Have you inadvertently arranged things in a way that actually presents some comments out of context?

Computer

For video editing, the general rule about computer purchases applies—you ideally want to have the fastest most recent computer that you can afford. Apart from a fast processing chip, you want a computer with as much RAM (random access memory) as you can get. If you have an older computer or if your current machine is not already maxed out, adding the maximum RAM is pretty affordable and you can often do it yourself on many machines. The other thing you want in an editing machine (i.e. computer) is a good fast graphics card to ensure smooth and fast video playback and rendering during editing. You should store your video projects and raw footage on an external drive anyway, so hard drive space isn't as big a factor. You just need a computer with enough hard drive space to hold all your programs and non-video data. Many of today's laptops are more than capable of handling routine video editing duties.

The more RAM (random access memory) and the faster your graphics card the better for editing.

Hard Drives

When it comes to hard drives you're probably also best off getting the largest capacity external hard drive that's within your budget. The reason I say the biggest is because depending on which camera and codec you're shooting on, HD digital data eats up **a lot** of space. The higher quality the format, the more space it will eat up. Specifically, if you're shooting an uncompressed format like RAW or anything shot in 2K or 4K resolution it's going to take up an insane amount of hard drive space, so make sure you do the math to calculate how much footage you'll need to store. No worries, there are plenty of apps and sites that will help you do the HD math such as **videospaceonline.com**.

It's also important to make sure that any hard drive you get not only has the proper port to connect to your computer, but also has connections that are compatible with any other hard drives that you may wish to daisy-chain together as well as the fastest and most recent types of connection such as E-Sata and Thunderbolt. Even though your current computer may not have a Thunderbolt connection, your editor, colorist, or sound mixer's computer, or the next computer you get *may* have one. It's never bad to buy

Thunderbolt and USB 3.0 are fast superior connections for editing.

hardware that's future-ready with the latest connection ports. (See my "Cable Guide" on page 211 for a list of different types of ports to consider.)

People often ask me what are the most reliable *brands* of hard drives they should get—*Lacie, G-Tech, Maxtor,* etc.? I don't have a reassuring answer, because for every single brand that one trusted and knowledgeable filmmaker I've consulted told me was "great" and "all they ever use" another trusted and knowledgeable filmmaker told me that very same brand of hard drive "sucks" and they'd "never use it again" . . . What's up with *that?!*

Here's the deal, from my observation: it's all based on personal bad experience. Whatever brand of hard drive fails on *you* is likely to be deemed "sucky for life". I say use whatever seems to work for most of your friends or stick to the brands with the best customer reviews on film vendor websites. All hard disks, especially those with moving parts—can and do sometimes break down. As the saying goes—*It just be's like that sometimes, homie.* The main thing you can do to protect yourself against catastrophic data loss is to always always always back up your video footage and projects on two different physical drives or alternatively you can use a special type of multi-disk drive called a RAID drive—which does just that.

RAID Drives

One type of storage system you may wish to consider is a RAID drive that actually has two or more hard drives in it. A RAID drive can have one of two big advantages for editing depending on which one of several possible configurations you choose when you first set it up:

1. **It can store data twice as fast by splitting the pipeline of data between multiple hard drives or**

2. **It can function as a dual drive and make multiple copies of all files *simultaneously*—one on each hard drive.**

And another benefit of many models of RAID drives is that the two different drives themselves are often in swappable "cartridges", so when they fill up or when you switch projects, you can just switch out the modular drives and not have to purchase a whole new RAID drive. Although the RAID drives and docks are more costly, these individual removable hard drive "cartridges" are generally less expensive than regular hard drives.

Monitor

Any size monitor will work for editing—even a little laptop screen—but the bigger and more resolution the monitor has the better now that we are in an HD/2K/4K world. It's preferable to see your image as close to the audience experience as possible. Since I am an admitted Apple enthusiast, my personal preference is a super-sharp 21" (or larger) Apple retina display monitor—available as a stand-alone monitor for any system or built into the iMac machines.

When it comes to monitors, the bigger the better and two is always better than one.

And not only is bigger better in this case, but it's also preferable to have two monitors instead of just one when possible. And if you can get two really big monitors with a super-sharp retina-display, you're really balling! The big advantage and convenience of having two monitors is that you can set-up your display system to treat them as one big desktop, so you'll now have twice as much screen real estate and can seamlessly glide your cursor from monitor to the next. Because you often have multiple windows open when you edit—edit bin, timeline, preview window, playback window, graphic programs, email, web browser, etc.—having double the screen real estate saves you a lot of time clicking and moving windows around and makes it easier to see and jump back and forth between all the windows that you need to access.

Keyboard Overlays

Using drop down menus is slow and the preferred method—*for amateurs*. If you want to become fast and efficient in the edit room, you've gotta do what the pros do and use keyboard shortcuts instead. So another item you may wish to add to your set-up once you have all the basics, is a keyboard overlay for your particular edit system. Whether you're cutting on AVID, Premiere, FCP X, or something else, there's probably a little rubber keyboard overlay or special keyboard you can purchase that shows you all the editing keyboard short cuts with color-coded keys and symbols for common functions like setting in and out points, fast-forward, stop, etc.

Keyboard overlays are great "cheat sheets" that can help you better learn and speed up the editing process.

WORKING WITH EDITORS

SAM POLLARD, PRODUCER/EDITOR

(4 Little Girls, Jim Brown All-American, Eyes on the Prize II, When the Levees Broke)

You know, I was very fortunate with Victor Kanefsky [Sam's Mentor]. What Victor Kanefsky taught me from the very beginning as a young editor, young assistant, young apprentice, was that part of my responsibility as an editor was to have no preconceived notions about the material that a director or producer brings to you. Well I wasn't looking for it to be perfectly shot or every camera angle to be perfectly right, what he or she brought to me as producers was material that said here's material with realms of possibility.

Some producers will come in and say, "Here's material with realms of possibility and here's an outline to help you understand how I think the film should go together."

Then there are some producers who will come in and say, "Here's material with realms of possibility, here's a script—a really thought out script—of how I think the film should come together."

Then there are some producers who come in and say, "Here's material with realms of possibilities, but to tell you the truth Sam, I don't have a clue how to put the damn thing together, I need your help."

Personally for me, because of the way I was taught by Victor, my ego prefers the third. I say, "Oh, now I can show you what I can do." But I'm open to work any way a producer wants to work. Part of my job is . . . to excavate from that material and find again, that word . . . the *story*.

This is perhaps the single most important decision you will make on your doc. Think it over long and hard, because the essence of documentary is *editing*. This is where the story is actually told. Up until this point, you've only got a collection of pretty pictures and talking heads. How you juxtapose that material, what info you leave out, what shots and comments you put in, the music you use, the prevailing viewpoints, pacing, all of these things are decided in editing and will make or break your story in the end. This isn't a decision to be taken lightly.

You have three basic choices when it's time to edit your project: cut it yourself, work with a technical editor, or hand it off to a creative editor. Just like many choices in filmmaking, there aren't necessarily right or wrong decisions, simply choices that will or won't work best for your particular project, skill level, and/or resources. Here's my advice, pros and cons. Decide for yourself.

Cutting It Yourself

Pros:
- ❏ Work from comfort of home
- ❏ You know the footage better than anyone
- ❏ You can save money by not hiring an editor
- ❏ No pressure to finish
- ❏ You can edit anywhere on a laptop

Cons:
- ❏ Will take 2 to 10 times longer than a pro editor
- ❏ No second opinion on crucial decisions
- ❏ Need a good computer and large hard drive
- ❏ All the distractions of home
- ❏ Need at least average computer skills
- ❏ You may get stuck for months or never finish at all

Recommended Tools: Premiere, Avid or Final Cut Pro. (iMovie or Windows Media is ok for small projects.) Dedicated large-capacity hard drive.

Preparation: Learn the software, practice editing, write script/outline, organize, log, and digitize media.

Advice: This is a realistic option for those with previous editing experience. If you've never edited before in your life and have no formal training, it's a bad idea to *start* with a major project. Cut your teeth on some home movies or helping a friend edit their DV project. Keep your footage organized! Even if you edit yourself, regularly show segments to trusted colleagues and friends and get feedback. The best suggestions often come from the simplest of outside observations. It's common for new filmmakers to get frustrated editing their own work and let their project languish on a shelf for months or even years. There are probably hundreds of half-documentaries buried in closets around the world that will never see the light of day. If you get stuck, consult an experienced editor or filmmaker. Be honest with yourself if it's just not coming together and consider working with or handing your project over to someone with more experience.

Working Closely with a Technical Editor

Pros:

- ❏ Much faster than doing it yourself
- ❏ Provides a second opinion
- ❏ You can just think and be creative
- ❏ Companionship on those long editing shifts
- ❏ Editor can cut some sequences without you

Cons:

- ❏ Your editing sensibilities may clash
- ❏ Two people in a small room
- ❏ Will probably have to pay them
- ❏ Will probably travel to edit in *their* space

Best Person for the Job:

- ❏ An assistant editor
- ❏ An intermediate or advanced film student
- ❏ A bored corporate editor
- ❏ Professional editors with small egos

Recommended Tools: Final Cut Pro, Avid Xpress, Premiere with edit deck or camera.

Preparation: Write script/outline. Organize and log tapes. Meet to discuss edit style, influential films, and story beforehand.

Advice: You basically need someone who is technically proficient with one of the major DV editing programs such as Avid, Final Cut Pro, Liquid, Premiere, etc. You also want someone who understands your doc project and your goals. Make sure they understand that you're primarily looking for someone to do the "mechanical" edit work and that you'll be present for most sessions to direct most of the edits. You should still allow them some space to do their thing and offer advice. Nobody wants to be just a robot taking orders. Give them first crack at a few scenes. You may be pleasantly surprised. Many editors will hate to work this way, but some will love it because it's easy for them and they're getting paid. Also, make sure they are comfortable with your subject matter if it's controversial. And don't forget, you're going to be spending several long days, if not weeks or months, in a small room with this person. Personality and hygiene definitely count.

Handing It Off to a Creative Editor

Pros:

❏ A good editor will take the ball and run
❏ Pros work much faster than amateurs
❏ Can easily analyze and solve edit problems
❏ More familiar with broadcast standards
❏ Access to high-end systems
❏ Access to more post-production tools
❏ May work wonders with mediocre material

Cons:

❏ You're a control freak and it kills you to hand over your project
❏ Good editors usually cost good money
❏ Editor may be making a very different film
❏ You may have different editing sensibilities

Best Person for Job:

❏ An experienced editor
❏ Someone who fully understands your project goals
❏ Someone with new ideas about presenting the material
❏ Someone with a demo reel that kicks butt
❏ Someone who cut a film/video that you liked
❏ Someone whose creative judgment you trust
❏ An exceptional advanced film student

Preparation: Write script, outline, or detailed notes. Organize and log tapes. Meet to discuss edit style, influential films, and story beforehand.

Recommended Tools: High End Final Cut Pro or Avid System with Deck

Advice: Don't just look at reels, interview people, more than once if necessary. Look for an editor that's excited about the project and has creative ideas about how to communicate with the footage you've got. You want an editor with enthusiasm for the project who brings thoughtful debate and questions to the table. Be realistic and discuss deadlines and how often you'll meet to review sequences. Stay true to your vision, but give them some room to experiment and run with it and bring new storytelling ideas. That's what the best editors do—take your vision, in whatever state it's in, and make it *better*. If it's whack to begin with, they can make it okay. If it's okay to begin with, they can make it good. And if it's already good, they can really make it great!

WORKING WITH AN EDITOR...
REMOTELY

MIKE ATTIE & MEGHAN O'HARA, CO-DIRECTORS

incountryfilm.com

(*In Country*, a documentary film about Vietnam War re-enactors)

Meghan: We knew we were going to need an outside voice once we got to structuring it and making a story out of it and having to make those hard choices about who is an important character, who has a story, who is going to be cut. We knew we wanted someone else. We pretty much finished everything we could think to shoot and logged it all ourselves in Final Cut and then we did a Kickstarter in the fall and raised about $26,500.

One of the things that's very contemporary about our process, that a lot of old school documentary people can't imagine is that we're in three different cities. Our Editor, Lindsay Utz, is in Chicago. I'm in San Francisco and Mike's in Seattle.

When we started out we had logged everything and I think it's very important that we had seen every frame of our film. We knew it very well before we handed it off to the editor.

We sat with her for five days and basically gave her a tour of the footage. We told her who the people were, showed her about 12 scenes we had rough cut the summer before just to see if they were scenes, if there was anything there.

Mike: Each one of us has a duplicate drive of the entire project so we have three 4 TB drives because I'm in Seattle, Meghan's in San Francisco, and Lindsey's in Chicago.

With that drive, she can just share the project file with us over Dropbox. It's about 100 MB, it's not huge. This way we can always see where she is or she can share something with us at any given moment without even really outputting it. So it's pretty good.

We want to give her her space, but we also recognize that we need to find other times when we can work together. We did do a ten-day intensive session in San Francisco where she had basically gone through and pulled out her selects and cut down little scenes.

She had done an amazing amount of work and then she said, "Let's start putting this together. Let's start moving the pieces around and see where the film is." That's something that we would have to do together.

Once you've shot all your interviews, B-roll, and cutaways, you may find that you still have a number of visual "holes" in your story. That's where stock and archival footage can come in. This is essentially any media that wasn't originally shot for your documentary. It can be anything from relevant still photos from a local newspaper to clips of old movies that tie in to your topic. Here are just some examples commonly featured in docs.

Suggested Archival Footage

- ✔ **Childhood photos of subjects**
- ✔ **Photos of subjects family members**
- ✔ **Home movies**
- ✔ **Footage from other docs and movies**
- ✔ **Television news stories**
- ✔ **Newspaper Articles**
- ✔ **Government film/TV archives**
- ✔ **Historical paintings and illustrations**
- ✔ **Stills of relevant historical relics**
- ✔ **Digital maps and charts**

Any or all of these can be sources of compelling and illustrative visuals to help tell your story. The real question is where do you get them and how much do they cost? Like almost everything else in filmmaking the answer depends on where you look and who you deal with among other factors.

There are three main sources for stock footage: your subject(s), stock footage houses and many major cable and broadcast networks which license raw and finished footage from their own news and documentary programs. Some stock footage houses now offer all or part of their libraries online. Not only can you preview clips of their footage, you can actually purchase and download a broadcast-quality digital file and start editing—all without leaving your computer. Ask your subjects if they have any photos they will allow you to use. (You'll probably get better results if you wait later into shooting after you've built up a good level of trust with them.) Ideally you want them to give you shoeboxes and albums of photos. Handle these with care. If necessary, set up and shoot the photos at your subject's home so you never even have to take them. Another effective technique is to have your subject flip through photo albums and comment on relevant pictures. Similarly, yearbooks, scrapbooks, and old diaries may all help your subjects to tell their stories better—with greater recollection and visual detail.

7 COMMANDMENTS OF ARCHIVAL FOOTAGE

RICK PRELINGER

The last decade has been good to film archives and stock footage libraries. Increased interest in archive and library holdings has exposed many hidden treasures. At the same time, the artifacts have stimulated reexamination of this century's history and preconceptions. Some independent film and videomakers make good use of these resources, but many others are intimidated by high prices, arcane policies, and complex procedures. Here are a few navigational hints designed to demystify the process of locating and using archival footage.

Many difficulties producers encounter in trying to locate and use archival footage can be avoided through careful planning and a willingness to be flexible. When starting any project that may employ archival footage, it's imperative to obey seven basic commandments:

1 If the success or failure of the production depends on the inclusion of specific scenes or images, determine at the outset whether the images actually exist, who holds them, and whether you can afford to duplicate and license them.

Some "famous" stock shots don't in fact exist, including Khrushchev's shoe-banging at the United Nations and the bespectacled 3-D movie audience (which are actually both still photographs). If feature film clips are necessary for your portrait of an activist actor, make sure that the actor's studio(s) will release the clips and get an idea of the costs involved.

2 Seriously consider hiring an archival researcher with expertise in the area of your production.

Quite frequently researchers can find more alternatives more quickly for less money. Their experience can make them valuable collaborators and even reshapers of your original concept.

3 Negotiate your licensing deals as soon as you think you know the footage you want to use.

Film libraries dislike extending discounts after a production is finished, and they have no incentive to do so.

4 Before your final cut, define your primary distribution media, markets, and territory. Decide which rights you can afford to clear.

As the number of distribution outlets have multiplied, rights have too. Contracts now cite such rights such "nonstandard television," "laser disc," "pay-per-view," "audio visual," and "multimedia." Territory is also a consideration in pricing rights. Distribution territory may be broadly defined to cover the United States or North America/Europe, or one may choose to narrowly target an audience, such as French-speaking Belgium. Many rights holders require full payment before releasing master material. A production with foreign sales or home video potential is useless if it must be shelved for want of license fees.

5 Get all the rights and clearances you need.

In order to reuse certain footage, you may need to obtain special rights. This is especially important when reusing footage from feature films, television programs, and musical and theatrical performances. Remember to clear music rights, get the consent of recognizable individuals appearing in the footage (or their estates), and possibly that of certain unions (Directors Guild of America and Writers Guild of America). Ultimately, you must decide between putting everything you want in your show and having it sit on the shelf, or clearing what you can afford and having a product to distribute legally.

6 Investigate the actual costs of research and duplication.

Libraries charge for their research time and generally mark up duplication costs. Costs may be surprisingly high if the footage you need is dispersed in several repositories, if your editing ratio is high, or if master material is expensive to duplicate.

7 Filmmakers: Choose your duplication format and, in cooperation with your lab, flowchart the handling procedure for different kinds of original material.

The preproduction phase is the time to decide between negative and positive, 35 mm and 16 mm, black and white and color, and all other options.

(From the article "Archival Survival: The Fundamentals of Using Film Archives and Stock Footage Libraries" by Rick Prelinger. More info is available at www.archive.org/details/ prelinger.)

HOW TO FIX IT IN POST: COVERING UP COMMON MISTAKES

by Greg Payton
c3stories.com

Generally, when I hear the term, "we'll fix it in post", it either means the development/production side of any project became lazy, careless or just didn't think the mechanics through of what would be needed to properly execute their concept. Here's where the Editor or Post-Production Team comes in to try to make sense of and salvage some of the things that were done, done wrong, or never even thought about during production.

Most of the post tips I cover below are general editing techniques that you can nuance in your own editing software, whether it be **Avid**, **Final Cut**, **Premiere**, **iMovie** or a basic consumer editing program. These tips are meant to be the first steps of "triage", to make sense of and even add production value to a project that may not have been initially executed that well. The goal is to always shoot as carefully as possible, so you can avoid expending additional time, expense and labor in post-production. But on those occasions when it's unavoidable or simply after the fact, somebody has to fix it in post. Here are ten techniques to cover up some common mistakes . . .

1. Fixing Soft-Focused Shots

Focus issues DO seem to happen with more and more footage these days in the age of DSLR's and large sensor video cameras which offer extreme shallow depth of field . . . and much higher chances of shooting things out of focus when the margin of error and the monitor on set is so small. So how do we fix it? When is it too soft to fix?

Generally, what you first want to do, if you are able, is find out how much you will be using the "soft" focus footage and if there is a way to minimize the usage of it with other shots. Once you've determined that, then proceed with **sharpening**. I say this only because applying sharpening to all of a particular clip may be very render intensive, time consuming, and not the most efficient way to get your edit done.

Next, when you're applying a sharpening filter, don't go too heavy handed with the actual effect. Remember, this is all just digital now and software will only fix a piece a footage so much. (This tip pretty much applies to most editing software effects.)

Set a visual reference for yourself when applying the sharpening filter. It's important to use more than one if possible. Take hair or eyebrows for instance. If hair or eyebrows begin to look "fake" or begin to look shiny or pixelated when applying the sharpening filter—you've gone too far. You might be surprised at just how effective a sharpening effect can be if done right, especially if you combine that effect with some simple color correcting. (More on that below.)

Take into consideration where your video is going to be shown. If it is for broadcast, cutting around it, covering it with B-roll (if the audio is more important) or re-shooting (if the picture is more important) may be necessary if there is time, money and the original subject or on-screen talent available.

SOFT FOCUS FIX

Before

The Fix

After

2. Extending Shots That Aren't Long Enough

Sometimes you'll have footage that just misses that moment you need to really punctuate a scene. It could be a couple seconds, or even a few frames. The point is, you DON'T HAVE IT.

Editing is about finding or creating the pace, a *rhythm* if you will. Whether it be a music video, documentary, narrative or experimental piece, anything visual will usually carry it's own pace, it's own beat, a pattern which tells the audience what kind of flow to expect from one scene to the next.

However, there are moments that pacing can be interrupted when you're unable to get the most out of a particular shot because it ends too soon. If you've already blown your "non-budget" and can't recreate the conditions necessary to extend the shot in the time you need there are several methods to resolve this problem. The first deals with adjusting the speed of your clip or making it appear a bit slower than it was originally shot. Now I'm not saying to make a shot look like it IS moving in slow motion, because that isn't the point of this technique. The point of this technique is to maintain your pacing and storytelling integrity without giving away your editing "slight of hand". If done right, slowing down a shot by say 90% even down to 68%, may be the solution to saving the pacing of your overall piece.

Another method I've enlisted when a shot just isn't long enough is to, at the very END of the clip, take a portion of it CLOSEST TO THE END, DUPLICATE IT and INSERT it right after the end of the SAME SHOT. The difference? Try applying a REVERSE effect on it, or −100% as it may appear. This may NOT work in all cases, particularly clips with dialogue at the end, so you need to use your best creative and critical editing judgment as to whether a technique like this helps or hurts your overall pacing. (That's the beauty of the UNDO button, baby.)

A third method you can enlist in dealing with shots that are too short is creating STILL FRAMES from the very LAST FRAME of the clip. By doing this, it allows you to quickly cut away to your next scene and maintain pacing.

You may have to use a combination of these methods at the same time in order to solve the problem. But remember, whatever you decide, be deliberate and make it a part of your overall edit so that one mistake you fix, doesn't appear to be a *the* mistake that brings an edit down. Create a "pattern", a "motif", and raise the production value of your overall edit.

3. Fixing a Boom Mic in the Frame

One of the simplest ways to get rid of a boom mic dipping into frame is by simply "scaling" or increasing the size of the video clip until you no longer see the boom mic. Find the further most point at which you see the mic dip into frame, and be sure to "blow-up" the video clip until you no longer see it.

But what about video quality? Well, generally video does give you SOME, and I stress SOME, flexibility to how far it can be blown up until the image becomes "soft", "fuzzy", or "grainy", none of which are very pleasing to the eye. You may find yourself blowing up a clip from it's original 100% to 110%, even 120% and that could be for broadcast. For the Internet, you may even be able to get away with blowing up a frame upward of 160%!

4. Faking Camera Coverage by Reframing a Shot

Speaking of "blowing up" shots, you may be working with footage such as an interview on a real set, location or against green screen where even though you have different images or B-roll to cut away to you still need more shots of your subject. What do you do when all you have is that ONE master shot?

Start with your master shot. Once you've begun shaping your overall piece, cut back to your subject's master shot, but this time blow it up to 110%, for example. The difference can be dramatic enough to not only further the visual story telling, but to potentially make a scene appear to have more camera coverage than how it was originally shot. You may actually make the original shooter (who may or may not be you), look better than they actually were on the day, which in turn, can only help you.

But again, what about video quality? As I mentioned earlier, video does have A LITTLE flexibility regarding how far you can blow it up, and that is also dependent on the final deliverable format your piece is going to be shown in. For the web, you may find yourself having far more flexibility than if it were for broadcast, because the compression of Internet video is such that video is at an amazing quality right now, but still nowhere near broadcast quality; at least NOT YET.

In the meantime though, it is important to note that should you happen to be working with footage from some of the current professional 4K digital cameras on the market from RED, Arri or Blackmagic, then you don't necessarily have to worry at all about blowing up a shot, since these cameras offers resolutions greater than the standard of Full HD (1920 pixels by 1080 pixels), thus allowing you in many cases to blow-up a shot without any immediate concern of video degradation.

Obviously, you DO NOT want to blow-up a shot unless you have to. Doing so if it is unmotivated is as useless as overshooting a simple scene. Eventually it will annoy you and inevitably annoy any producer or director you're working with if it doesn't further along the storytelling. As long as your blow-ups and reframes enhance the visual story and "hold-up" visually when displayed on your computer monitor or another HD monitor, you'll be able to create a sense of coverage that will elevate the production value of your edited piece.

5. Fixing Bad White Balance

If you receive footage that is too red, blue, or green, then chances are a WHITE BALANCE may not have been correctly adjusted during shooting. Once again thanks to human error (ie: laziness/carelessness/lack of attention to detail), you now have yet another problem to "fix in post".

The way to approach this is as simply as possible. Trust your eye and your instincts. Similar to attaining the right level of a sharpness filter to sharpen a "soft" image, the same eye for detail is necessary for making off-color footage look normal.

From my experience, color can work in complementary pairs. If a shot is too orange or red, within your editing software consider setting your color correction filter to the opposite side of the spectrum, moving it to the deep BLUES or PURPLES. You'll notice how quickly someone's orange skin becomes fairly normal.

Continue to tweak as necessary in order to really "normalize" a specific shot before you begin editing.

Another example is if a shot is too blue. What do we do? Guess? Using the color correction tool, slide the color dials in the opposite side of the spectrum, to orange or red, whatever need be, until "that blue wall-that SHOULD BE white" looks as close to white as possible.

Generally these techniques will work for most situations where a camera may have been incorrectly white-balanced for tungsten (indoor) light when it should have been set for daylight or vice versa.

FIXING FOOTAGE THAT'S TOO WARM

Before

The fix

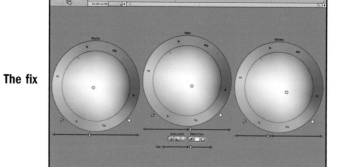

After

FIXING FOOTAGE THAT'S TOO COOL

Before

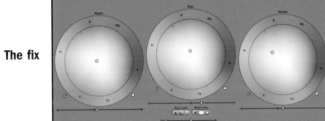

The fix

After

6. Fixing Low Resolution Video and Stills

If you've ever seen a documentary by either Ken Burns, Spike Lee or any documentarian who utilizes stills and/or actual archival film footage within their current work, you'll notice a particular *way* it is used. You too can incorporate your own style. I, as well as many other editors, producers, etc., have developed our own methods.

LOW RES FOOTAGE TREATMENTS

Particularly when dealing with old low-resolution images and footage that cannot be easily blown up or resized into our current HD, IMAX, and Uber-giant formats, sometimes a workaround is necessary.

When dealing with standard-definition footage, which can typically be described as 720 pixels by 480 (or 486) pixels, it is significantly SMALLER than our current standard high definition of 1920 pixels by 1080 pixels and obviously growing larger from there. So, a good method of still incorporating such SD footage into a HD or larger format, is to keep the video or still (if that also is too small) in it's original size, as long as it's viewable. Generally, because the image/footage is smaller, you'll have a significant area of black within the rest of the frame.

For some, the black is fine, for others it is a glaring visual that, "something is missing and needs to be filled in!" So a method I often enlist is creating multiple video layers with the lower or bottom most layer being the original image or archival footage. Because it's been blown up to fill the black spaces in the frame, the video is definitely going to be fuzzy and poor to view, so a workaround is to apply a general "blur" effect or filter on the image, and then lower the opacity or "dim" the image down so it isn't distracting to the main video you wish to see on your top most layer.

This particular method allows you to again further progress your editing style and further your visual storytelling without sacrificing a necessary piece of archival footage or stills.

7. What do I do if my Audio is Out of Sync?

Sync issues deal mainly with not having a "sync point" or a place to line up a specific sound in audio, with the corresponding image in video. Footage that doesn't have a clap slate or provide a distinct sound like a "clap" can often make lining up audio with picture difficult and time consuming.

Resolving audio sync issue requires looking through the footage, scanning for any distinct movements that may carry with them distinct sounds. For instance, seeing a driver honking a horn on camera may be perfect for lining up the corresponding audio. If someone is on camera shouting or saying a specific phrase on camera, that can then be matched up to the sound of that word or phrase.

Obviously this is frustrating and tedious, but an important lesson in why it is important to slate interviews, scenes, or any visual requiring sound when shooting **double system audio**.

Relating to footage taken from the Internet, oftentimes video and audio can fall out of sync due to the severely compressed nature of the video file from the web. One solution is to first convert this footage into something similar to what you are using in your edit. If the audio is still out of sync, it may be a good idea to bring the video clip into your editing software. Line up the audio to the picture so that it IS in sync, re-export the clip in your sequence to make a BRAND NEW clip and then RE-IMPORT it into your editing software. Tedious? Yep! Time consuming? Indeed! So if you're going to grab clips from "wherever" there is video, there may be a price to pay.

8. Fixing Coughs, "Ums", and "Ahs"

Often when we have footage of a scene that involves dialogue or an interview, it may be interrupted by natural things we do, as well as by nature itself.

For example, we may never really "hear" how many times we say, "um", "ah" or just cough in a normal conversation. But for some reason, the moment the camera turns on us and the mic is pointed towards us, we clam up, stutter, stammer, etc. This may be acceptable in reality, but when watching a film, or an interview, it can be distracting.

If you were wise enough to shoot room tone (either from an indoor or outdoor location or set), you can often replace that bit of someone's "um", "cough" etc, with a carefully placed bit of room tone. You may tempted to just delete the audio and "keep it moving". However, it's important to know the difference between having "no audio" and having *no sound* during a scene. Deleting the audio entirely will be noticeable and pull your audience out of an engaging scene or interview of your piece.

So consider covering these natural human flubs with room tone that has no discernible sound, but DOES keep your scene or interview moving. This technique is ESPECIALLY useful, when dealing with a scene or interview that involves any adult language that you wish to avoid in your screened project. Sometimes a "BEEEEEP" can be too distracting and anyone who's seen enough reality/TV shows knows it can be a little overbearing. Sometimes, again depending on the nature of your piece, covering a curse with a little room tone can be helpful.

BUT, sometimes, you just don't have room tone. In cases like these, we'll need to go through a scene or an interview and really dig for a moment, a breath, a pause, where there is no talking or noise, and most times, if we're lucky, we can use that in lieu of room tone. A little bit of aural sleight of hand can go a long way to polish a finished piece.

If lip movements still make the offending word or sound too obvious to the audience, another pretty fail-safe method to remove "ums" and "ahs" is to just chop them out cleanly, being careful to space the remaining words on the timeline, so they still sound like a natural flow of speech. Lay-in room tone to fill in any gaps of audio silence then strategically insert a cut-away or some B-Roll to cover the visual jump cut.

9. Reducing Wind Noise

Sometimes nature just doesn't want to behave and sometimes wind can be an annoying distraction, not only for a scene or interview, but in the very ability to just hear what our subject is saying.

Some audio filters like "EQ", "High Pass", or "Low Cut" will filter out as much of the bassy or "low end" audio noise from a scene or interview as possible. The same goes for any high-pitched noises that need to be filtered out to really bring the subject audio to the forefront. So as long as you don't filter out your important subject audio or make it sound like it's coming out of a tin can, you'll be in good shape.

Obviously if you have access to software like ProTools, Sound Soap, or anything comparable, there is a whole slew of other tricks you can pull out to fix wind and other noises. But if you don't have access to yet another potentially costly software, oftentimes you have to work with what you've got and most editing software will have some basic audio filtering tools even if they exist under slightly different names.

But the one thing I've learned over the years is that any strong or persistent wind noise can really only be minimized, but never completely eliminated, mainly because it exists on the same or similar frequency of your important subject audio and you don't want to filter that out.

Apply these effects one by one, tweaking and adjusting each one slightly and you'll be surprised how much you can improve your subject's audio.

These audio tricks are also very tedious and something I'd recommend be left until the end of you cutting for overall video content. Once you "lock" or finalize your picture, then you can address these sound issues. Because audio mixing and engineering can be so time consuming, you'd be wasting your own time by trying painstakingly to fix a piece of audio that may eventually be cut for pacing or time. Wait for picture lock, then lock your audio, THEN dive in and do your best to fix it in the sound mix!

10. Fixing Over and Underexposed Shots

It's first important to know the different between using the tools of Brightness and Contrast Versus Blacks/Mids/Whites or Low/Mids/Highs.

When many people start out editing they tend to fix an underexposed/overexposed shot by just relying on using the "Brightness/Contrast" tool, in either Final Cut, Avid, or Premiere. It will "work" sometimes, but you can often lose a lot of information in the image because it may either become too "milky" by adding brightness to a shot that was too dark, or lack any detail, because you've drained out all the brightness.

Elements like "blacks" that exist in shadows, some hair, some skin tones and clothing; "mids" typically in skin tones, clothing, furniture; "whites" like clouds, skies, white walls and sometimes highlights in skin tones can help you understand how to save a shot's clarity without sacrificing the lights, mids and darks within.

There is not necessarily a "right" or "wrong" way of adjusting exposure, only an *appropriate* way for what you need it to accomplish for your piece.

Some key things to remember is to BE CONSISTENT. If you are going to do ANY color correction to *fix exposure* (not adjusting or fixing color, as mentioned before), be consistent throughout for mood, pacing and story. You never want your attempt to fix exposure to distract from the story you're trying to tell.

Looking at the examples, there are some ways to go about enhancing or bringing out someone's skin tone, color, skin highlights, and overall "presence". By doing what you may have heard called "crushing the blacks" or making the "blacker" elements of your shots darker and making the "whiter" elements of your shots brighter to make your subjects "pop" you really can enhance and bring attention to the crisp detail of a shot.

Conversely, if you *don't* want to make an image pop, you can adjust the exposure in a very different way to make your image look more "dream-like" or faded. But in the end, the range in which you can play with and fix a shot is limited by how badly it is under or over exposed.

Due to the wide variety of digital video cameras, each of them varying in levels of image quality, you can either be very limited or unlimited in how much you can fix an under or overexposed shot.

If a shot is too under/overexposed, you run the risk of having either a very grainy shot (which may work for your overall piece) since you are artificially forcing light into the "blacks" or darks into a shot that doesn't naturally exist. Or, you may have a shot that lacks detail because it is too bright and even bringing the "highs" or "whites" down may not give you back the detail initially lost when it was shot.

Just about every editing application on a desktop, laptop, tablet, and even *smartphone* is capable of adjusting brightness and contrast, and some can adjust "highs, mids and lows"/"whites, mids, blacks". They can be found in your Effects or Image Control settings.

Elements like increasing/decreasing brightness and contrast (to enhance overall exposure) of a shot, will also effect how significant the color correct effects are noticed, which may help or hurt your shot. Tread creatively and use your best judgment.

The better you are at color correcting and adjusting exposure, the more effective your edit can be, especially when dealing with a piece using multiple cameras that all look very different.

OVEREXPOSURE FIX

Before

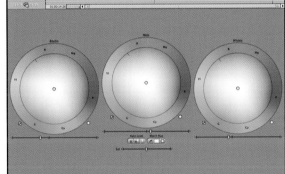

The fix

After

Before

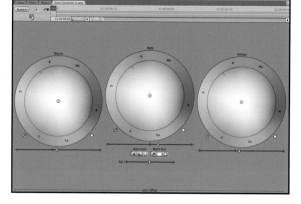

The fix

After

Lucky Bonus Tip #11!: Fixing a Shaky Shot

If you *don't* have access to an expensive compositing program, there is an option in the old stalwart Adobe After Effects. Like much of the rest of Adobe's Creative Suite, the options keep getting better and better with every new version. Image stabilization is one of those new options in particular.

Via **After Effects**, one of the more tedious ways to stabilize a shot is to use After Effects **Motion Tracker**. Found by going to the "Window" option and selecting "Tracker", you'll want to go to the Motion Source option, clicking on your specific shaky clip.

Moving on to the "Track Type" option, you then click "Stabilize". Don't forget to click the Position and Rotation options since your shot probably deals with a specific angle or orientations.

You'll find a series of boxes, an inner and outer box. These are where you'll make your tracking selections. When it comes to image stabilization whether it be in editorial programs like Final Cut, Avid, Premiere or After Effects they rely on high contrast areas in the frame and areas with little to no motions to "lock-on" or "anchor" themselves to.

Resize the outer box so that it's big enough to find a tracking point. Let the software analyze the shot. Once the software is done analyzing the clip, apply the tracking data to your shot. Click on the "edit target" button and choose the clip we just finished tracking and hit "Apply." After rendering your video, you can see just how smooth the movement has become.

Since motion tracking will always create these moving edges of black on the outer edge of your frame, you need to "blow-up" the shot a little so we won't see the black frayed edges. This means your frame is going to be changed, often making a wide shot or medium shot into a medium shot or close up shot, respectively. With this in mind, if you know a shot is going to be handheld or otherwise potentially shaky in production, try to make sure that that shot is framed a bit wider than you need, so that any image stabilization won't hurt the framing and composition of the shot you want to use.

Okay, so you went to After Effects and realized you really need this "image stabilization to fix my shaky shot" thing done, and done FAST without me having to learn a whole new software! OTHER options do exist. **Avid**, **Premiere Final Cut Pro 7**, and some versions of **Final Cut Pro X**, all contain image stabilizers that are simpler and just require you to apply them and render. But image stabilization can be brutally long to "render" and as a result can slow down your post process. So I recommend you wait until you "lock" your picture and THEN go in and stabilize shots.

In Final Cut Pro X, though, you can just right-click on your footage in your timeline and choose the "Analyze and Stabilize" option. Final Cut Pro X will then stabilize your footage in the background while you edit your project. So, some NLE's have better or faster rendering solutions than others. But regardless, always plan ahead for time to render your digital effects.

Final Advice for Aspiring Editors

Some final bits of advice I would give any Editor. Get involved and stay involved. If you have the chance to be brought in during development to consult on how a project will look in the editing process, BE THERE AND BE THERE EARLY. If you have the opportunity to be on-set, BE ON SET. It is not your job to second guess anyone in their departments, however. Your job is to be a Post Production resource; answering questions and providing solutions that will ultimately make *your* job easier.

If you remain collaborative, respect the on-set production hierarchy, and work with professionals who are concerned about the best product and not their egos, you'll be amazed how often they ask you whether something will "cut together", "blow up well", or "look clear enough" for the post process. Once that bond of trust and respect is established, it is a calling card to a great finish to any project.

However, oftentimes you are merely the "hired-gun", tasked on a project that was conceived long before you even knew there was a job. In those cases, my advice is to try and remain as flexible, cool, and calm as possible. Provide as much consolation, professional know-how, and experience possible to those who clearly have made missteps that you as the Editor now has to resolve. We're only human and flare ups can, have and will continue to happen. Just be sure to keep it professional and plan for the next job to go more smoothly—hopefully, with you more involved in the process.

Having worked through the ins and out of post production for a number of years, I've heard and understood all of the "excuses" as to why the Editor now has to absorb the heavy lifting of a production's screw-ups. Ultimately, I believe the term "we'll fix it in post" can breed terribly bad habits. DON'T BREED BAD HABITS. Learn what it means to have to usher an idea through development, pre-production, production and onto post. By doing this, even if it's just for one project, you'll have a new appreciation and respect for those who may have to one-day "fix" *your* filmmaking mistakes.

Think C.L.A.A.P. Before You Apply

Clout: All festivals are not created equal. Some are magnets for distributors and press and others are barely a blip on the industry radar screen. There are more industry players, perks, better networking, and better press coverage at the prestigious film fests. Making contacts for your current and future projects is a vital part of any long-term filmmaking strategy. Do your homework. Find out what caliber of industry folk are most likely to attend. Festival clout is the difference between an article in the *Hollywood Reporter* and the *Skankville Gazette*.

Location: Hustling your festival team and subject(s) downtown, a few states away, or all the way to Europe makes a big difference in cost, logistics, and how many people you can afford to bring with you. Less people means less promotion manpower. Choose wisely.

Awards: What types of awards or prizes might you win? Best Director? Best Foreign Film? Jury Award? And don't underestimate the attention-grabbing power of an Audience Award for best film. If you win what do you get? $30,000? (Doubtful.) A free rental or post-production package? The newest 4K camera? A gift certificate to Red Lobster? Even digital guerrilla success has its rewards. And even if you don't win a single prize, remember that you beat out a bunch of people just to get nominated and you always have bragging rights!

Application Fee: Although there are festivals that are free to apply to, most film festivals have entry fees that range from $25 to $75. (And, no, you don't get your money back if your film is rejected.) Tack on the cost of mailing submissions and applying to just 10 festivals could easily run you well over 500 bucks! Apply to the festivals that will be most worthwhile for your project according to the goals of your festival strategy. Beware of scam film fests that just collect large entry or screening fees to make money.

Perks: Will the festival cover airfare? A 5-star hotel room? Are there numerous events with free food and drinks? Is there a $500 goodie bag? Does the fest have a reputation for being *fun*? This industry is all about the perks, baby. The food, the drinks, the free tickets, the lavish parties, the celebrity access, the hotels. they all help take the sting out of your exhaustion, overwhelming debt, and battered ego. Even if your screening is half empty and you don't win a single award, you've still got some free stuff and a nice room with a view to enjoy. This part of the filmmaking experience is the 1% of what we do in the course of making a film that actually *is* a little glamorous. Enjoy it and take pictures.

PASSION, BUSINESS, & FILMMAKING

ADRIAN BELIC, CO-DIRECTOR/PRODUCER

(Genghis Blues, Beyond the Call)

The way you nurture a film, the way you get allies on your side, is you go to festivals. And a lot of people think that festivals are about business, that's hocking yourself, that's being a salesperson. No, it's not. It's getting your passion out to the audience. I make films not for myself. I have a great time traveling around the world, but it's really hard to edit the film. So, I make films because I want *the audience* to see them.

At places like Sundance, they spend millions of dollars, every year, 365 days a year, to bring the world's top distributors here—business people, financiers, press people. And all I've got to do is show up, sleep on my friend's floor, and hustle from dawn to dusk, and all night long to get my film out to as many people as I can.

The other thing is to gain allies. We need to get allies, people who believe in our film and believe in *us*. And the only way that that happens is to go out. Some may call it business. I call it filmmaking. That's part of the whole filmmaking process. I spend three, four years making a film. To hell if I'm gonna let it just fall dead on the ground when I'm done! For me, it's about extending my passion. I just extend my passion through thinking of the film, and preproduction and production, and post, to distribution.

One of the things we realize is that, frankly, most people are lazy. You know how I know? Because, *I'm* lazy. So one of the things I try to do for distributors or programmers or film festivals or the press is to make it as *easy* as it can be for them.

So, if we find out about a magazine that we want to get into, we learn something about that magazine, and then we try to figure out how to pitch our story to that magazine so that they'll pick it up. If there is a distributor that we want to get into, or some film festival, we learn a little bit about that film festival. What did they show last year? So, when we go and talk to that distributor, we actually know what the hell we're talking about.

7 WAYS TO WORK A FILM FESTIVAL

Okay, you've poured your heart out into making your doc, it's finally finished, and you even got accepted into a few festivals. So, now it's time to sit back and let the accolades, awards, and applause roll in, right? Wrong! Now it's time to hustle just as hard as you did for all the other steps of the filmmaking process to make sure that people know about, see, and report about your film. Here's an overview of how to get the most out of a festival experience:

1. Do Your Homework

Any information that you can gather could give you an edge over the competition (or at least keep you from putting your foot in your mouth). So find out as much as you can about the particular festival you are attending. Read and print out all the info on their web site. Look it up in the festival guides. Talk to past attendees and filmmakers. Try to figure out what films did well there and why. Find out what the audience responded to in the past. Research the programmers' tastes and stated festival goals.

2. Apply Early

Filmmakers are notorious procrastinators. However, this often isn't because we're irresponsible. It's because we're perfectionists and the indie filmmaking process is such that things always seem to be twice as hard and take twice as long as we anticipated. However, with film festivals, procrastination is an ill-advised practice.

As someone who has organized a few festivals, I can tell you that the vast majority of entries come in during the *last few days* before the entry deadline. If your project is lumped in with all the rest of the last-minute entries, it has less of a chance of standing out from the crowd. Weary festival organizers and screeners are more tempted to hit the fast forward or eject button at the first sign of flaws or boredom. So I strongly advise submitting your project several weeks before any deadline while the judges are still fresh and not glazed over from hours of viewing bad movies.

A site worth investigating for film festival applicants is Withoutabox.com. This site allows filmmakers to streamline the festival submission process by filling out and submitting one universal festival application and digital press kit to multiple film fests at once. According to their site, there are more than 5,000 participating film fests worldwide including many of the major festivals. This online one-stop-shopping approach to applying ultimately makes life easier for the festivals *and* the filmmakers.

Withoutabox.com simplifies the festival application process.

3. Put Together a Guerrilla Festival Team

You can't adequately promote your project all by yourself at a film festival. You need to enlist the help of your producers, crew members, friends, and family to help assemble promo materials then hit the festival streets and hang posters, hand out fliers, drum up press and interviews, pull wacky publicity stunts, and otherwise talk up, hype, and push your project. This is a great opportunity to bring your core filmmaking team back together for a celebratory reunion and one last hustle. If at all possible, try to bring the main subject(s) of your documentary. Audience and press are *much* more attracted to doc screenings where the actual subjects will be present and accessible. Inspiring or colorful subjects of well-received docs can become instant festival celebrities and easily double your promotion without even trying.

4. Put Together a Hot Press Kit and Promo Materials

There's crazy competition for eyeballs and attention at any film festival. Your posters, promotional materials, and trailer are the most important tools for luring audience members and press to your film. It helps if you have a decent budget, but creativity can help make up the difference. You'll need postcards, posters, a press release, video trailers, giveaways, production photos, and more. Originality, creativity, and grabbing attention counts more than your budget. You can do many

ingenious things with paper alone. To take your guerrilla promotions to the next level, enlist some friends with advertising, design, or art backgrounds to come up with something that is affordable, clever, and, most important, *memorable*.

5. Get Your Hustle On

If you're a filmmaker with a film in a festival, you can't afford to be shy. You have to hustle to get butts in seats. You've **gotta** get out there, meet the festival attendees, and hype your film. Don't be a raving lunatic, but let anyone who will listen know about your film and when it's playing. A good-natured publicity stunt doesn't hurt either. The goal is to pack your screening to capacity and hopefully sell out. Get as many people handing out fliers as possible. Entertainment people hate to be "out of the loop." If there's a buzz, people want to know what it's about. Even if they don't actually see your project, the mere *buzz* created by sold out screenings, people discussing the project and admiring your clever and original promotional campaign will create a positive impression and familiarity in their heads . . . "If people are talking about it, it must be good."

6. Mix at the Parties and Panels

The panels and parties are where people are most approachable and sociable. While many corporate business deals begin on the golf course, many film deals begin with a casual conversation over cocktails or at industry events. If you aren't likable, engaging, and pleasant to be around socially, who's going to seriously entertain the notion of entangling themselves with you in deals or projects that play out over months or even years? Oscar-nominated director, Adrian

One of many panels at Sundance.

Belic of *Genghis Blues* fame, summed it up best when he said, "**Until people see your film, all they see is *you*.**" Given a choice, anyone would choose to work long-term with someone they enjoy being around rather than those they don't, so go to the parties and attend some filmmaking panels and let people know who you are and what you do. Filmmaking opportunities and alliances often start with a simple social conversation. So get out to those events and mix and mingle, even if it hurts.

7. Don't Just Network, Follow Up

Don't make the mistake of thinking that the only thing to be gained at a film festival is distribution and publicity. The cold truth is that a distribution deal is a long shot for most films at any festival, but it's far from the only prize. A single chance (or orchestrated) meeting could hold the key to your filmmaking future. Know this: Networking *is* the film and TV industry. Don't be intimidated by the word "networking." All it really means is meeting and connecting with people in your industry and trading info and resources. It's getting out there and putting yourself out there. The goal of networking is not to see how many people you can pitch your project to or hit up for favors. Networking is a two-way street. It's as much about what you can *give* as what you get. Lasting relationships are based on mutual giving whether it's trading advice, information, services, or connecting someone with one of your contacts. (Notice I didn't distinguish between "business" and "personal" relationships. The rules are one in the same.) If you genuinely connect and look to help other people, the rest will follow. If you're willing to help people, people will be willing to help you. People in this business can easily tell when you're desperate or just want to get something from them and it's a major turn off. Once you connect and you have a card, e-mail address, or phone number, you should follow up within two weeks tops. A short e-mail to say hello, point to an article, update them on your project, or asking what's going on with their project is sufficient. If you can meet up in person for lunch or coffee it's all the better. Once there's a human connection you will have another ally to help you achieve your future filmmaking goals.

HOW TO HUSTLE AT SUNDANCE

REBEKAH SINDORIS AND CHRISTIE PESICKA

(Paper Chasers, Paper Dolls, Rovin' Gamblers, Mr. Arizona)

Rebekah: It's really good to go to the panels on any of the festivals— Slamdance or Sundance or any of the surrounding festivals. When you go to a panel discussion (and a lot of them are free) you get access to people afterwards. That is when people are very approachable. Read the publication about the people sitting on the panel. If you see any panelist that you want to talk to, you go afterwards with your business card and they're very approachable versus when they're in LA or New York or elsewhere.

I find my more valuable connections are earlier in the evening when there are more panels or earlier receptions. Because that's when you really talk more. They're a lot of fun and you never know who you're gonna meet . . . The panels are the most valuable resource, even if you don't see any movies. If you go to some panels up here and meet a couple of people who can help you fund your film or start your film, you've done better than most people.

So, I definitely recommend the panels. I recommend some of the receptions, the parties are great too, but go to some of the panels, especially the early evening ones, before everyone is out partying, because you'll be able to get some of your stuff out there and they will remember who you are.

Always write down on the back of people's business card who they are and where you met them, so you'll remember them. The most important part about all the connections you make up here is follow up. Most people don't follow up. What good is a connection in a month or two if you don't follow up?! Make sure you follow up or it's worthless . . .

Christie: If you don't have the money for a publicist, which can be tough, because truthfully, people spend more on publicity than they do their films. When you're talking about films being done for 10, 15, 20 thousand dollars, people are spending that on publicity just for a ten-day festival. So, how do you compete with them and get your film out there? You have to seek out smaller indie film podcasts, blogs and media. Seek out people that really want to sit down and talk to you and hear what you have to say.

You want to make connections with some of the smaller shows, the smaller publications, that need you as much as you need them. Some people are seeking out Spielbergs and George Lucas to get help . . . No, you need to find people who are on *your* level, who are going through the same thing, who can help you. But, if you go to people who are kinda doing the same thing that you are doing, and maybe in a different area . . . If you can partner up with people like that, I think you're better off than trying to get a sound bite with a station that may or may not ever use it.

Rebekah: My recommendations on how to publicize your film if you don't have a lot of money and you're at a festival is to bring tons of DVDs, meet every distribution-type person you can. Go to the panels and Q&As . . . Talk to other filmmakers that have had success. Find out who their producer's reps are. Find out who is doing their distribution. Poster the town. Bring friends. Get a condo. Bunk up. It's not expensive if you book ahead of time. Get a bunch of people together. Some can sleep on the floor . . . It's not expensive if you do it that way. Get friends and family with you to help you spread the word. Set up your own screening if you want. It's a lot harder to do, but there are avenues. There are places where you can sign up for a screening time. Just really get to the people who are going to be able to help you sell it.

WORDS OF WISDOM FOR YOUNG FILMMAKERS

CLIFF CHARLES, DIRECTOR OF PHOTOGRAPHY
cliffcharles.com
(When the Levees Broke, Good Hair, Venus and Serena, etc.)

Personally, I wish that I would have been taught that the film business is business first and art later. That's not something that's emphasized in school, perhaps rightfully so. But there's not enough talk about the fact that, hey, this is a business, and it's approached as a business by all the power brokers in this industry. Your creative vision is not going to be at the fore-front of a financier's mind, and that's something that is important to grasp in your maturity in the film business. That's something that I really didn't fully grasp when I was a film student, but I totally get it now.

You grow as a person, and you take your youth for granted. So I think that when a person is young, they should do what young people do—be completely selfish, and be able to be completely *immersed* in what they're doing. Because once you start pushing 40 years old and you have other realities in your life, you're really not going to be able to be that selfish, and even beyond that, you're not going to be able to be physically prepared to handle all the demands of what it takes to be really good. We used to work ridiculous hours when we were in school, and as a kid you can go without sleep and eat constant junk food all day long and be able to get up and keep going. When you get older, your body is not as forgiving. So it's a young person's game, in terms of when you're learning how to do this. So if you're a young student—not saying that you can't be an old student—but if you are a young student, embrace that youthful zeal, that youthful energy, that love of learning, and that never-say-die attitude, because that's one of the great-est things about being young. You're revolutionary, simply by nature. So embrace it, because it's not going to last . . . Use it while you've got it.

ANTHONY'S RECOMMENDED READS

The *Shut Up and Shoot Documentary Guide* is just a starting point for a film education. You've still got a long way to go to true filmmaking enlightenment. First you must understand this: Learning the craft of filmmaking is a *lifelong* process. It doesn't stop after you finish a given book, class, or project . . . There's an ever deeper and evolving world of visual storytelling, technology and techniques to learn and comprehend. (There's a reason why most of the people at the top of the film game have gray hair—it takes that long to master it.)

Some things you read don't make sense until you shoot, but some things you screw up shooting don't make sense until you read. I'm all about maximizing your resources. And the number one resource that can help you make the most of any budget is knowledge. Whether you're in a film school, workshop, or self-teaching, you should begin building a filmmaking reference library. Simply clicking around the Internet alone ain't gonna cut it. Here are some of my personal recommendations to help you get the ball rolling:

The Shut Up and Shoot Freelance Video Guide

by Anthony Q. Artis

This is my second book for filmmakers. It covers more intermediate camera, audio, and lighting techniques in 300+ pages with 700+ illustrations and picks up from where the *Shut Up and Shoot Documentary Guide* leaves off. If you haven't figured it out by now—personal filmmaking simply doesn't pay the bills. (It actually becomes yet another bill.) Corporate and freelance filmmaking, on the other hand, is a great way to not only further your filmmaking skill set, but to also *get paid* while you're doing it. I'll teach you my Down and Dirty approach to creating successful corporate, music, wedding, and live event videos that will keep paying clients coming back while helping you still achieve your loftier long-term filmmaking goals.

Bare Bones Camera Course for Film and Video

by Tom Schroeppel

I highly recommend this book to anyone brand-new to cinematography. It's a self-published, underground classic not in too many stores but available online. True to its name, this book offers simple, clear, cartoon-illustrated instructions on the fundamentals of screen grammar and cinematography. I never fully "got" a lot of the things I read in other film books and heard in lectures until after I read this book. God bless Tom for finally explaining it to the rest of us.

What They Don't Teach You At Film School: 161 Strategies to Making Your Own Movie No Matter What

by Camille Landau and Tiara White

These smart women, who have obviously already been there and done that, have compiled a great collection of ultra-practical tips on the countless little things that frequently trip up filmmakers in the process. These are purely practical tips on the psychology, reality, and delicate daily minutia of filmmaking that you would only pick up from painful experience or by having the foresight to study a book of practical wisdom like this.

The Guerilla Film Makers Movie Blueprint

by Chris Jones

This is one the most practical and comprehensive film books I've ever read. It breaks down who does what, explains equipment packages, and lays out the filmmaking process step-by-step. It also features some very informative interviews from industry insiders who we don't usually hear too much from . . . and it's all in plain English. It's an invaluable reference guide for anyone making an indie feature.

The Lean Forward Moment: Create Compelling Stories for Film, TV, and the Web

by Norman Hollyn

The Shut Up and Shoot Documentary Guide is a video production primer, *The Lean Forward Moment* by veteran Hollywood editor and USC professor Norm Hollyn on the other hand, is a visual *storytelling* primer. Whether it's pacing, editing, shot choice, or sound design. Norm breaks down all the tried, true, and new techniques to engage an audience and move them to laughter, tears, fears, or anything else you want them to feel . . . Don't just tell 'em. Make 'em feel it, baby! This book will show you how.

Documentary Storytelling: Making Stronger and More Dramatic Nonfiction Films

by Sheila Curran Bernard

Now that you've got an overview of the process and a technical grasp of the genre, you need to dig deeper into the meaning and nuances of documentary. This book will help you understand the many visual, aural, and cerebral techniques and subtleties of telling a documentary story. It also features in-depth interviews with several notable names in docs.

Directing the Documentary

by Michael Rabiger

This is the definitive comprehensive text on documentary filmmaking. It's a bit thick, but it pretty much has to be to thoroughly cover all aspects of documentary filmmaking from history to theory to production practices. Includes student exercises.

Ultimate Film Festival Guide

by Chris Gore

Not many film books live up to their title, but this one really is the "ultimate" book on film festivals and festival strategy. Apart from the standard contact info and deadlines, Chris gives you tips on the flavor of each fest, self-promotion, and the application process. If you're planning on entering festivals, you should start with this book.

The Filmmakers Tool Kit

by Jason Tomaric

This is another book that's jam-packed with practical filmmaking knowledge and advice. From lens choices to production techniques, Jason has put together a comprehensive tome to help you get your first feature off to a running start.

Television Production

by Gerald Millerson

This is the definitive book for the practices of television. From three-camera shoots to blocking and editing, this book lays out and illustrates the entire world of TV production. The practices of TV are very similar but far from the same. If you want to work in "the little screen," you'll want to read this book.

The Documentary Filmmakers Handbook: A Guerilla Guide

by Genevieve Jolliffe

The latest entry in the guerrilla filmmaking handbook series turns the focus to docs. Heavy on interviews with industry insiders from directors to distributors and all the players in between, Genevieve shares detailed doc knowledge of the process that picks up where this book leaves off.

The IFILM Digital Video Filmmaker's Handbook

by Maxie Collier

From my fellow Down and Dirty filmmaker and good colleague, who was one of the very first authorities on DV filmmaking, this title gives beginning filmmakers an inspirational overview of the digital filmmaking process. It covers the creative and technical aspects and features a candid case study of the digital guerrilla documentary, *Paper Chasers*.

Development Girl: The Hollywood Virgin's Guide to Making It in the Movie Business

by Hadley Davis

If you have any inclination at all to work in the industry in any type of office setting, you can't afford not to read this humorous book, which chronicles the ins and outs of Hollywood workplace culture. Following Hadley's advice, you can avoid the most common newbie mistakes and go from Office Runner to Department Head in half the time.

Spike Lee's Gotta Have It

by Spike Lee

This is Spike's first film book and still my favorite of his series. It contains a script, interview, and diary of his struggle to make his first feature. While it's not about docs, it's a real study in the intense hustle, focus, and hard work it takes to pull off a low-budget indie.

How I Made a Hundred Movies in Hollywood and Never Lost a Dime

by Roger Corman

It's not about documentaries and I'm not even sure if this book is still in print, but it is a great autobiographical text by one of my idols, the B-film Godfather, Roger Corman. Before I was even born, Roger was keeping it Down and Dirty and cranking out quality films on ridiculously low budgets. Ron Howard, Martin Scorsese, and Francis Ford Coppolla all started with Roger, and if they all had lessons to learn from him, so do we. Hunt down a copy and don't loan it out.

Direct Your Own Damn Movie

by Lloyd Kaufman

This is another great book by one of the B-Movie greats—Lloyd Kaufman, who's best known as the CEO of Troma Films and the director of the legendary cult classic *Toxic Waste Avenger* among many many others. But don't sleep on this book just because over-the-top comedy-horror-sex isn't your thing. Lloyd is an astute and well-studied director whose deep knowledge of the industry and film history is shared in this book, which is full of practical wisdom and advice for filmmakers of all genres. Dare I say, it's even more fun to read than this book.

GLOSSARY

1-shot	A shot with only one person in frame.
3-point lighting	Traditional lighting setup using three lights: key light, fill light, and hair light.
4-point lighting	Traditional lighting setup using four lights: key light, fill light, background light, and hair light.
720p	High-definition (HD) video that has 720 lines of vertical resolution. The "p" refers to progressive scan HD video.
1080p or 1080i	High-definition (HD) video that has 1080 lines of vertical resolution. When followed by "p," it refers to progressive scan HD video. When followed by "i," it refers to interlaced scan HD video.
access	Your ability to get up close and inside the world of your subject. This is the golden ticket to documentary making.
ADR	Acronym for "additional dialogue recording," which refers to the technique of having on-screen talent lipsync a section of their dialog in postproduction because it was not captured well during location recording.
AGC	See **auto gain control**.
ambassador	Another term for a "stringer." Someone who acts as a liaison between your production and another community or culture. Someone who knows their way in the society you wish to film.
amp	A unit that measures electricity. Most household circuits are 15–20 amps.

anamorphic	A technique for capturing a 16:9 widescreen picture on standard 4:3 aspect ratio camera. Uses an electronic process or a special lens that squeezes the 16:9 widescreen image into a 4:3 aspect ratio, which can be later unsqueezed in postproduction.
aperture ring	The spinning ring on a camera lens that controls exposure. Prosumer camera models may have a small aperture dial instead of an aperture ring.
approach	How you choose to tell your documentary story. Using re-enactments, your style of camera work, narration, editing techniques, viewpoint, etc., are all parts of your overall approach.
archival footage/photos	Any footage/photos that you use that was not originally shot for your documentary. This includes news segments, movie clips, etc.
aspect ratio	This is a ratio that simply refers to the shape of your image. In video there are two aspect ratios to choose from: 4:3 = standard TV and is more square; 16:9 = widescreen and is more rectangular. The numbers represent units of width:height.
audience	This is the people you are actually making this film for. Don't ever forget about them.
autogain control	Commonly abbreviated as "AGC." This is a camera feature that automatically adjusts sound levels for you.
A/V screenplay format	Industry script format that splits picture and audio into two columns so that visuals can be described with their corresponding dialog, music, and sound FX displayed side by side. Commonly used for corporate video and commercials.
Avid	One of the leading professional computer editing programs available for PC and Mac.
back light	A light usually placed above and behind your subject, used to separate them from the background by using a rim of light to outline them. Also synonymous with a hair light, which is positioned the same but focused more on the hair.
background plates	The scenes, photos, or animations that are to be inserted as the background when compositing a greenscreen scene.

barn doors

The metal flaps mounted on the front of professional film lights that open and close to control the shape of your light and prevent unwanted light from spilling in undesirable places.

bars and tone

The industry standard reference tools for adjusting color and audio: SMPTE color bars and 1 kilohertz audio tone. It's important to include bars and tone at the beginning of every media card, tape, and every finished project so that editors, projectionists, audio engineers, and other film and TV professionals know how to adjust your color and audio to accurately reproduce what you intended.

black wrap

Extra heavy-duty aluminum foil coated in a special heat-resistant black paint. This is used to shape and control light much like barn doors, but black wrap is completely customizable.

blown out

Overexposed video. This is the video kiss of death. If important parts of your video such as your subject's face or the entire background are blown out, it sucks to be you. Blown-out white blotches in video simply can't be fixed in post. Use zebra stripes to avoid this issue.

BNC

Video cable commonly used to connect cameras to monitors, projectors, and other A/V equipment.

breakaway cable

Special sound cable that combines two XLR cables and a headphone cable into one cable that connects between the camera and the mixer or microphone. There is a twist-apart connector in the middle to allow camera people to quickly "break away" from sound people.

bus drive

These are small high-capacity mini-hard drives that are powered by plugging them into a computer via a USB or FireWire cable. Because they don't require AC power, they are an ideal choice for offloading HD video footage at remote locations and run-and-gun shooting.

C47s

Common, ordinary clothes pins. Used to secure gels to the barn doors of lights.

character studies

Films centered around a single person. The content is heavily driven by that person's personality and character traits.

cheat

To move a prop or person to a new or staged position for a more favorable shot.

chimera	Special heat-resistant tent-like housing for light instruments that provides soft, evenly diffused light. Popular for interviews.
China ball	See **Chinese lantern**.
Chinese lantern	Common, round household paper lanterns that produce soft, warm light. Often used as soft key lights and as fill lights for interviews. Also known as "China balls."
circuit breaker	An automatically operated electrical switch designed to protect an electrical circuit from damage caused by overload or short circuit.
clapper board	Also known as a "slate," this item is used to mark the beginning or end of each take, but more importantly the clapper board is used for syncing up visuals to sound by using the exact frame where the board claps as a visual and audio reference point in editing.
closing down	See **stopping down**.
CMOS chip	CMOS stands for "complementary metal oxide semiconductor."
coaxial	Type of video cable used to connect cameras, decks, monitors, and other video equipment to each other. Most commonly recognized on your cable box, VCR, or TV.
compact flash card	Digital media card used by some cameras including the RED camera.
contingency	This is all-purpose emergency money that is built into your budget. Industry standard is 15 percent set aside for contingency. Don't shoot without some amount of contingency money.
cookie	A cutout pattern used to cast interesting shadows that add texture to the background of scenes. A cookie may also mimic the pattern of light shining through a window or blinds.
craft services	The snacks, drinks, and sometimes food department on a film set. These people are responsible for keeping caffeine, sugar, and nourishment flowing at all times.
crane	Piece of equipment used to raise a camera and/or camera operator to get high-angle shots and cool swooping camera moves.

crop out	To adjust your frame by tightening a shot or panning or tilting the camera so that an undesirable element such as a sign or jerk waving at the camera is no longer in the frame.
CTB gel	Stands for "color temperature blue." Put this gel on a light source to make it appear the same color temperature as daylight.
CTO gel	Stands for "color temperature orange." Put this gel on a light source to make it appear the same color temperature as tungsten (indoor) light.
dailies	Refers to the footage shot the previous day (i.e., the crew's daily output). In an ideal world, this footage is viewed by the director, cinematographer, and other crew members to make sure that everything is coming out okay and all necessary shots are being covered.
DB	Stands for "decibel." These are units for measuring sound levels.
dead cat	Film slang for furry coverings used to block wind noise from boom mics. Also known as "windjammers."
depth of field	A term that refers to how much of your frame is in focus at any given time. If your subject is in focus and the background and foreground are out of focus, then you have a shallow depth of field. If everything in the frame is in focus, then you have a deep depth of field.
digitize	To convert video into a digital format so that it can be edited. Done by hooking up a camera or tape deck to your computer and importing the video footage in a nonlinear editing program such as Final Cut Pro, iMovie, Premiere, or Avid.
dimmer box	A small electrical accessory that uses a dial or sliding switch to quickly control the brightness of any light instrument plugged into it.
dirty track	A low-quality track of audio that is not suitable for the final project, but recorded just for reference, so that better quality audio from a separate source can be synched up or recreated in post-production.
dolly	Any camera movement or piece of equipment used that rolls the camera. If it has wheels and you put the camera on it to shoot, it's a dolly.

double system audio   Audio that is recorded with a separate audio recorder apart from the camera. When shooting double system, the audio is synched up with the picture by using a clapper slate, so the sound of the clap can be aligned with physical clap seen on camera. It is also common when shooting video to record a "dirty" reference track with a camera mic to assist with synching.

dramatic reading   Storytelling convention where actors are used to read a document and/or portray the voice of a subject. Used to breathe life into letters, diaries, or other documents.

dramatic zoom-in   The act of zooming in or out slowly on a subject to give dramatic emphasis to what is being said. These are generally done at the most important or compelling parts of an interview to bring the audience physically and emotionally closer to the subject.

dropouts   Apart from people who quit film school early, this term also refers to breaks and omissions in the audio, usually caused by a cable short, wireless interference, or power issues that result in no sound being recorded for a few seconds here and there. This can't be fixed in post.

DSLR   Short for digital single lens reflex camera, which is a popular form of professional still camera. The "single-lens" part simply means the picture you see in the viewfinder is the actual picture the camera is taking through the lens. The important distinction about these cameras is that they are basically *still photo cameras* that have *added* HD video capability. However, they were never meant to be dedicated video cameras so lack some common (and vital) professional features found even in dedicated prosumer video cameras.

Dutch angle   A shot tilted diagonally to communicate tension or an edgy extreme attitude.

DV Rack   PC-only computer software that can record live footage directly to a hard drive via a laptop computer. Also has other features for image analysis and color correction.

end roll   The term for the wise practice of letting the camera roll for an extra few seconds after each take so that there is adequate room at the end of a scene for an editor to make a cut without losing the end of the take.

equipment package	The entire list of equipment that you need to make a film. Includes your lights, camera, sound, and all the trimmings.
fast lens	A fast lens refers to a lens that is capable of opening to a very low f-stop, generally lower than 2.8, and therefore let's more light into the lens. Fast lenses can better handle low-light shooting situations and are generally more versatile and faster to shoot with, since you have less lighting hassles and can use filters more freely. Naturally, fast lenses are more expensive than other lens.
filament	The little delicate spring that glows hot to produce the light inside light bulbs.
fill light	A light whose function is to bring up the light level some to fill in dark shadows so that details are visible on a subject's face or a lit scene. Fill light should be soft and even. Fill lights are often bounced off a wall or ceiling.
Firestore	A particular brand of small battery-powered camera-mountable hard drives that capture live video via FireWire as a DV camera records it. The captured video files are immediately ready to be edited, saving you tons of time digitizing and logging tapes.
FireWire 400/800	Also known as "IEEE 1394" and "iLink," these are super-fast connections for transferring video data to or from a camera, computer, or hard drive. FireWire 800, used in computers and hard drives, is about twice as fast as FireWire 400, which transfers data at 400MBps. At the time of publication, DV cameras only use FireWire 400.
flood	To widen a beam of light so that it is less intense and more diffused and even. Focusable professional film lights have controls to allow you to flood or spot the light beam.
fluorescent light	Long tubular mercury-vapor lights that require a ballast to regulate the flow of power. Professional fluorescent lights such as Kinoflos may come as tungsten or daylight balanced. However, most household and industrial fluorescents give off light with an unattractive green or bluish tint.

follow focus	A device that attaches to a lens focus ring that's used to more smoothly and precisely focus shots. Using the dial on a follow focus, an operator does not have to touch the lens and can accurately repeat focus moves by marking focal points directly on the dial. Very useful for controlling cameras with very shallow depth of field.
format	Refers to the type of video you are shooting as expressed by vertical pixels and frame rate, typically in terms such as 1080/60i or 720/24p. May also be more generally referred to as "standard definition" or "high definition" as determined by the lines of vertical resolution.
frame line	The imaginary line that marks the top of a framed shot. If a boom mic drops below this line, it will be in the shot.
frame rate	Refers to the number of frames of video you are shooting each second. Frame rates are usually shown in camera specs followed by a designation of "p" for progressive or "i" for interlaced scanning. Typical frame rate specs are expressed in terms such as 24p, 30p, and 60i.
frame-within-a-frame	A shot composition that includes some other element of a scene, such as a doorway or window, that forms a second "frame" around a subject already in the camera's frame.
Franken-Camera	Slang term for DSLR cameras that have been outfitted with all the third-party accessories necessary to make them fully functional for professional video shooting. Includes any combination of support rods, a field monitor, follow focus, audio recording device, matte box, and more.
f-stop	F-stops are numbers that refer to the size of the hole that lets light into the lens, otherwise known as the "aperture." It's counterintuitive, but the larger the f-stop number, the less light is allowed in the lens, the darker the image will be.
gaffer's tape	Professional film industry tape, which is easy to rip by hand, but still very strong. It is also designed not to rip off paint or leave a sticky residue. This is a must-have for any shoot.

gain	This is just another word for "level." There are two types of gain in video: audio gain and video gain. Audio gain adjusts the volume level of audio signals. Video gain adjusts the voltage of the video signal to make an image brighter.
gels	Transparent or translucent sheets of material used to color lights or correct the color of lights.
ghetto-flectors	Homemade reflectors fashioned out of cardboard, aluminum foil, and paper. They aren't pretty or impressive, but reflect light just as effectively as their $30–$100 "professional" reflectors.
HDMI	Stands for "High Definition Multi-Interface." A connection or cable that allows you to hook up video devices such an HD camera and monitor to transmit high-quality high-definition images. Look for these on high-definition cameras, monitors, and TVs.
iMovie	Simple easy-to-use, but powerful editing program that is bundled standard with Mac computers.
in point	The starting timecode point of a shot or edit.
incandescent	An incandescent light passes electricity through a thin filament that heats up inside the vacuum of a bulb to provide light. Most household and professional film lights are incandescent. The other common type of lighting is fluorescent.
insurance certificate	An insurance certificate is a representation of the insurance policy that covers a particular project or production company. At your request, your insurance company will issue certificates naming locations and equipment rental houses as "additional insured" as proof that they are also protected by your insurance policy.
intensity	A term that simply refers to the quantity of light. Light intensity can be controlled in a number of ways, including moving the light closer or farther away, using ND or other light-reducing filters, or spotting or flooding the light beam.
interview subjects	The people who will be interviewed for your project.

interlace

Refers to how a video picture is captured or displayed. Interlaced scanning skips every other vertical row of pictures–making one pass on the odd-numbered pixel rows (1, 3, 5, etc.) and then a second pass on the even-numbered pixel rows (2, 4, 6, etc.) and alternating between these two half images known as video "fields" to form a single interlaced frame of video. Interlaced video is not as detailed and smooth as progressive video.

jam sync

Jamming sync is the act of using a SMPTE time code generating device to send continuous matching free run timecode to one or multiple cameras or recorders. Time code is fed from one device (the master) to a second device (the slave), which then syncs up to the master device's time code so they are exactly the same. The time code generating device may be an electronic smart slate, time code generator or other video or audio recording device capable of sending time code.

jib

A mechanical arm balanced with a camera on one end and a counterweight and camera controls on the other end. Often mounted on tripod legs. Works similar to a seesaw, but the balance point is closer to the end with the controls so that the camera is at the long end of the arm and can make sweeping vertical or horizontal moves.

jump cuts

Refers to a cut made in editing where two shots of the same subject, but taken from different angles, are cut back to back to create a jarring "jump" in screen composition.

jump-cut style shooting

My own terminology for the "jumpy" style of cinematography most popular in some reality, music tv, and mockumentary projects that consists of rapid manual zooming (i.e. push-ins and pull-outs) to switch composition from a wide shot to close-up, or vice-versa, during a scene. "The Office" is a popular American show that's shot in this style.

Ken Burns Effect

A popular visual effect for animating digital still photos that smoothly pans, zooms in, zooms out and otherwise adds life by performing digital "camera moves" on simple still photos. It was popularized by documentary filmmaker, Ken Burns. It's commonly found on many non-linear editing programs, photo slideshow programs like iPhoto and mimicked on computer screen savers.

Kinoflo	Popular brand of professional fluorescent lights used in filmmaking. Known for their light weight; soft, even light; and low power consumption and heat output.
kit rental	A standard industry "rental fee" charged by professionals who also provide special equipment or supplies, such as makeup artist or sound, camera, and lighting people with their own equipment. They get their day rate for their labor plus a smaller kit rental for use of their gear and/or supplies that you would otherwise have to rent or buy separately.
lavs (aka lavalieres)	Small mics designed to be worn close to the body on the chest or neck. Because of their small size, they can also be hidden on location to pick up sound in wide shots.
location	Any real-life environment not created specifically for film production, such as an office, a park, or someone's home, where you are shooting.
location release	Legal agreement between a location owner and filmmaker that grants a filmmaker permission to shoot in and publicly show a location in their film. Also spells out any fees and obligations to the location owner in the event of damage or injury.
lock down	To secure a tripod's pan-and-tilt function so that it does not move and keeps the shot on camera locked into place.
log sheet	A form used to make notes about the location of scenes and quality of your footage. A log sheet typically includes information such as timecode, scene description, length, and whether a shot was good or bad.
logging	Going through all your footage to note the starting timecode, contents, and other vital information that will be necessary for locating scenes and making decisions during editing. Usually written out in a log sheet (see **log sheet**).
MCU	Shorthand for "medium close-up." Basically a shot from the shoulders up.
Magic Lantern	Third-party firmware that can be installed on some models of DSLR cameras to add some basic video camera features such as zebra stripes, audio meters, etc.

mark slate	To call the information on a slate out loud, typically including title of the production, scene number or name, and take number.
matte box	A box-like apparatus that mounts onto the front of a camera lens used to avoid unwanted lens flare from the sun and artificial lights. Matte boxes also allow you to mount multiple filters on the front of the lens.
metadata	Information about your video that is embedded within a digital file that can be accessed in playback mode or in post-production. Typically includes things such as important camera settings, date, time or day, or custom information that a user enters via the menu. Some new cameras can even include geographic location.
mini-stereo connector	Another term for an 1/8" stereo sound connector like the one on your iPod.
money shots	The most important shots of a given project that will have the most impact on your audience. The shots that mean you are screwed if you don't get them. For a wedding, it's the kiss; for a race, it's the winner crossing the finish line; for a concert, it's the moment the lead singer leaps into the audience to crowd surf in the middle of the finale. These are the most iconic shots that tell the story of the scene or event almost by themselves. Know what they are ahead of time and be ready to capture every one.
monopod	A device that serves the same function as a tripod but is made up of only a single extending and locking leg. Monopods are highly portable and easy to move and reset quickly.
Movie Magic Budgeting	A powerful and widely used software program designed specifically for budgeting movies. MMB makes it easy to create, rearrange, and compare different versions of a budget.
narration	The oral telling of a story. In documentary filmmaking, narration is often laid in as a voice-over the picture.
narrative filmmaking	Filmmaking genre that tells a story. Narrative is almost always scripted but can be improvised as well. If there are actors and a script, it's a narrative.
ND gel	Clear gray lighting gel used to cut down the intensity of lights.

neutral cutaways	Very useful shots that can be inserted almost anywhere in a scene because they aren't very time or action specific. For example, a cutaway to a picture on the wall, a subject's hand gestures, or a reaction shot of someone listening are all examples of neutral cutaways that could be used just about anywhere in a scene to help you condense time, cover up a mistake, or just make it more visually interesting.
NLE	Short for "nonlinear editor." Final Cut Pro, Avid, Premiere, and iMovie are all NLEs.
noise	Video static and artifacts caused by using the camera's gain, digital zoom feature, or other electronic function that results in poor image quality.
on the D.L.	Short for "on the down low." Means to travel and shoot as low-key as possible and not draw any unnecessary attention to yourself when shooting without permission or in hostile areas.
open up the lens	To increase the camera's aperture so that more light comes into the lens.
out point	The ending timecode of a shot or edit.
overmodulate	When sound levels are set so high that they distort, sound rumbly, or are unintelligible. Overmodulation can't be fixed in postproduction.
P2 card	Digital media cards used by some Panasonic cameras including the Panasonic HVX-200.
paper edit	A preliminary editing of material by cutting and arranging sections of transcripts into the order they will appear in the film and then using this paper version of your project to make the rough cut.
pelican cases	Popular industry-standard hard plastic cases designed to store and protect film and video equipment during transit. Pelican cases are water resistant and are typically used with foam.
pickup pattern	Outlines the direction(s) in which a microphone best captures and records sound. Common pickup patterns are cardioid, hypercardioid, and omni.
pixels	The little red, green, and blue microdots that make up the image on a TV or monitor screen. The more pixels there are, the sharper and clearer the picture will be.

Plan B	This is what you plan to do when your first idea doesn't work out. To be successful at guerrilla filmmaking, you always need a Plan B, C, and D when things go wrong.
play back	The act of viewing or listening to previously recorded video or audio.
pots	Another name for the knobs on audio gear. If someone says, "Turn up the pot on channel 2," they are not referring to the drug.
practical lights	Any lights that appear on camera as part of your scene. They may or may not actually be contributing to the main lighting of your scene.
pre-amp	An audio device similar to but simpler than a mixer that is used to boost, control, and/or transform audio signals.
preproduction	All the thought, preparation, planning, and budgeting that takes place before you start to shoot.
pre-roll	Refers to the few seconds of tape that need to roll off before a camera or deck is up to proper recording speed.
production insurance	Insurance that covers you and your crew from liabilities as a result of any property damage, theft or loss, and personal death or injury caused by your production.
production value	The professional look or polish of a production. Production value is affected by such factors as the quality of your lighting, video, audio, camerawork, sets, graphics, and number of mistakes. The term "putting your money on the screen" means raising production value wherever possible.
progressive	Refers to how a video picture is captured or displayed. Progressive video scanning goes straight down the vertical rows of pixels to form a complete picture on each frame of video. Progressive cameras and TVs have smoother, more film-like images.
raccoon eyes	The effect created when you're shooting subjects in bright daylight when the sun is high in the sky, which puts their eye sockets in complete shadow.
rate cards	A rental house's or other vendor's price list.
RCA	Also known as "phono." The very common yellow, white, and red cables/connections used with video equipment. Yellow=Video, White=Left, and Red=Right. However, they are completely interchangeable.

rack focus	To shift focus either to or from a person or object in the foreground to or from another person or object in the background of a shot when shooting with a very shallow depth of field. This move forcibly shifts the audience's attention from one thing to another.
reaction shot	A shot showing how another participant is responding to an event. In interviews, this is the occasional shot of the interviewer responding to the subject. For a performance, a reaction shot would focus on audience members.
re-enactments/re-creations	A dramatic acting out of some significant event. May be performed by actors or the actual persons involved in the original event. Often presented in documentary style similar to flashbacks in narrative filmmaking. Re-enactments are common in crime and historical documentaries.
refresh rate	The number of times per second an image is scanned on a screen to form the picture. This number is measured in units called Hertz (Hz). A screen with a 60Hz refresh rate scans the image on-screen 60 times per second to form an image.
research	Any and all work you do to learn more about your subject as you prepare to shoot your documentary. Research encompasses reading books, surfing the web, watching videos, visiting locations, talking to experts, etc. Research is doing homework on your subject.
resolution	The size of the image in pixels. In camera and TV specs, resolution is listed as the number of horizontal pixels x vertical pixels. For HD, there are usually 1080 or 720 vertical pixels.
reverse shot	Very similar to a reaction shot, a reverse shot is just the same action captured from the opposite angle to show another viewpoint.
rolling shutter	Rolling shutter refers to the method that CMOS cameras use to scan an image by "rolling" or moving the shutter across part of the image, so that not all parts of the image are recorded at the same time, even though they are played back as a single frame. Issues that commonly result from rolling shutter particularly when the camera or objects move quickly are smears, diagonal skews or bending of images, and wobbly images known as the "jello effect".

rotoscoping	The technique of manually creating a matte for an element on live-action footage so it may be composited over another background. The matte masks certain parts of the image on a layer of video allowing you to show just a single object or person from a scene and then lay that object or person on top of another scene. You are essentially "cutting out" parts of a video or still photo and putting them on top of another scene.
rove	A loose style of handheld camerawork, most common in reality TV and some scripted dramas where the camera is continually moving and shifting slightly (as if hovering) as opposed to traditional handheld camerawork where the objective would be to hold the camera as steady as possible. Also a common technique for POV camerawork to give the psychological feeling that we are watching through someone else's eyes.
rule of thirds	Rule of composition that dictates if the screen is divided into thirds horizontally and vertically forming a tic-tac-toe pattern, your subjects should be framed so that they are positioned on the intersection of any two or more lines.
run and gun	Guerrilla shooting style that generally refers to any hectic, unpredictable, fast, and unfolding shooting condition that requires you to cover a lot in a little time often at various locations. Local news is almost always a run-and-gun shooting situation.
S.A.G. paperwork	The simple, but very important forms required by the Screen Actors Guild (aka S.A.G.) whenever an actor in their professional union works on a production. This paperwork verifies the hours they worked, rate agreed upon and that S.A.G. rules regarding lunch breaks and turnaround were followed by the filmmakers.
SxS card	Digital media cards used by some Sony model cameras, including the Sony EX-1, Sony EX3, and the Sony F3.
scene detection	The ability of some edit programs to automatically divide footage into video clips by detecting the timecode when the record button was pressed to start each new shot.
screen captions	Titles placed at the bottom of the frame to spell out dialog or subtitles.

scrims	Specially fitted round metal screens of various thicknesses that come as full or half circles placed in front of a light to reduce intensity.
SSD	Stands for solid state drive. These are hard drives that use flash memory similar to P2 and SxS cards. They have no moving parts, so they are sturdier and not as susceptible to the malfunctions that can more easily occur with hard disk drives which have spinning disks and moving parts.
SDHC card	Small, relatively inexpensive reusable flash media cards used to record audio and video. Common media for many models of consumer and prosumer video cameras.
short	A loose or bad connection in any cable that results in the cable not clearly and consistently carrying an audio or video signal, which generally will result in static, pops, and dropouts of the signal.
shotgun	Another name for hypercardioid mics, which have a very narrow pickup pattern and focus only on sound in the direction they are pointed.
shutter speed	This term refers to the amount of time the camera's shutter stays open to expose each frame of video. Shutter speed affects how motion is portrayed–sharp or blurry– and how much light enters the lens.
single system audio	Audio that is recorded on the camera at the same time as picture.
slate	This is a device used to synchronize picture and sound and mark particular scenes and takes recorded during production. Can be as simple as someone clapping their hands in front of the camera or as complicated as a battery-operated slate with electronic timecode display. Also commonly used as a verb. Alternatively known as a "clapper board," "marker," or "smart slate."
Slug	Text that is edited into a project as a note or reminder for those working in post-production, projection or broadcast usually to denote things such as titles, audio tracks used, or unfinished elements. Slug text is not intended to be ever seen by the audience.

SMPTE	Pronounced /*simp-tee*/. Stands for the "Society of Motion Picture and Television Engineers." This long-standing group of film and TV engineers develops industry standards. Best known for their SMPTE color bar test pattern, which is used to adjust video colors on monitors.
spill light	Any excess, unwanted, or uncontrolled light that appears in a shot. Barn doors, flags, and black wrap are all common tools for blocking spill light.
snoots	Can-like cylindrical inserts that go in front of lights to reduce the width of the beam to highlight a specific subject or object in a scene.
sound blankets	Thick quilted movers' blankets used to dampen echoes caused by hard room surfaces.
speed	Term referring to the moment a second or two after you press the record button when a camera has finished its pre-roll and reached the necessary speed to properly record video and audio signals.
spill	Undesired light that is illuminating any area other than the targeted area. Barn doors, black wrap, and snoots are used to control excess spill light.
spot	To adjust a light's spot/flood control so that the light is at its narrowest, most intense beam.
staging area	An area set aside on a set or location for a department to exclusively use as homebase to store and set-up all their equipment and supplies. Camera, audio, make-up, etc. all need separate staging areas.
statement of work	A document that describes the work that you are proposing to do and clearly spells out what you will do as a producer/director, the basics of how it will be accomplished (such as locations, number of shooting days, etc.), and how much it will cost your clients. Presented after you have an initial meeting or conversation with a client to discuss their needs.
SteadiCam	An industry standard and very expensive camera-stabilizing device used to get smooth, fluid, handheld camera shots. The professional models require a trained operator.
sticks	Another word for "tripod."

stills	Refers to digital or film still photographs.
stock footage	Stock footage is essentially any footage that was not originally shot for your documentary. It can be anything from relevant stills from a local newspaper to clips of old movies that deal with your topic. Stock footage houses sell historical and current video footage.
stopping down	To make a shot darker by closing the lens aperture so that less light comes into the lens.
style sheet	A general term for the written description of the look and feel of various visual and graphic elements such as lower thirds and main titles, transitions, on-screen graphics, how interviews are framed and lit, color palette, style of cinematography, etc. This simple document ensures that your project has a consistent look and style throughout.
surveillance video	Video that is recorded without a subject's knowledge. Usually done from afar using telephoto lens or with hidden or unmanned cameras to capture criminal activity.
S-video	Analog connection/cable used to transmit high-quality video signals between cameras, monitors, and videotape decks. Does not carry audio.
tally light	The little red light that comes on whenever the camera is recording. Found on the front and sometimes also on the rear of video cameras.
take	Every time you call "cut" or start a shot over again is considered a take. To successfully capture a single shot, you may do multiple takes.
telephoto	The longest lens setting achieved by zooming all the way in to a subject. Subjects that are very far away will have to be shot with a telephoto lens to get a medium or close-up shot.
timecode	A digital signal recorded as a track on a DV tape that maintains consistent playback by digitally marking the precise time and tape position down to seconds and frames (1 second = 30 DV frames). This is what editing programs use to mark the exact start and stop points of an edit.

timecode break   The common anomaly that can occur when there is an error in recording that results in the timecode track not recording.

tone   See bars and tone

transcript   The line-for-line written conversion of a videotaped interview or conversation into a "script." For doc filmmaking purposes, transcripts should also denote the timecode of interview questions and dialog so they can be easily located during editing.

translucent powder makeup   Makeup used to smooth and even out complexions as well as diminish the appearance of common blemishes such as wrinkles, acne, freckles, and moles. Particularly useful for counteracting the unflattering effects of HD video on close shots.

tungsten   Light that is orange in color temperature. Most quartz bulbs and standard household lights are tungsten.

USB/USB 2.0   Stands for "Universal Serial Bus." These data cables/ connectors are used to connect digital equipment such as cameras, computers, and hard drives.

USB drives   Also known as "thumb drives," these are popular, sturdy flash media storage devices a little bigger than a pen cap that plug into a computer's USB port. USB stands for "Universal Serial Bus."

verbal release   Recording a subject giving you verbal permission to use their image in your project. Not as trusty as a written talent release but will still offer some proof of a subject's cooperation and consent should there be a legal dispute in the future. This is a runner-up when you can't get a written release right then.

video noise   Undesirable static, dots, and graininess in a video picture. Most common when shooting in low light or with the gain turned up.

VFX   Short for "visual effects."

visual FX   General term used to describe a wide array of special effects accomplished using computer software such as Adobe After Effects or Apple's Motion. Spinning metallic text, muzzle fire added for a fake gun, or digital snow are all examples of common visual FX.

warm cards	Special pale green or blue "white cards" made to give your image a warmer look when you white balance your camera on them instead of pure white.
watts	A unit used to measure electricity. Typical household light bulbs are 40–100 watts. Professional film lights are typically 250–2000 watts.
whip pan	A quick pan move that's so fast that it causes the image to blur in the middle of the move until the lens rests on the final shot.
whip zoom	A quick manual zoom move in or out that's so fast that it causes the image to blur in the middle of the move until the lens rests on the final shot. This move is common in reality, sports, music videos and other high energy productions.
white balance	A video camera function that adjusts your image to correct variations in color temperature.
white cards	A special pure white card used as a reference to set a camera's white balance function to adjust for the lighting conditions. Pure white sheets of paper or T-shirts are a common substitute for white cards in the field.
wild sound	Recording of the natural sound of a room or environment to help you smooth out audio problems and re-create the original sound quality of the location during postproduction.
wind shield/windjammer	Also known as a "dead cat." A faux fur cover that's custom-fitted to a mic or zeppelin (aka blimp) and used to provide significant reduction of wind noise above and beyond a zeppelin or wind filter alone .
wipe	To erase a digital media card by reformatting it which clears all video and or audio clips from the card . . . *forever*. This function is usually found in the camera's menu and likely at the very bottom of the menu set. Never wipe a card until you've verified your footage by playing it back and listening to it.
wrap out	When everything is packed up and put back in place at the end of a shoot.
XLR	The most common high-quality sound cables/connectors used for professional sound applications. The connectors are three-pronged (male) or three-holed (female).

zebra stripes	Vibrating diagonal stripes that are superimposed on the overexposed parts of the image on a viewfinder or LCD screen. Zebra stripes are not recorded to tape.

zeppelin	A microphone housing that resembles its namesake, designed to shield boom mics from wind noise.

INDEX

Government grants 17–18
Grey Gardens 6, 12, 13, 259
Guerrilla festival team 326

H
Handheld
    camera positions 136
    camerawork 144
    editing 135
    mic 191
    shooting 135
Hard drives 296–7
HDMI cable 212, 343
HDV image size 39
Head room 219
Headphones 184, 206, 277
Histogram 120
Hollywood Creative Directory 20
Hospital 152

I
IDA 20
If God is Willing 36, 37
IFP 20
Image
    control of 114
    exposure 118, 119–20
    focus 115–17
    gain effects 119–20
    lighting 117, 118
    sharpness and detail 43
iMovie 300, 343
In Country 33, 225, 303
In-camera vs post 140
Incandescent bulbs 121, 343
Indiwire.com 20
Instructional DVDs 4
Insurance
    certificate 110, 343
    location 109
    shooting without 110
Interlaced image 38
Internet 8
Internet Movie Database 20
Interview
    arrival 250
    at press conference 269

backgrounds 251, 252
celebrities 275
exploitation 273
feedback 272
final preparation 249
hazards 278
interrupting 276
listening skills 271
one-on-one 269
pre-preparation 248
preparation/warm up 270
questions 265–7, 274
remote 279–81
resistant subjects 268
responding to subject 272
technical issues 276–7
Interview subject 343
    briefing 260
    clothing 254, 255
    description 11
    eyeline 253
    facial appearance 256, 257
    instructing 261
    positioning 253
    powder makeup 257
    talent release form 258, 259
    tips 262
    walking away 263
Inventory of equipment 245
iPhones *see smartphones*
ISO function 171

J
Jim Brown All-American 14, 299
JVC, GY-HM750 58

K
Key light 163
Keyboard overlays 298
Kickstarter 33–4

L
Lalee's Kin 6, 259
Lancaster, Kurt 60
Lavalier Mic 191, 193, 194, 262
LCD screen 117
LED light 159

Anthony Q. Artis (*ant-nee kew art-iss*) is a 20-year veteran of the film and TV industry and a passionate teacher, public speaker and trainer of aspiring filmmakers. He has written *The Shut Up and Shoot Documentary Guide* and *The Shut Up and Shoot Freelance Video Guide* by Focal Press, as well as numerous filmmaking video courses on **Lynda.com**. Anthony is also the lively co-host of *The Double Down Film Show* podcast and creator of the *Indie Film Boot Camp* filmmaking workshop and DVD series.

(Photo by Lucas Deming)

He has worked professionally in positions as diverse as producer, director, cinematographer, gaffer, sound mixer and location manager amongst others. His features and shows have been screened at the Tribeca Film Festival, the IFP Feature Market, Slamdance, and on MTV. Most notably, Anthony produced the IFP Feature Market grand prize-winner, *Shelter*, Associate Produced and gaffed the IFC feature documentary, *Paper Chasers*, and served as a segment producer for the popular MTV reality series *Flipped*.

For more than a decade Anthony managed the Production Center in the Film and TV department of New York University's legendary Tisch School of the Arts which houses some 200+ film and video cameras and serves more than 1000 grad and undergrad students. He has since retired from that position to pursue his passions for filmmaking, public speaking, and training aspiring filmmakers full-time.

Known for his candid, yet inspirational and humorous approach to teaching filmmaking, Anthony is a proud alumni and adjunct instructor at NYU, where he's taught hundreds of students camera, lighting, sound and practical filmmaking wisdom for the last 11 years.

His blog and website for filmmakers is **DownAndDirtyDV.com**.

Project Coordinator
Anthony Q. Artis
Associate Project Coordinators
Jenny Chun
Nathan Kensinger
Lisa Kjerulff
Meghan O'Hara
Project Consultant
Pete Chatmon
Additional Copy Editor
Darren C. Hackett
Interview Subjects
Mike Attie & Meghan O'Hara
Adrian Belic
Alrick Brown
John Canemaker
Cliff Charles
Christina DeHaven
Albert Maysles
Christie Pesicka
Sam Pollard
Rose Roseblatt & Marion Lipschutz
Micah Schaffer
Rebekah Sindoris
Safiya Songhai
Additonal Articles
Stjepan Alaupovic
Michelle Coe
Jon Harris
Cybel Martin
Rick Prelinger
Models
Marlyne Afflack
Sonya Artis
Dustin Chang
Eddie Cunha
Ina Franck
Cruce Grammatico
Sorayya Kassamali
Frank Monteleone
Kathleen Monteleone
Hannah Schluder
Danielle Velkoff
Timothy Wong
Yekaterina Yakubov
Crew as Themselves

Videography for Photos
Fruto Corre
Ahmed Hawari
Freddie Jackson
Gary Jean
Rich Joneleit
Kian Najmabadi
Max Nova
Sophie Shepard
Lori Majewski
Greg Pickard
Doug Crawford
Clair Harlam
Tyler Wilson
Kevin Darnell Walker
Zoe Salicrup Junco
Robert Blake
Brian Thomson-DiPalma
Chris Thomson-DiPalma
Eliza McNitt
Mary Schmidt-Campbell
"Black Magic" Tim
Additional Crew
Sean Charlesworth
Andrew Engbert
Maggie Langalinais
Kristin Wynn
Bonus Website Video Editor
Dan Shipp
DVD Trailer Editor
Greg Payton
Bonus Video Music
B26 for Bshani Media Group
Maurice Carr
D&D Website Design
Cidney Hue
Logo Design
Brian and Sarah Gallarello
Hand-Camera Graphic Design
Ian Kim
Additional Photos
Death of Two Sons
In Country
Paper Chasers
The Education of Shelby Knox
Sonya Artis
Canon
Glidecam

Google.com
JVC
Losmandy
Lowel Lighting
Panasonic
Sony
WithoutABox.com
Kessler Crane
Lite Panels
Leyla T. Rosario
Double 7 Images
Black Magic Design
Susan Chen
Interview Transcripts
Skye Dent—24/7 Transcriptions
Lisa Kjerulff
Kristin Wynn
Special Thanks
The NYU Film and TV Community
Student Filmmakers Magazine
Double 7 Images
CCC Manhattan
The Down and Dirty DV Nation
The Treitley Family
Lou LaVolpe
Sheril Antonio
Rosanne Limoncelli
Rob and Alyce Benevides
The Drumadics
Dave DiGioia
Brandon Kiggins
Yuri Densynko
Creative Letterpress
lynda.com
Greg Pickard
Inspiration and Motivation
Charles Blackwell
Pete Chatmon
Maxie Collier
The Playa Haters
Bennie Randall "The Motivator"
Johnny Rice II
The Original *Paper Chasers* Crew
My Production Center Family
My Family
Fat Joe
God